FREE Test Taking Tips Video/DVD Offer

To better serve you, we created videos covering test taking tips that we want to give you for FREE. **These videos cover world-class tips that will help you succeed on your test.**

We just ask that you send us feedback about this product. Please let us know what you thought about it—whether good, bad, or indifferent.

To get your **FREE videos**, you can use the QR code below or email freevideos@studyguideteam.com with "Free Videos" in the subject line and the following information in the body of the email:

a. The title of your product

b. Your product rating on a scale of 1-5, with 5 being the highest

c. Your feedback about the product

If you have any questions or concerns, please don't hesitate to contact us at info@studyguideteam.com.

Thank you!

Test Prep Books

SCAN HERE

IELTS Academic and General Training Study Guide

3 Practice Tests and IELTS Book for Exam Prep
[Includes Audio Links for the Listening Section]

Joshua Rueda

Written and edited by TPB Publishing.

ISBN 13: 9781637754894
ISBN 10: 1637754892

Table of Contents

Welcome

Dear Reader,

Welcome to your new Test Prep Books study guide! We are pleased that you chose us to help you prepare for your exam. There are many study options to choose from, and we appreciate you choosing us. Studying can be a daunting task, but we have designed a smart, effective study guide to help prepare you for what lies ahead.

Whether you're a parent helping your child learn and grow, a high school student working hard to get into your dream college, or a nursing student studying for a complex exam, we want to help give you the tools you need to succeed. We hope this study guide gives you the skills and the confidence to thrive, and we can't thank you enough for allowing us to be part of your journey.

In an effort to continue to improve our products, we welcome feedback from our customers. We look forward to hearing from you. Suggestions, success stories, and criticisms can all be communicated by emailing us at info@studyguideteam.com.

Sincerely,
Test Prep Books Team

FREE Videos/DVD OFFER

Doing well on your exam requires both knowing the test content and understanding how to use that knowledge to do well on the test. We offer completely FREE test taking tip videos. **These videos cover world-class tips that you can use to succeed on your test.**

To get your **FREE videos**, you can use the QR code below or email freevideos@studyguideteam.com with "Free Videos" in the subject line and the following information in the body of the email:

a. The title of your product
b. Your product rating on a scale of 1-5, with 5 being the highest
c. Your feedback about the product

If you have any questions or concerns, please don't hesitate to contact us at info@studyguideteam.com.

SCAN HERE

Quick Overview

As you draw closer to taking your exam, effective preparation becomes more and more important. Thankfully, you have this study guide to help you get ready. Use this guide to help keep your studying on track and refer to it often.

This study guide contains several key sections that will help you be successful on your exam. The guide contains tips for what you should do the night before and the day of the test. Also included are test-taking tips. Knowing the right information is not always enough. Many well-prepared test takers struggle with exams. These tips will help equip you to accurately read, assess, and answer test questions.

A large part of the guide is devoted to showing you what content to expect on the exam and to helping you better understand that content. In this guide are practice test questions so that you can see how well you have grasped the content. Then, answer explanations are provided so that you can understand why you missed certain questions.

Don't try to cram the night before you take your exam. This is not a wise strategy for a few reasons. First, your retention of the information will be low. Your time would be better used by reviewing information you already know rather than trying to learn a lot of new information. Second, you will likely become stressed as you try to gain a large amount of knowledge in a short amount of time. Third, you will be depriving yourself of sleep. So be sure to go to bed at a reasonable time the night before. Being well-rested helps you focus and remain calm.

Be sure to eat a substantial breakfast the morning of the exam. If you are taking the exam in the afternoon, be sure to have a good lunch as well. Being hungry is distracting and can make it difficult to focus. You have hopefully spent lots of time preparing for the exam. Don't let an empty stomach get in the way of success!

When travelling to the testing center, leave earlier than needed. That way, you have a buffer in case you experience any delays. This will help you remain calm and will keep you from missing your appointment time at the testing center.

Be sure to pace yourself during the exam. Don't try to rush through the exam. There is no need to risk performing poorly on the exam just so you can leave the testing center early. Allow yourself to use all of the allotted time if needed.

Remain positive while taking the exam even if you feel like you are performing poorly. Thinking about the content you should have mastered will not help you perform better on the exam.

Once the exam is complete, take some time to relax. Even if you feel that you need to take the exam again, you will be well served by some down time before you begin studying again. It's often easier to convince yourself to study if you know that it will come with a reward!

Test-Taking Strategies

1. Predicting the Answer

When you feel confident in your preparation for a multiple-choice test, try predicting the answer before reading the answer choices. This is especially useful on questions that test objective factual knowledge. By predicting the answer before reading the available choices, you eliminate the possibility that you will be distracted or led astray by an incorrect answer choice. You will feel more confident in your selection if you read the question, predict the answer, and then find your prediction among the answer choices. After using this strategy, be sure to still read all of the answer choices carefully and completely. If you feel unprepared, you should not attempt to predict the answers. This would be a waste of time and an opportunity for your mind to wander in the wrong direction.

2. Reading the Whole Question

Too often, test takers scan a multiple-choice question, recognize a few familiar words, and immediately jump to the answer choices. Test authors are aware of this common impatience, and they will sometimes prey upon it. For instance, a test author might subtly turn the question into a negative, or he or she might redirect the focus of the question right at the end. The only way to avoid falling into these traps is to read the entirety of the question carefully before reading the answer choices.

3. Looking for Wrong Answers

Long and complicated multiple-choice questions can be intimidating. One way to simplify a difficult multiple-choice question is to eliminate all of the answer choices that are clearly wrong. In most sets of answers, there will be at least one selection that can be dismissed right away. If the test is administered on paper, the test taker could draw a line through it to indicate that it may be ignored; otherwise, the test taker will have to perform this operation mentally or on scratch paper. In either case, once the obviously incorrect answers have been eliminated, the remaining choices may be considered. Sometimes identifying the clearly wrong answers will give the test taker some information about the correct answer. For instance, if one of the remaining answer choices is a direct opposite of one of the eliminated answer choices, it may well be the correct answer. The opposite of obviously wrong is obviously right! Of course, this is not always the case. Some answers are obviously incorrect simply because they are irrelevant to the question being asked. Still, identifying and eliminating some incorrect answer choices is a good way to simplify a multiple-choice question.

4. Don't Overanalyze

Anxious test takers often overanalyze questions. When you are nervous, your brain will often run wild, causing you to make associations and discover clues that don't actually exist. If you feel that this may be a problem for you, do whatever you can to slow down during the test. Try taking a deep breath or counting to ten. As you read and consider the question, restrict yourself to the particular words used by the author. Avoid thought tangents about what the author *really* meant, or what he or she was *trying* to say. The only things that matter on a multiple-choice test are the words that are actually in the question. You must avoid reading too much into a multiple-choice question, or supposing that the writer meant something other than what he or she wrote.

5. No Need for Panic

It is wise to learn as many strategies as possible before taking a multiple-choice test, but it is likely that you will come across a few questions for which you simply don't know the answer. In this situation, avoid panicking. Because most multiple-choice tests include dozens of questions, the relative value of a single wrong answer is small. As much as possible, you should compartmentalize each question on a multiple-choice test. In other words, you should not allow your feelings about one question to affect your success on the others. When you find a question that you either don't understand or don't know how to answer, just take a deep breath and do your best. Read the entire question slowly and carefully. Try rephrasing the question a couple of different ways. Then, read all of the answer choices carefully. After eliminating obviously wrong answers, make a selection and move on to the next question.

6. Confusing Answer Choices

When working on a difficult multiple-choice question, there may be a tendency to focus on the answer choices that are the easiest to understand. Many people, whether consciously or not, gravitate to the answer choices that require the least concentration, knowledge, and memory. This is a mistake. When you come across an answer choice that is confusing, you should give it extra attention. A question might be confusing because you do not know the subject matter to which it refers. If this is the case, don't eliminate the answer before you have affirmatively settled on another. When you come across an answer choice of this type, set it aside as you look at the remaining choices. If you can confidently assert that one of the other choices is correct, you can leave the confusing answer aside. Otherwise, you will need to take a moment to try to better understand the confusing answer choice. Rephrasing is one way to tease out the sense of a confusing answer choice.

7. Your First Instinct

Many people struggle with multiple-choice tests because they overthink the questions. If you have studied sufficiently for the test, you should be prepared to trust your first instinct once you have carefully and completely read the question and all of the answer choices. There is a great deal of research suggesting that the mind can come to the correct conclusion very quickly once it has obtained all of the relevant information. At times, it may seem to you as if your intuition is working faster even than your reasoning mind. This may in fact be true. The knowledge you obtain while studying may be retrieved from your subconscious before you have a chance to work out the associations that support it. Verify your instinct by working out the reasons that it should be trusted.

8. Key Words

Many test takers struggle with multiple-choice questions because they have poor reading comprehension skills. Quickly reading and understanding a multiple-choice question requires a mixture of skill and experience. To help with this, try jotting down a few key words and phrases on a piece of scrap paper. Doing this concentrates the process of reading and forces the mind to weigh the relative importance of the question's parts. In selecting words and phrases to write down, the test taker thinks about the question more deeply and carefully. This is especially true for multiple-choice questions that are preceded by a long prompt.

9. Subtle Negatives

One of the oldest tricks in the multiple-choice test writer's book is to subtly reverse the meaning of a question with a word like *not* or *except*. If you are not paying attention to each word in the question, you can easily be led astray by this trick. For instance, a common question format is, "Which of the following is...?" Obviously, if the question instead is, "Which of the following is not...?," then the answer will be quite different. Even worse, the test makers are aware of the potential for this mistake and will include one answer choice that would be correct if the question were not negated or reversed. A test taker who misses the reversal will find what he or she believes to be a correct answer and will be so confident that he or she will fail to reread the question and discover the original error. The only way to avoid this is to practice a wide variety of multiple-choice questions and to pay close attention to each and every word.

10. Reading Every Answer Choice

It may seem obvious, but you should always read every one of the answer choices! Too many test takers fall into the habit of scanning the question and assuming that they understand the question because they recognize a few key words. From there, they pick the first answer choice that answers the question they believe they have read. Test takers who read all of the answer choices might discover that one of the latter answer choices is actually *more* correct. Moreover, reading all of the answer choices can remind you of facts related to the question that can help you arrive at the correct answer. Sometimes, a misstatement or incorrect detail in one of the latter answer choices will trigger your memory of the subject and will enable you to find the right answer. Failing to read all of the answer choices is like not reading all of the items on a restaurant menu: you might miss out on the perfect choice.

11. Spot the Hedges

One of the keys to success on multiple-choice tests is paying close attention to every word. This is never truer than with words like *almost*, *most*, *some*, and *sometimes*. These words are called "hedges" because they indicate that a statement is not totally true or not true in every place and time. An absolute statement will contain no hedges, but in many subjects, the answers are not always straightforward or absolute. There are always exceptions to the rules in these subjects. For this reason, you should favor those multiple-choice questions that contain hedging language. The presence of qualifying words indicates that the author is taking special care with his or her words, which is certainly important when composing the right answer. After all, there are many ways to be wrong, but there is only one way to be right! For this reason, it is wise to avoid answers that are absolute when taking a multiple-choice test. An absolute answer is one that says things are either all one way or all another. They often include words like *every*, *always*, *best*, and *never*. If you are taking a multiple-choice test in a subject that doesn't lend itself to absolute answers, be on your guard if you see any of these words.

12. Long Answers

In many subject areas, the answers are not simple. As already mentioned, the right answer often requires hedges. Another common feature of the answers to a complex or subjective question are qualifying clauses, which are groups of words that subtly modify the meaning of the sentence. If the question or answer choice describes a rule to which there are exceptions or the subject matter is complicated, ambiguous, or confusing, the correct answer will require many words in order to be expressed clearly and accurately. In essence, you should not be deterred by answer choices that seem excessively long. Oftentimes, the author of the text will not be able to write the correct answer without offering some qualifications and modifications. Your job is to read the answer choices thoroughly and completely and to select the one that most accurately and precisely answers the question.

13. Restating to Understand

Sometimes, a question on a multiple-choice test is difficult not because of what it asks but because of how it is written. If this is the case, restate the question or answer choice in different words. This process serves a couple of important purposes. First, it forces you to concentrate on the core of the question. In order to rephrase the question accurately, you have to understand it well. Rephrasing the question will concentrate your mind on the key words and ideas. Second, it will present the information to your mind in a fresh way. This process may trigger your memory and render some useful scrap of information picked up while studying.

14. True Statements

Sometimes an answer choice will be true in itself, but it does not answer the question. This is one of the main reasons why it is essential to read the question carefully and completely before proceeding to the answer choices. Too often, test takers skip ahead to the answer choices and look for true statements. Having found one of these, they are content to select it without reference to the question above. The savvy test taker will always read the entire question before turning to the answer choices. Then, having settled on a correct answer choice, he or she will refer to the original question and ensure that the selected answer is relevant. The mistake of choosing a correct-but-irrelevant answer choice is especially common on questions related to specific pieces of objective knowledge.

15. No Patterns

One of the more dangerous ideas that circulates about multiple-choice tests is that the correct answers tend to fall into patterns. These erroneous ideas range from a belief that B and C are the most common right answers, to the idea that an unprepared test-taker should answer "A-B-A-C-A-D-A-B-A." It cannot be emphasized enough that pattern-seeking of this type is exactly the WRONG way to approach a multiple-choice test. To begin with, it is highly unlikely that the test maker will plot the correct answers according to some predetermined pattern. The questions are scrambled and delivered in a random order. Furthermore, even if the test maker was following a pattern in the assignation of correct answers, there is no reason why the test taker would know which pattern he or she was using. Any attempt to discern a pattern in the answer choices is a waste of time and a distraction from the real work of taking the test. A test taker would be much better served by extra preparation before the test than by reliance on a pattern in the answers.

Introduction to the IELTS

Function of the Test

The International English Language Testing System (IELTS) has served as a standardised test of English-language proficiency for non-native English speakers for around twenty-five years. It is jointly owned by the British Council, IDP: IELTS Australia, and the Cambridge English Learning Assessment and is intended to measure English-language proficiency for people who want to study or work in an English-speaking country or environment. It is intended to treat all "standard" varieties of English as equally valid, including North American, British, Australian, and New Zealand.

The IELTS is offered in two versions. The first is the Academic version, intended for individuals applying for admission to a college, university, or professional registration. The second is the General Training version, intended for individuals emigrating to Australia, Canada, or the United Kingdom, individuals seeking admission to secondary school, or individuals seeking direct employment

The IELTS is very commonly used overseas and particularly in the United Kingdom. However, it is also accepted by over 3,000 institutions in the United States, including almost all colleges that enroll a large number of international students.

Close to three million individuals take the test each year, with the number increasing steadily in recent years. Around 80% of IELTS takers opt for the Academic version of the test, with the rest taking the General Training version.

Test Administration

The IELTS tests are offered in over 1,000 locations including around 50 in the United States. Each test center may offer the exam up to four times per month, for a total of 48 sessions per year. There are no particular restrictions on retaking the IELTS; test takers may reapply as soon as they feel ready to do so, though the testing agency recommends that test takers engage in new study rather than simply taking the test again to achieve a higher score.

Test takers with disabilities or special requirements for taking the exam may receive accommodations by request. Individuals in need of a modified version of the exam must make their request to their test center at least three months in advance. Individuals in need of special arrangements such as additional time must give the test center at least six weeks notice.

Test Format

Both versions of the IELTS are comprised of four sections: Listening, Speaking, Reading, and Writing. The Listening and Speaking sections are the same on the Academic and General Training tests, but the material in the Reading and Writing sections differs. A summary of the sections follows:

Section	Description	Number of Questions	Time
Listening	Test takers hear four recordings of spoken English in varying settings and then answer questions about each conversation.	40	30 minutes
Speaking	Test takers speak to an examiner, answering questions and addressing subjects verbally.	3 tasks	11-14 minutes
Reading	Test takers read texts and excerpts and then answer questions about the material they read.	40	60 minutes
Writing	Test takers write two separate essays on assigned topics.	2 tasks	60 minutes

Scoring

IELTS scores are reported in nine "bands," ranging from 1 ("non-user," a test taker with no ability to use English aside from a few isolated words) to 9 ("expert user," a test taker with full operational command of English). Each test taker receives a band score in each of the four sections as well as an overall band score consisting of the average of the four section band scores. Each of the four sections is individually scored according to its own criteria, with the Listening and Reading sections scored by a total number of correct answers out of the 40 questions delivered, and the Writing and Speaking sections scored subjectively by examiners according to stated criteria.

Listening Section

We have recorded audio to go along with the listening practice questions. You can find all of our audio recordings by going to testprepbooks.com/bonus/ielts or by scanning the QR code below. The audio is only online. There is no CD.

SCAN ME

Study Prep Plan for the IELTS

1 **Schedule** - Use one of our study schedules below or come up with one of your own.

2 **Relax** - Test anxiety can hurt even the best students. There are many ways to reduce stress. Find the one that works best for you.

3 **Execute** - Once you have a good plan in place, be sure to stick to it.

One Week Study Schedule

Day 1	Listening
Day 2	Writing
Day 3	Speaking
Day 4	Practice Test #1
Day 5	Practice Test #2
Day 6	Practice Tests #3 & #4
Day 7	Take Your Exam!

Two Week Study Schedule

Day 1	Listening	Day 8	Answer Explanations #1
Day 2	Identifying Information from Printed...	Day 9	Practice Test #2
Day 3	Analyzing Nuances of Word Meaning...	Day 10	Answer Explanations #2
Day 4	Writing	Day 11	Practice Test #3
Day 5	Sentences	Day 12	Answer Explanations #3
Day 6	Speaking	Day 13	Practice Test #4
Day 7	Practice Test #1	Day 14	Take Your Exam!

One Month Study Schedule

Day 1	Listening	Day 11	Analyzing Nuances of Word Meaning...	Day 21	Speaking
Day 2	Reading	Day 12	Authors Use of Evidence to Support...	Day 22	Practice Test #1
Day 3	Analysis of History/ Social Studies Excerpts	Day 13	The Purpose of a Passage	Day 23	Answer Explanations #1
Day 4	Analysis of Science Excerpts	Day 14	Rhetoric	Day 24	Practice Test #2
Day 5	Non-Fiction	Day 15	Writing	Day 25	Answer Explanations #2
Day 6	Making Inferences	Day 16	Writing the Essay	Day 26	Practice Test #3
Day 7	Identifying Information...	Day 17	Parts of Speech	Day 27	Answer Explanations #3
Day 8	Using Legends and Map Keys	Day 18	Sentences	Day 28	Practice Test #4
Day 9	Understanding the Use of Affixes, Context...	Day 19	Punctuation	Day 29	Answer Explanations #4
Day 10	Meaning of Words in Context	Day 20	Various Homonyms	Day 30	Take Your Exam!

Build your own prep plan by visiting:
testprepbooks.com/prep

Listening

The Listening section of the IELTS™ test lasts 30 minutes and consists of four recordings of native English speakers with a series of ten questions that follow each listening clip. Before the recording begins, test takers are given approximately 30 seconds to skim the questions that pertain to that clip. This is a good opportunity to briefly familiarize oneself with key words to listen for such as places, names, or prices. Test takers are encouraged to take notes while listening and are granted ten additional minutes beyond the 30-minute section window to transfer any answers in the form of notes onto the answer sheet. It should be noted that proper spelling and grammar are expected on the answer sheet; mistakes will be penalized so test takers should exercise care when finalizing their answers.

The first recording is a casual conversation between two speakers about everyday topics encountered in normal social situations. While the topics are similar in the second recording, instead of being a dialogue, it is a monologue—a single person talking about a common life topic such as a description of services offered at the local library or information about a public event. The third recording is another conversation, but this time, there may be up to four speakers and the setting and topic revolve around academics or university matters. Questions are typically more difficult than those pertaining to the first conversation and may also ask test takers to identify speakers' attitudes or opinions. The final recording is another monologue; this time it is likely an academic lecture excerpt or other educational contexts.

We have recorded audio to go along with the listening practice questions. You can find all of our audio recordings by going to testprepbooks.com/bonus/ielts or by scanning the QR code below. The audio is only online. There is no CD.

SCAN ME

There are six task types that test takers will encounter on the IELTS Listening Section. The following list provides the basic details of each type:

- **Multiple-choice**: There are a couple of multiple-choice question formats on the Listening section. In one type, there is a question followed by three possible answers, A, B, or C, and test takers must select the one best choice. Other questions will be followed by a longer list of possible answers and ask test takers to select more than one choice. Test takers must read the question and directions thoroughly to ensure they properly fulfill the task. Lastly, test takers may be presented with a sentence followed by three possible options to complete the sentence, again, selecting the single best answer. In addition to the variety of multiple-choice forms, the content of these questions runs the gamut from addressing the overall topic or main point of the recording to requiring test takers to identify specific details from the clip.

- **Matching**: Matching questions require test takers to match a numbered list of items from the listening passage or dialogue to a set of options presented on the question and answer sheet. This type of task assesses the test taker's ability to listen for details, follow varied conversations, and correctly understand information or connections between ideas or facts provided via spoken language.

- **Plan, map, diagram labeling**: These questions ask test takers to complete labels on a plan, map, or diagram such as a building blueprint, a map of campus or town, or a parts diagram of a piece of equipment or science illustration. In most cases, test takers are provided with an answer bank from which they can select the appropriate choices for the given blank labels. This question type assesses the test taker's ability to understand and follow spoken information regarding directions or spatial relationships and translate it into an accurate visual representation.

- **Form, note, table, flow-chart, summary completion**: These questions require test takers to identify main ideas or facts from the text and fill them into the appropriate blanks in a provided outline. The outline may be of a variety of types such as a form necessitating test takers to fill in names or other details, a set of notes or a table to summarize the relationships between different items or categories, or a flow-chart to represent the steps in a process. Like the labeling questions, test takers are usually provided with a word bank from which they can select the appropriate missing words. In some cases, words will be missing from the recording that test takers must deduce and fill in. In these instances, a word limit will be provided, such that test takers can only answer the question with the allocated number of words. Answers that fail to adhere to the word limit will incur a penalty. It should be noted that hyphenated words count as a single word but contractions are invalid responses.

- **Sentence completion**: These questions typically assess the test taker's ability to understand cause and effect relationships and necessitate completing gaps in a sentence or set of sentences that summarize material from the listening clip. Again, a strict word limit will guide the response.

- **Short-answer**: In this task, the ability of the test taker to listen for and correctly identify specific details or facts such as locations, times, or prices is assessed. He or she is asked to list two to three points within the allocated word limit. Again, it is crucial for test takers to carefully read the instructions regarding the word limit; failure to adhere to the guidelines will penalize one's score.

It should be noted that not all of the speakers in the audio recordings in the Listening section may speak with native North American English accents. Test takers may encounter English speakers with native accents from the United Kingdom, New Zealand, and Australia.

ETS test administrators model the IELTS™ Listening section exercises after typical classroom lectures, discussions, or common administrative tasks that test takers will encounter in real-world settings long after passing the IELTS™. Lecture topics pull from a variety of academic disciplines in the arts and sciences, such as history, psychology, earth science, economics, and sociology. Some lecture exercises will be delivered by a single speaker, or they may feature several speakers in a classroom discussion format, often between the instructor and a handful of students. For example, the instructor may give a short lecture about architecture and then pause to call on a couple of students to answer questions pertaining to the material just presented, or a student may ask the instructor a clarifying question. After the instructor answers the student's question, he or she may continue with the lecture or segue into an organic conversation that deviates from the original lecture topic but more fully answers the student's question.

The conversations revolve around typical interactions encountered in daily life or around a university setting between a variety of individuals such as coaches, students, secretaries, administrators, and friends. Academic topics may include conversations about registering for classes, purchasing textbooks, asking for directions or locating buildings around campus, meeting a roommate, receiving feedback on an assignment, and asking for academic support, among many others. The daily life topics can include any sort of everyday activity or context such as grocery shopping, visiting a friend, organizing an event, seeing a doctor, or getting a car repaired. The speech in the conversations is meant to sound natural and duplicate that which normally occurs between people, including imperfections and pauses. Characters may stumble over their words or even use the wrong word sometimes; in the questions that follow the recording, test takers may be asked to point out these errors.

Test takers are allowed to listen to each exercise only one time, but they are encouraged to take notes while they listen. They can refer to these notes that follow the clip. If headsets are provided, they will have adjustable volume that test takers can experiment with prior to listening to the scored exercises. Some centers use sound systems with speakers for the Listening section of the exam.

Test takers often find the Listening section daunting, particularly because exercises can only be played once. However, the following are a couple of helpful strategies that successful test takers employ to achieve high scores in this section:

- **Skim**: Test takers are advised to quickly look over the questions prior to listening to get a sense of what to listen for. During the recording, test takers can glance at the next question in line, essentially looking at two questions at once, because questions fall in the order in which they will be delivered in the recording. This will keep the listener one step ahead so he or she hopefully will not miss any answers.

- **Take notes**: Test takers can, and should, take notes while they listen to the recording to refer to while answering questions. While it is most important to devote attention towards critical listening, jotting down a few key points or details that seem important can help jog one's memory after the recording is over and the questions are presented. Some questions ask very specific information and this is where careful listening to details and a couple of key notes can be quite helpful. For example, from a conversation between two roommates buying course textbooks at the campus store, test takers may be asked to recall the specific subjects for which one speaker was buying books.

- **Practice**: The importance of practice cannot be overstated. Successful test takers listen to spoken English every chance they get and try to understand the main points, supporting details, and the emotions and attitudes of the speakers. There are a variety of media that present listening opportunities from television programs and movies to podcasts and audio books. In-person opportunities include class lectures, conversations with peers and friends, interactions with customer service agents, among others. While formal questions aren't presented after most listening opportunities, candidates can assess their understanding by listening to recordings several times or asking speakers of in-person conversations clarifying questions to verify understanding.

- **Listen for verbal cues**: Listeners can gather clues by appreciating the verbal cues from the recordings. Word emphasis, tone of voice, pauses interjected for effect, and changes in voice inflection can communicate implicit information such as the speaker's emotion (surprise, worry, frustration, etc.) or emphasize that something important is about to happen. Again, understanding these nuances in spoken language will help test takers to more fully grasp the meaning of the conversation or lecture in the recordings.

- **Predict**: While difficult, it can be useful to try and predict what the speakers will say by following along in the conversation. It is also possible to try and predict what the questions will ask, based on details in the conversation. For example, if a speaker starts explaining the steps needed to register for classes, it is likely that this will appear in a question, which can signal to the test taker that it's a good idea to start jotting down notes.

- **Guess**: Each question is worth one point and test takers are not penalized for incorrect answers, so it is better to guess than to leave a question unanswered. It is also recommended that test takers skip the questions that they do not know the answers to and simply move on to the next question without dwelling on the information they did not catch. Because the questions will be addressed in order during the recording, if test takers note the clip addressing a later question, they can be assured that they have missed the answer and should move down the list of questions to the next one. At the end of the recording, test takers can quickly circle back and try to fill in any blank responses with an educated guess.

- **Check your work**: Spelling and grammar count, so responses should be checked for errors before the section is up. Even if a test taker is unsure of a spelling, it is better to try and sound the word out and make an educated guess than leave the answer blank. Partial credit is awarded for correct answers that are just misspelled, while no credit is given for blank responses. Entirely wrong answers are not penalized.

Reading

The Reading section is one of the two sections that is slightly different between the two versions of the IELTS™. For both tests, the Reading section is 60 minutes and contains three sections with a total of 40 questions. The reading exercises test skills such as identifying the theme, main idea, language usage, or supporting details; understanding logical arguments or the author's opinion, attitude, and purpose; or the ability to draw conclusions, inferences, or relationships among facts and ideas in the texts.

In the Academic test, each text section is one long passage of 2,150–2,750 words taken from various books, newspapers, journals, or magazines. They may be descriptive, factual, argumentative, or analytical, and while test takers do not need prior knowledge on the particular subject of a given passage, the text selections are designed to assess the test taker's ability to understand university-level academic texts. Texts may be pulled from any number of subjects such as biology, sociology, business, and literature, but again, test takers do not need prior experience or knowledge of the subject to answer the questions successfully; all necessary information is contained within the passages themselves. The test taker only needs to demonstrate their ability to comprehend academic texts, rather than convey an advanced understanding of the specific subject matter. Texts may contain graphic materials such as diagrams, graphs, or illustrations. Glossaries are provided when texts contain technical jargon or specific vocabulary.

For the General Training exam, the texts tend to be less formal and are pulled from materials that one would encounter in everyday life such as books, magazines, newspapers, memos, manuals, advertisements, and company policies. On the General Training exam's Reading test, there are three sections. Section 1, "social survival," contains two or three short texts—often from memos, schedules, advertisements, and notices—that are relevant to basic linguistic survival in English-speaking contexts. There are two texts in Section 2, "workplace survival" that focus on workplace texts like job descriptions, contracts, and employment materials. In Section 3, "general reading," there is one long descriptive or instructional text with a more complex structure, often drawn from daily life texts like newspapers, journals, books, or public notifications.

In both IELTS™ test iterations, the Reading sections will contain the following varied task types:

- **Multiple-choice**: These questions assess a variety of reading skills, ranging from understanding the overall main topic or opinion to grasping the specific details in the text. Some questions may ask test takers to complete the sentence while others are fully stated questions with related answer options. Test takers should carefully read the instructions for each question, as some will involve selecting one correct response, while others require choosing two or more best responses.

- **Identifying information**: Used mostly with factual texts, in this task, test takers are provided with several statements and asked to determine whether the given statements agree with the information provided only in the text and not from any prior knowledge. Test takers are to write "true" if the information was in fact stated in the passage, "false" if the statement contradicts what was presented in the passage, or "not given" if the statement's content was not covered in the text.

- **Identifying writer's views/claims**: As in the "identifying information task," test takers are provided with several statements and asked to determine and write "yes," "no," or "not given" in regard to whether the given statements agree with the views and claims of the text's writer.
- **Matching information**: The texts provided on the exam have lettered paragraphs or sections. In this task, test takers must use this identifying information to locate and pull out specific parts of the text such as a word's meaning, a description, a reason or cause, a comparison, or an effect. The letter denoting the paragraph or section that contains the appropriate information would serve as the letter for the answer. It should be noted that in these tasks, not all paragraphs may be used and one paragraph may contain the answer for multiple questions, in which case the letter ascribed to that section would be used more than once on the answer sheet.
- **Matching headings**: Compared with the "matching information" task (which tends to focus on specific details, language use, or explanations), the "matching headings" task generally assesses one's understanding of the overall theme, topic, main idea, or argument in the passage. In this exercise, a list of headings with lower-case Roman numerals is provided that each refer to the main idea of one of the paragraphs or sections (denoted with alphabetized letters) of the text. Test takers are tasked to match the heading to the correct text sections, while considering that some headings will not be used because there are more headings provided than text sections and some paragraphs may not be included in the assigned questions.
- **Matching features**: This exercise assesses one's ability to recognize relationships and connections between facts or opinions and theories in a passage. It requires skill in skimming to locate information, careful reading for detail, reasoning to understand connections, and logical thinking to accurately link various ideas or thoughts together. The task usually necessitates matching pieces of information or a set of statements or ideas to a list of options from the text identified by letters. The instructions should be read carefully because this task type may take on several different forms. For example, a question may ask test takers to use the information in the passage to match different outcomes from a research study with the different experimental groups in the study. However, some of the options for outcomes may apply to more than one group and be used numerous times, while others may be distractions that are not to be used.
- **Matching sentence endings**: Like the multiple-choice questions, these questions address the material in the order in which it appears in the passage and require skill in scanning for specific details. Each question of this type will provide several sentence stems or first clauses, and test takers must use the passage information to match the correct ending from the provided list of options, bearing in mind that not all options will be used as there are more ending choices than sentence stems.
- **Sentence completion**: It is prudent for test takers to take great care when reading the instructions for sentence completion tasks because the question will state a specific word limit that must be strictly followed or the response will be penalized. Test takers must complete the sentence using just the allotted number of words, such as "one word only" or "no more than three words and a number." As in the Listening section, hyphenated words count as one word, numbers can be spelled out or represented by their figure, and contractions are not to be used. These questions also are presented in the order in which their answers appear in the text.

- **Summary, note, table, flow-chart completion**: Test takers must complete a partial summary, table, or flow-chart that is presented by using information from the text. This question type is used especially frequently with descriptive texts and not only assesses text comprehension and the ability to connect ideas, but also one's understanding language usage and grammar, by sometimes asking for answers to be of specific parts of speech (nouns, adjectives, etc.). There may be sentences to connect in summary form, or boxes and cells to fill in from a table or sequence of events. The content will somehow organize, summarize, or paraphrase part or all of the passage, but more commonly they pull material from a particular section of the text. It is important to note that the correct answers will not necessarily occur in the same order as they appeared in the text. In some cases, a word bank from which test takers should select their answers is provided, while other times, test takers must simply scan the passage and choose the designated number of words or phrases from the passage and use those to fill in the blanks.

- **Diagram label completion**: Test takers are presented with a diagram that relates to a description of something in the text with various blank labels that must be completed with a certain number of words. Diagrams can be of a variety of types, but often are parts of a building, machine, or other descriptive element that can take on a pictorial representation.

- **Short-answer**: Usually these are reserved for factual passages, and require test takers to write a word, phrase, or number answers on their answer sheets.

For either exam, test takers should be prepared to critically analyze the point of view and structure of the passage, as there are often multiple perspectives presented, and typically at least one question per passage addresses the organizational structure of the reading exercise. The information in the following sections should be used to review salient features of different texts and to improve one's reading comprehension and critical analysis skills. While some sections may pertain more to one test version or the other (Academic Test versus the General Training), it is recommended that all test takers review this section in its entirety to optimize success on the Reading section. Following the information in this section, there is a full-length practice test for each of the two exam versions.

Analysis of History/Social Studies Excerpts

The IELTS™ Reading section may include historically-based excerpts. The test may also include one or more passages from social sciences such as economics, psychology, or sociology.

For these types of questions, the test taker will need to utilize all the reading comprehension skills discussed below, but mastery of further skills will help. This section addresses those skills.

Comprehending Test Questions Prior to Reading

While preparing for a historical passage on a standardized test, first read the test questions, and then quickly scan the test answers prior to reading the passage itself. Notice there is a difference between the terms **read** and **scan.** Reading involves full concentration while addressing every word. Scanning involves quickly glancing at text in chunks, noting important dates, words, and ideas along the way. Reading the test questions will help the test taker know what information to focus on in the historical passage. Scanning answers will help the test taker focus on possible answer options while reading the passage.

When reading standardized test questions that address historical passages, be sure to clearly understand what each question is asking. Is a question asking about vocabulary? Is another asking for the test taker to find a specific historical fact? Do any of the questions require the test taker to draw conclusions, identify an author's topic, tone, or position? Knowing what content to address will help the test taker focus on the information they will be asked about later. However, the test taker should approach this reading comprehension technique with some caution. It is tempting to only look for the right answers within any given passage. However, do not put on "reading blinders" and ignore all other information presented in a passage. It is important to fully read every passage and not just scan it. Strictly looking for what may be the right answers to test questions can cause the test taker to ignore important contextual clues that actually require critical thinking in order to identify correct answers. Scanning a passage for what appears to be wrong answers can have a similar result.

When reading the test questions prior to tackling a historical passage, be sure to understand what skills the test is assessing, and then fully read the related passage with those skills in mind. Focus on every word in both the test questions and the passage itself. Read with a critical eye and a logical mind.

Reading for Factual Information

Standardized test questions that ask for factual information are usually straightforward. These types of questions will either ask the test taker to confirm a fact by choosing a correct answer, or to select a correct answer based on a negative fact question.

For example, the test taker may encounter a passage from Lincoln's Gettysburg Address. A corresponding test question may ask the following:

> Which war is Abraham Lincoln referring to in the following passage?: "Now we are engaged in a great civil war, testing whether that nation, or any nation so conceived and so dedicated, can long endure."

This type of question is asking the test taker to confirm a simple fact. Given options such as World War I, the War of Spanish Succession, World War II, and the American Civil War, the test taker should be able to correctly identify the American Civil War based on the words "civil war" within the passage itself, and, hopefully, through general knowledge. In this case, reading the test question and scanning answer options ahead of reading the Gettysburg Address would help quickly identify the correct answer. Similarly, a test taker may be asked to confirm a historical fact based on a negative fact question. For example, a passage's corresponding test question may ask the following:

> Which option is incorrect based on the above passage?

Given a variety of choices speaking about which war Abraham Lincoln was addressing, the test taker would need to eliminate all correct answers pertaining to the American Civil War and choose the answer choice referencing a different war. In other words, the correct answer is the one that contradicts the information in the passage.

It is important to remember that reading for factual information is straightforward. The test taker must distinguish fact from bias. Factual statements can be proven or disproven independent of the author and from a variety of other sources. Remember, successfully answering questions regarding factual information may require the test taker to re-read the passage, as these types of questions test for attention to detail.

Reading for Tone, Message, and Effect

The Reading section does not just address a test taker's ability to find facts within a reading passage; it also determines a reader's ability to determine an author's viewpoint through the use of tone, message, and overall effect. This type of reading comprehension requires inference skills, deductive reasoning skills, the ability to draw logical conclusions, and overall critical thinking skills. Reading for factual information is straightforward. Reading for an author's tone, message, and overall effect is not. It's key to read carefully when asked test questions that address a test taker's ability to identify and analyze these writing devices. These are not questions that can be easily answered by quickly scanning for the right information.

Tone

An author's **tone** is the use of particular words, phrases, and writing style to convey an overall meaning. Tone expresses the author's attitude towards a particular topic. For example, a historical reading passage may begin like the following:

> The presidential election of 1960 ushered in a new era, a new Camelot, a new phase of forward thinking in U.S. politics that embraced brash action and unrest and responded with admirable leadership.

From this opening statement, a reader can draw some conclusions about the author's attitude towards President John F. Kennedy. Furthermore, the reader can make additional, educated guesses about the state of the Union during the 1960 presidential election. By close reading, the test taker can determine that the repeated use of the word *new* and words such as *admirable leadership* indicate the author's tone of admiration regarding President Kennedy's boldness. In addition, the author assesses that the era during President Kennedy's administration was problematic through the use of the words *brash action* and *unrest.* Therefore, if a test taker encountered a test question asking about the author's use of tone and their assessment of the Kennedy administration, the test taker should be able to identify an answer indicating admiration. Similarly, if asked about the state of the Union during the 1960s, a test taker should be able to correctly identify an answer indicating political unrest.

When identifying an author's tone, the following list of words may be helpful. This is not an inclusive list. Generally, parts of speech that indicate attitude will also indicate tone:

- Comical
- Angry
- Ambivalent
- Scary
- Lyrical
- Matter-of-fact
- Judgmental
- Sarcastic
- Malicious
- Objective
- Pessimistic
- Patronizing
- Gloomy
- Instructional

- Satirical
- Formal
- Casual

Message

An author's **message** is the same as the overall meaning of a passage. It is the main idea, or the main concept the author wishes to convey. An author's message may be stated outright, or it may be implied. Regardless, the test taker will need to use careful reading skills to identify an author's message or purpose.

Often, the message of a particular passage can be determined by thinking about why the author wrote the information. Many historical passages are written to inform and to teach readers established, factual information. However, many historical works are also written to convey biased ideas to readers. Gleaning bias from an author's message in a historical passage can be difficult, especially if the reader is presented with a variety of established facts as well. Readers tend to accept historical writing as factual. This is not always the case. Any discerning reader who has tackled historical information on topics such as United States political party agendas can attest that two or more works on the same topic may have completely different messages supporting or refuting the value of the identical policies.

Therefore, it is important to critically assess an author's message separate from factual information. One author, for example, may point to the rise of unorthodox political candidates in an election year based on the failures of the political party in office while another may point to the rise of the same candidates in the same election year based on the current party's successes. The historical facts of what has occurred leading up to an election year are not in refute. Labeling those facts as a failure or a success is a bias within an author's overall message, as is excluding factual information in order to further a particular point. In a standardized testing situation, a reader must be able to critically assess what the author is trying to say separate from the historical facts that surround their message.

Using the example of Lincoln's Gettysburg Address, a test question may ask the following:

> What message is the author trying to convey through this address?

Then they will ask the test taker to select an answer that best expresses Lincoln's message to his audience. Based on the options given, a test taker should be able to select the answer expressing the idea that Lincoln's audience should recognize the efforts of those who died in the war as a sacrifice to preserving human equality and self-government.

Effect

An author may want to challenge a reader's intellect, inspire imagination, or spur emotion. An author may present information to appeal to a physical, aesthetic, or transformational sense. Take the following text as an example:

> In 1963, Martin Luther King stated "I have a dream." The gathering at the Lincoln Memorial was the beginning of the Civil Rights movement and, with its reference to the Emancipation Proclamation, Dr. King's words electrified those who wanted freedom and equality while rising from hatred and slavery. It was the beginning of radical change.

The test taker may be asked about the effect this statement might have on King's audience. Through careful reading of the passage, the test taker should be able to choose an answer that best identifies an effect of grabbing the audience's attention. The historical facts are in place: King made the speech in 1963 at the Lincoln Memorial, kicked off the civil rights movement, and referenced the Emancipation Proclamation. The words *electrified* and *radical change* indicate the effect the author wants the reader to understand as a result of King's speech. In this historical passage, facts are facts. However, the author's message goes beyond the facts to indicate the effect the message had on the audience and, in addition, the effect the event should have on the reader.

When reading historical passages, the test taker should perform due diligence in their awareness of the test questions and answers up front. From there, the test taker should carefully, and critically, read all historical excerpts with an eye for detail, tone, message (biased or unbiased), and effect. Being able to synthesize these skills will result in success in a standardized testing situation.

Analysis of Science Excerpts

The Reading section may include passages that address the fundamental concepts of Earth science, biology, chemistry, or other sciences. Again, prior knowledge of these subjects is not necessary to determine correct test answers; instead, the test taker's ability to comprehend the passages is key to success. When reading scientific excerpts, the test taker must be able to examine quantitative information, identify hypotheses, interpret data, and consider implications of the material they are presented with. It is helpful, at this point, to reference the above section on comprehending test questions prior to reading. The same rules apply: read questions and scan questions, along with their answers, prior to fully reading a passage. Be informed prior to approaching a scientific text. A test taker should know what they will be asked and how to apply their reading skills. In this section of the test, it is also likely that a test taker will encounter graphs and charts to assess their ability to interpret scientific data with an appropriate conclusion. This section may use the identification of hypotheses, the reading and examination of data, and the interpretation of data representation passages to determine the skill levels of test takers in the comprehension of scientific data.

Examine Hypotheses

When presented with fundamental, scientific concepts, it is important to read for understanding. The most basic skill in achieving this literacy is to understand the concept of hypothesis and, moreover, to be able to identify it in a particular passage. A **hypothesis** is a proposed idea that needs further investigation in order to be proven true or false. While it can be considered an educated guess, a hypothesis goes more in depth in its attempt to explain something that is not currently accepted within scientific theory. It requires further experimentation and data gathering to test its validity and is subject to change, based on scientifically conducted test results. Being able to read a science passage and understand its main purpose, including any hypotheses, helps the test taker understand data-driven evidence. It helps the test taker to be able to correctly answer questions about the science excerpt they are asked to read.

When reading to identify a hypothesis, a test taker should ask, "What is the passage trying to establish? What is the passage's main idea? What evidence does the passage contain that either supports or refutes this idea?" Asking oneself these questions will help identify a hypothesis. Additionally, hypotheses are logical statements that are testable and use very precise language.

Review the following hypothesis example:

> Consuming excess sugar in the form of beverages has a greater impact on childhood obesity and subsequent weight gain than excessive sugar from food.

While this is likely a true statement, it is still only a conceptual idea in a text passage regarding how sugar consumption affects childhood obesity, unless the passage also contains tested data that either proves or disproves the statement. A test taker could expect the rest of the passage to cite data proving that children who drink empty calories gain more weight and are more likely to be obese than children who eat sugary snacks.

A hypothesis goes further in that, given its ability to be proven or disproven, it may result in further hypotheses that require extended research. For example, the hypothesis regarding sugar consumption in drinks, after undergoing rigorous testing, may lead scientists to state another hypothesis such as the following:

> Consuming excess sugar in the form of beverages as opposed to food items is a habit found in mostly sedentary children.

This new, working hypothesis further focuses not just on the source of an excess of calories, but tries an "educated guess" that empty caloric intake has a direct, subsequent impact on physical behavior.

When reading a science passage to determine its hypothesis, a test taker should look for a concept that attempts to explain a phenomenon, is testable, is logical, is precisely worded, and yields data-driven results. The test taker should scan the presented passage for any word or data-driven clues that will help identify the hypothesis, and then be able to correctly answer test questions regarding the hypothesis by using their critical thinking skills.

Identify Passage Characteristics

Writing can be classified under four passage types: narrative, expository, descriptive (sometimes called technical), and persuasive. Though these types are not mutually exclusive, one form tends to dominate the rest. By recognizing the *type* of passage you're reading, you gain insight into *how* you should read. If you're reading a narrative, you can assume the author intends to entertain, which means you may skim the text without losing meaning. A technical document might require a close read because skimming the passage might cause the reader to miss salient details.

1. **Narrative writing**, at its core, is the art of storytelling. For a narrative to exist, certain elements must be present. First, it must have characters. While many characters are human, characters could be defined as anything that thinks, acts, and talks like a human. For example, many recent movies, such as *Lord of the Rings* and *The Chronicles of Narnia*, include animals, fantastical creatures, and even trees that behave like humans. Second, it must have a plot or sequence of events. Typically, those events follow a standard plot diagram, but recent trends start *in medias res* or in the middle (near the climax). In this instance, foreshadowing and flashbacks often fill in plot details. Finally, along with characters and a plot, there must also be conflict. Conflict is usually divided into two types: internal and external. Internal conflict indicates the character is in turmoil and is presented through the character's thoughts. External conflicts are visible. Types of external conflict include a person versus nature, another person, or society.

2. **Expository writing** is detached and to the point. Since expository writing is designed to instruct or inform, it usually involves directions and steps written in second person ("you" voice) and lacks any persuasive or narrative elements. Sequence words such as *first, second,* and *third*, or *in the first place, secondly*, and *lastly* are often given to add fluency and cohesion. Common examples of expository writing include instructor's lessons, cookbook recipes, and repair manuals.

3. Due to its empirical nature, **technical writing** is filled with steps, charts, graphs, data, and statistics. The goal of technical writing is to advance understanding in a field through the scientific method. Experts such as teachers, doctors, or mechanics use words unique to the profession in which they operate. These words, which often incorporate acronyms, are called **jargon**. Technical writing is a type of expository writing but is not meant to be understood by the general public. Instead, technical writers assume readers have received a formal education in a particular field of study and need no explanation as to what the jargon means. Imagine a doctor trying to understand a diagnostic reading for a car or a mechanic trying to interpret lab results. Only professionals with proper training will fully comprehend the text.

4. **Persuasive writing** is designed to change opinions and attitudes. The topic, stance, and arguments are found in the thesis, positioned near the end of the introduction. Later supporting paragraphs offer relevant quotations, paraphrases, and summaries from primary or secondary sources, which are then interpreted, analyzed, and evaluated. The goal of persuasive writers is not to stack quotes but to develop original ideas by using sources as a starting point. Good persuasive writing makes powerful arguments with valid sources and thoughtful analysis. Poor persuasive writing is riddled with bias and logical fallacies. Sometimes logical and illogical arguments are sandwiched together in the same piece. Therefore, readers should display skepticism when reading persuasive arguments.

Non-Fiction

Nonfiction works are best characterized by their subject matter, which must be factual and real, describing true life experiences. There are several common types of literary non-fiction.

Biography
A **biography** is a work written about a real person (historical or currently living). It involves factual accounts of the person's life, often in a re-telling of those events based on available, researched factual information. The re-telling and dialogue, especially if related within quotes, must be accurate and reflect reliable sources. A biography reflects the time and place in which the person lived, with the goal of creating an understanding of the person and their human experience. Examples of well-known biographies include *The Life of Samuel Johnson* by James Boswell and *Steve Jobs* by Walter Isaacson.

Autobiography
An **autobiography** is a factual account of a person's life written by that person. It may contain some or all of the same elements as a biography, but the author is the subject matter. An autobiography will be told in first person narrative. Examples of well-known autobiographies in literature include *Night* by Elie Wiesel and *Margaret Thatcher: The Autobiography* by Margaret Thatcher.

Memoir
A **memoir** is a historical account of a person's life and experiences written by one who has personal, intimate knowledge of the information. The line between memoir, autobiography, and biography is often muddled, but generally speaking, a memoir covers a specific timeline of events as opposed to the

other forms of nonfiction. A memoir is less all-encompassing. It is also less formal in tone and tends to focus on the emotional aspect of the presented timeline of events. Some examples of memoirs in literature include *Angela's Ashes* by Frank McCourt and *All Creatures Great and Small* by James Herriot.

Journalism
Some forms of **journalism** can fall into the category of literary non-fiction—e.g., travel writing, nature writing, sports writing, the interview, and sometimes, the essay. Some examples include Elizabeth Kolbert's "The Lost World, in the Annals of Extinction series for *The New Yorker* and Gary Smith's "Ali and His Entourage" for *Sports Illustrated*.'

Informational Texts
Informational texts are a category of texts within the genre of nonfiction. Their intent is to inform, and while they do convey a point of view and may include literary devices, they do not utilize other literary elements, such as characters or plot. An informational text also reflects a **thesis**—an implicit or explicit statement of the text's intent and/or a **main idea**—the overarching focus and/or purpose of the text, generally implied. Some examples of informational texts are informative articles, instructional/how-to texts, factual reports, reference texts, and self-help texts.

Finding Evidence in a Passage

In order to identify factual information within one or more text passages, begin by looking for statements of fact. Factual statements can be either true or false. Identifying factual statements as opposed to opinion statements is important in demonstrating full command of evidence in reading. For example, the statement *The temperature outside was unbearably hot* may seem like a fact; however, it's not. While anyone can point to a temperature gauge as factual evidence, the statement itself reflects only an opinion. Some people may find the temperature unbearably hot. Others may find it comfortably warm. Thus, the sentence, *The temperature outside was unbearably hot,* reflects the opinion of the author who found it unbearable. If the text passage followed up the sentence with atmospheric conditions indicating heat indices above 140 degrees Fahrenheit, then the reader knows there is factual information that supports the author's assertion of *unbearably hot*.

In looking for information that can be proven or disproven, it's helpful to scan for dates, numbers, timelines, equations, statistics, and other similar data within any given text passage. These types of indicators will point to proven particulars. For example, the statement, *The temperature outside was unbearably hot on that summer day, July 10, 1913,* most likely indicates factual information, even if the reader is unaware that this is the hottest day on record in the United States. Be careful when reading biased words from an author. Biased words indicate opinion, as opposed to fact.

The following list contains a sampling of common biased words:

- Good/bad
- Great/greatest
- Better/best/worst
- Amazing
- Terrible/bad/awful
- Beautiful/handsome/ugly
- More/most
- Exciting/dull/boring

- Favorite
- Very
- Probably/should/seem/possibly

Remember, most of what is written is actually opinion or carefully worded information that seems like fact when it isn't. To say, *duplicating DNA results is not cost-effective* sounds like it could be a scientific fact, but it isn't. Factual information can be verified through independent sources.

The simplest type of test question may provide a text passage, then ask the test taker to distinguish the correct factual supporting statement that best answers the corresponding question on the test. However, be aware that most questions may ask the test taker to read more than one text passage and identify which answer best supports an author's topic. While the ability to identify factual information is critical, these types of questions require the test taker to identify chunks of details, and then relate them to one another.

Displaying Analytical Thinking Skills

Analytical thinking involves being able to break down visual information into manageable portions in order to solve complex problems or process difficult concepts. This skill encompasses all aspects of command of evidence in reading comprehension.

A reader can approach analytical thinking in a series of steps. First, when approaching visual material, a reader should identify an author's thought process. Is the line of reasoning clear from the presented passage, or does it require inference and coming to a conclusion independent of the author? Next, a reader should evaluate the author's line of reasoning to determine if the logic is sound. Look for evidentiary clues and cited sources. Do these hold up under the author's argument? Third, look for bias. Bias includes generalized, emotional statements that will not hold up under scrutiny, as they are not based on fact. From there, a reader should ask if the presented evidence is trustworthy. Are the facts cited from reliable sources? Are they current? Is there any new factual information that has come to light since the passage was written that renders the argument useless? Next, a reader should carefully think about information that opposes the author's view. Do the author's arguments guide the reader to identical thoughts, or is there room for sound arguments? Finally, a reader should always be able to identify an author's conclusion and be able to weigh its effectiveness.

The ability to display analytical thinking skills while reading is key in any standardized testing situation. Test takers should be able to critically evaluate the information provided, and then answer questions related to content by using the steps above.

Making Inferences

Simply put, an inference is an educated guess drawn from evidence, logic, and reasoning. The key to making inferences is identifying clues within a passage, and then using common sense to arrive at a reasonable conclusion. Consider it "reading between the lines."

One way to make an inference is to look for main topics. When doing so, pay particular attention to any titles, headlines, or opening statements made by the author. Topic sentences or repetitive ideas can be clues in gleaning inferred ideas. For example, if a passage contains the phrase *DNA testing, while some consider it infallible, is an inherently flawed technique,* the test taker can infer the rest of the passage will contain information that points to DNA testing's fallibility.

The test taker may be asked to make an inference based on prior knowledge but may also be asked to make predictions based on new ideas. For example, the test taker may have no prior knowledge of DNA other than its genetic property to replicate. However, if the reader is given passages on the flaws of DNA testing with enough factual evidence, the test taker may arrive at the inferred conclusion that the author does not support the infallibility of DNA testing in all identification cases.

When making inferences, it is important to remember that the critical thinking process involved must be fluid and open to change. While a reader may infer an idea from a main topic, general statement, or other clues, they must be open to receiving new information within a particular passage. New ideas presented by an author may require the test taker to alter an inference. Similarly, when asked questions that require making an inference, it's important to read the entire test passage and all of the answer options. Often, a test taker will need to refine a general inference based on new ideas that may be presented within the test itself.

Reading Strategies

A **reading strategy** is the way a reader interacts with text in order to understand its meaning. It is a skill set that a reader brings to the reading. It employs a reader's ability to use prior knowledge when addressing literature and utilizes a set of methods in order to analyze text. A reading strategy is not simply tackling a text passage as it appears. It involves a more complex system of planning and thought during the reading experience. Current research indicates that readers who utilize strategies and a variety of critical reading skills are better thinkers who glean more interpretive information from their reading. Consequently, they are more successful in their overall comprehension.

Pre-Reading Strategies

Pre-reading strategies are important, yet often overlooked. Non-critical readers will often begin reading without taking the time to review factors that will help them understand the text. Skipping pre-reading strategies may result in a reader having to re-address a text passage more times than is necessary. Some pre-reading strategies include the following:

- Previewing the text for clues
- Skimming the text for content
- Scanning for unfamiliar words in context
- Formulating questions on sight
- Recognizing needed prior knowledge

Before reading a passage, a reader can enhance their ability to comprehend material by **previewing the text for clues**. This may mean making careful note of any titles, headings, graphics, notes, introductions, important summaries, and conclusions. It can involve a reader making physical notes regarding these elements or highlighting anything they think is important before reading. Often, a reader will be able to gain information just from these elements alone. Of course, close reading is required in order to fill in the details. A reader needs to be able to ask what they are reading about and what a passage is trying to say. The answers to these general questions can often be answered in previewing the text itself.

It's helpful to use pre-reading clues to determine the main idea and organization. First, any titles, sub-headings, and chapter headings should be read, and the test taker should make note of the author's credentials if any are listed. It's important to deduce what these clues may indicate as it pertains to the focus of the text and how it's organized.

During pre-reading, readers should also take special note of how text features contribute to the central idea or thesis of the passage. Is there an index? Is there a glossary? What headings, footnotes, or other visuals are included and how do they relate to the details within the passage? Again, this is where any pre-reading notes come in handy, since a test taker should be able to relate supporting details to these textual features.

Next, a reader should **skim** the text for general ideas and content. This technique does not involve close reading; rather, it involves looking for important words within the passage itself. These words may have something to do with the author's theme. They may have to do with structure—for example, words such as *first, next, therefore*, and *last*. Skimming helps a reader understand the overall structure of a passage and, in turn, this helps them understand the author's theme or message.

From there, a reader should quickly **scan** the text for any unfamiliar words. When reading a print text, highlighting these words or making other marginal notation is helpful when going back to read text critically. A reader should look at the words surrounding any unfamiliar ones to see what contextual clues unfamiliar words carry. Being able to define unfamiliar terms through contextual meaning is a critical skill in reading comprehension.

A reader should also **formulate any questions** they might have before conducting close reading. Questions such as "What is the author trying to tell me?" or "Is the author trying to persuade my thinking?" are important to a reader's ability to engage critically with the text. Questions will focus a reader's attention on what is important in terms of ideas and supporting details.

Last, a reader should recognize that authors assume readers bring a prior knowledge set to the reading experience. Not all readers have the same experience, but authors seek to communicate with their readers. In turn, readers should strive to interact with the author of a particular passage by asking themselves what the passage demands they know during reading. If a passage is informational in nature, a reader should ask "What do I know about this topic from other experiences I've had or other works I've read?" If a reader can relate to the content, they will better understand it.

All of the above pre-reading strategies will help the reader prepare for a closer reading experience. They will engage a reader in active interaction with the text by helping to focus the reader's full attention on the details that they will encounter during the next round or two of critical, closer reading.

Strategies During Reading

After pre-reading, a test taker can employ a variety of other reading strategies while conducting one or more closer readings. These strategies include the following:

- Inferring the unspoken/unwritten text
- Clarifying during a close read
- Questioning during a close read
- Organizing the main ideas and supporting details
- Summarizing the text effectively

Inferring the unspoken or unwritten text demands the reader read between the lines in terms of an author's intent or message. The strategy asks that a reader not take everything he or she reads at face value, but instead, he or she will determine what the author is trying to say. A reader's ability to make inference relies on their ability to think clearly and logically about what he or she is reading. It does not ask that the reader make wild speculation or guess about the material but demands he or she be able to come to sound conclusion about the material, given the details provided and those not provided. A reader who can make logical inference from unstated text is achieving successful reading comprehension.

A reader needs to be able to **clarify** what they are reading. This strategy demands a reader think about how and what they are reading. This thinking should occur during and after the act of reading. For example, a reader may encounter one or more unfamiliar ideas during reading, then be asked to apply thoughts about those unfamiliar concepts after reading when answering test questions.

Questioning during a critical read is closely related to clarifying. A reader must be able to ask questions in general about what they are reading and about the author's supporting ideas. Questioning also involves a reader's ability to self-question. When closely reading a passage, it's not enough to simply try to understand the author. A reader must consider critical thinking questions to ensure they are comprehending intent. It's advisable, when conducting a close read, to write out margin notes and questions during the experience. These questions can be addressed later in the thinking process after reading and during the phase where a reader addresses the test questions. A reader who is successful in reading comprehension will iteratively question what they read, search text for clarification, then answer any questions that arise.

A reader should **organize** main ideas and supporting details cognitively as they read, as it will help them understand the larger structure at work. The use of quick annotations or marks to indicate what the main idea is and how the details function to support it can be helpful. Understanding the structure of a text passage is sometimes critical to answering questions about an author's approach, theme, messages, and supporting details. This strategy is most effective when reading informational or nonfiction texts. Texts that try to convince readers of a particular idea, that present a theory, or that try to explain difficult concepts are easier to understand when a reader can identify the overarching structure at work.

Post-Reading Strategies

After completing a text, a reader should be able to **summarize** the author's theme and supporting details in order to fully understand the passage. Being able to effectively restate the author's message, sub-themes, and pertinent, supporting ideas will help a reader gain an advantage when addressing standardized test questions. Employing all of these strategies will lead to fuller, more insightful reading comprehension.

Identifying Information from Printed Communications

While expository in nature, memorandums (memos) are designed to convey basic information in a specific and concise message. Memos have a heading, which includes the information *to, from, date,* and *subject,* and a body, which is either in paragraph form or bullet points that detail what was in the subject line.

Though e-mails often replace memos in the modern workplace, printed memos still have a place. For example, if a supervisor wants to relate information, such as a company-wide policy change, to a large group, posting a memo in a staff lounge or other heavily traveled area is an efficient way to do so.

Posted announcements are useful to convey information to a large group of people. Announcements, however, take on a more informal tone than a memo. Common announcement topics include items for sale, services offered, lost pets, or business openings. Since posted announcements are found in public places, like grocery or hardware stores, they include contact information, purpose, meeting times, and prices, as well as pictures, graphics, and colors to attract the reader's eye.

Classified advertisements are another useful medium to convey information to large groups. Consider using classified advertisements when you want to buy and sell items, or look for services. Classified ads are found in newspapers, or online through *Craigslist*, *eBay*, or similar websites and blogs. While newspapers rely on ads to help fund their publications and often provide only local exposure, online sites provide a statewide or even global platform, thus shipping costs are an important consideration when looking at the cost of the item.

Regardless of the medium, all advertisements offer basic information, such as the item in question, a description, picture, cost, and the seller's contact information. It may also note a willingness to negotiate on the price or offer an option to trade in lieu of a sale. As websites like *Craigslist* and *Buy/Sell/Trade* increase in popularity, more localities offer "safe zones," where purchases and trades are conducted in supervised environments.

Informational Graphics

A test taker's ability to draw conclusions from an informational graphic is a sub-skill in displaying one's command of reading evidence. Drawing conclusions requires the reader to consider all information provided in the passage, then to use logic to piece it together to form a reasonably correct resolution. In this case, a test taker must look for facts as well as opinionated statements. Both should be considered in order to arrive at a conclusion. These types of questions test one's ability to conduct logical and analytical thinking.

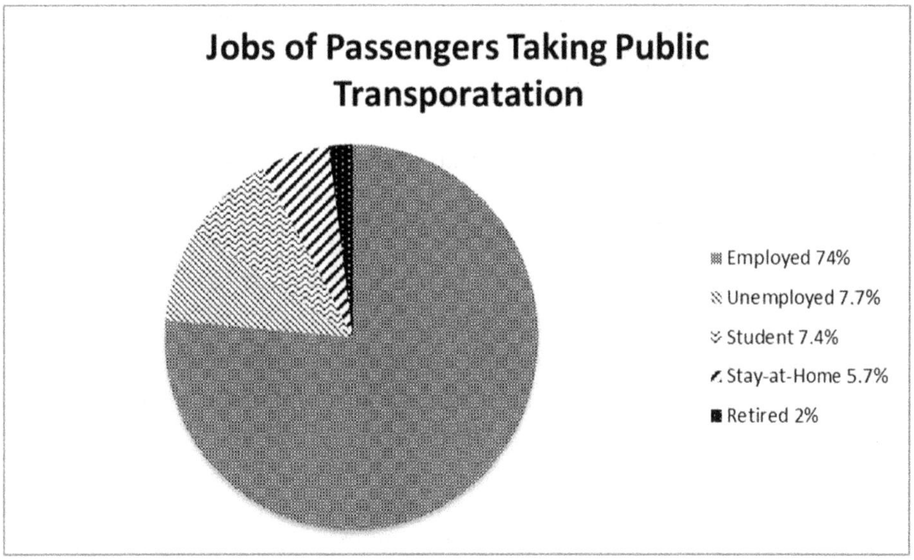

Identifying data-driven evidence in informational graphics is very similar to analyzing factual information. However, it often involves the use of graphics in order to do so. In these types of questions, the test taker will be presented with a graph, or organizational tool, and asked questions regarding the information it contains. Review the following pie chart organizing percentages of primary occupations of public transportation passengers in US cities.

This figure depicts the occupations of passengers taking public transportation in U.S. cities. A corresponding question may have the test taker study the chart, then answer a question regarding the values. For example, is the number of students relying on public transportation greater or less than the number of the unemployed? Similarly, the test may ask if people employed outside the home are less likely to use public transportation than homemakers. Note that the phrase *less likely* may weigh into the reader's choice of optional answers and that the test taker should look for additional passage data to arrive at a conclusion one way or another.

Identifying Information in an Index or Table of Contents

An index is an alphabetical listing of topics, such as people, works, or concepts that appear at the end of expository materials like textbooks, cookbooks, and repair manuals. When these key words are used in paragraphs, they sometimes appear in bold writing to indicate their importance and let the reader know that they're found in the index as well.

Index listings often discard articles like *a*, *an*, and *the*. Additionally, authors will be listed by their last names, not first. Topics may be further divided into subtopics. If you start by looking for the most basic topics first, you can quickly acquire information. For example, when looking for a cookie recipe in a cookbook, first find the word *cookie* in the index and then examine the indented list of cookie-related topics located directly beneath the original heading.

Some textbooks have multiple indexes arranged by different subjects. If, for instance, you're dealing with a weighty literature textbook, you might find one index that lists authors and another devoted to concepts. The lengthier the book, the more likely you are to find this format.

While an index is typically found at the end of a book, a table of contents is found at the beginning to help readers quickly locate information. A table of contents is arranged differently, however, because it provides a chronological listing of each chapter and a corresponding page number. Each entry may also include a description, summary statement, or objective.

When students first receive a textbook, they should take time to preview the table of contents to create a framework for mentally organizing information. By classifying the contents, the reader creates mental schemas and becomes more likely to retain the information longer.

Using Legends and Map Keys

Legends and map keys are placed on maps to identify what the symbols on the map represent. Generally, map symbols stand for things like railroads, national or state highways, and public parks. Legends and maps keys can generally be found in the bottom right corner of a map. They are necessary to avoid the needless repetition of the same information because of the large amounts of information condensed onto a map. In addition, there may be a compass rose that shows the directions of north, south, east, and west. Most maps are oriented such that the top of the map is north.

Maps also have scales, which are a type of legend or key that show relative distances between fixed points. If you were on a highway and nearly out of gas, a map's scale would help you determine if you could make it to the next town before running out of fuel.

Main Idea

It is very important to know the difference between the topic and the main idea of the text. Even though these two are similar because they both present the central point of a text, they have distinctive differences. A **topic** is the subject of the text; this can usually be described in a concise one- to two-word phrase. On the other hand, the **main idea** is more detailed and provides the author's central point of the text. It can be expressed through a complete sentence and can be found in the beginning, middle, or end of a paragraph. In most nonfiction books, the first sentence of the passage usually (but not always) states the main idea. Take a look at the passage below to review the topic versus the main idea:

Cheetahs

> Cheetahs are one of the fastest mammals on land, reaching up to 70 miles an hour over short distances. Even though cheetahs can run as fast as 70 miles an hour, they usually only have to run half that speed to catch up with their choice of prey. Cheetahs cannot maintain a fast pace over long periods of time because they will overheat their bodies. After a chase, cheetahs need to rest for approximately 30 minutes prior to eating or returning to any other activity.

In the example above, the topic of the passage is "Cheetahs" simply because that is the subject of the text. The main idea of the text is "Cheetahs are one of the fastest mammals on land but can only maintain this fast pace for short distances." While it covers the topic, it is more detailed and refers to the text in its entirety. The text continues to provide additional details called **supporting details**, which will be discussed in the next section.

Supporting Details

Supporting details help readers better develop and understand the main idea. Supporting details answer questions like *who, what, where, when, why,* and *how*. Different types of supporting details include examples, facts and statistics, anecdotes, and sensory details.

Persuasive and informative texts often use supporting details. In persuasive texts, authors attempt to make readers agree with their point of view, and supporting details are often used as "selling points." If authors make a statement, they should support the statement with evidence in order to adequately persuade readers. Informative texts use supporting details such as examples and facts to inform readers. Take another look at the previous "Cheetahs" passage to find examples of supporting details:

Cheetahs

> Cheetahs are one of the fastest mammals on land, reaching up to 70 miles an hour over short distances. Even though cheetahs can run as fast as 70 miles an hour, they usually only have to run half that speed to catch up with their choice of prey. Cheetahs cannot maintain a fast pace over long periods of time because they will overheat their bodies. After a chase, cheetahs need to rest for approximately 30 minutes prior to eating or returning to any other activity.

In the example above, supporting details include:

- Cheetahs reach up to 70 miles per hour over short distances.
- They usually only have to run half that speed to catch up with their prey.
- Cheetahs will overheat their bodies if they exert a high speed over longer distances.
- Cheetahs need to rest for 30 minutes after a chase.

Look at the diagram below (applying the cheetah example) to help determine the hierarchy of topic, main idea, and supporting details.

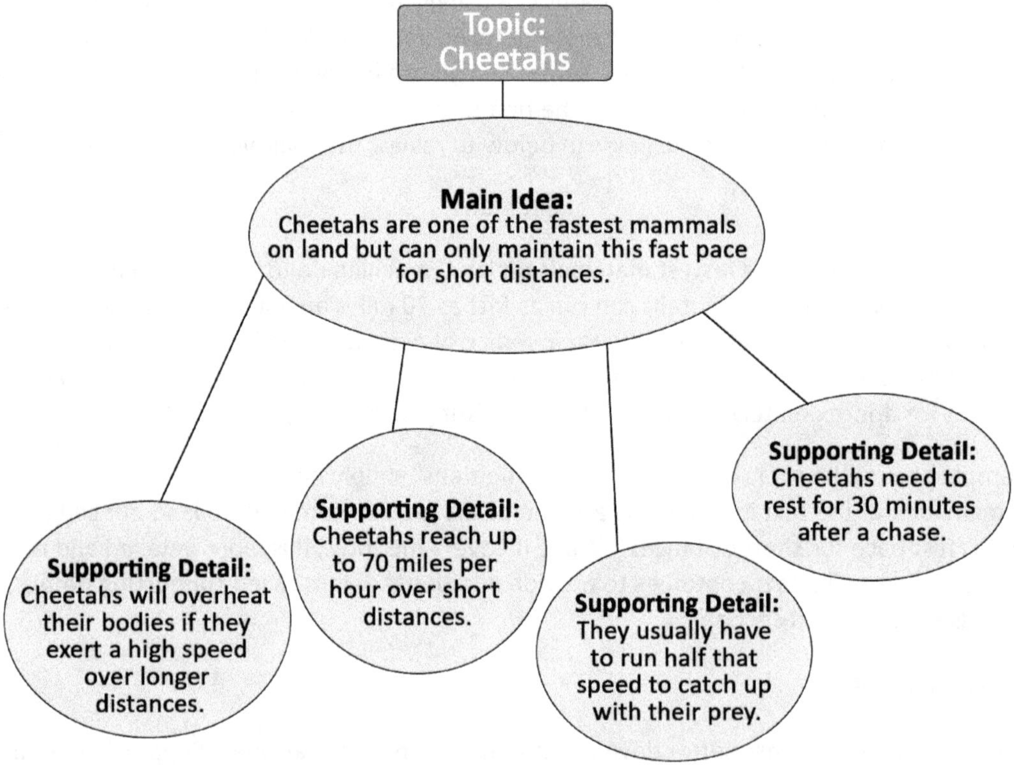

Understanding the Use of Affixes, Context, and Syntax

Affixes

Individual words are constructed from building blocks of meaning. An **affix** is an element that is added to a root or stem word that can change the word's meaning.

For example, the stem word *fix* is a verb meaning *to repair*. When the ending *–able* is added, it becomes the adjective *fixable*, meaning "capable of being repaired." Adding *un–* to the beginning changes the word to *unfixable*, meaning "incapable of being repaired." In this way, affixes attach to the word stem to create a new word and a new meaning. Knowledge of affixes can assist in deciphering the meaning of unfamiliar words.

Affixes are also related to inflection. **Inflection** is the modification of a base word to express a different grammatical or syntactical function. For example, countable nouns such as *car* and *airport* become plural with the addition of *–s* at the end: *cars* and *airports*.

Verb tense is also expressed through inflection. **Regular verbs**—those that follow a standard inflection pattern—can be changed to past tense using the affixes *–ed*, *–d*, or *–ied*, as in *cooked* and *studied*. Verbs can also be modified for continuous tenses by using *–ing*, as in *working* or *exploring*. Thus, affixes are used not only to express meaning but also to reflect a word's grammatical purpose.

A **prefix** is an affix attached to the beginning of a word. The meanings of English prefixes mainly come from Greek and Latin origins. The chart below contains a few of the most commonly used English prefixes.

Prefix	**Meaning**	**Example**
a-	Not	amoral, asymptomatic
anti-	Against	antidote, antifreeze
auto-	Self	automobile, automatic
circum-	Around	circumference, circumspect
co-, com-, con-	Together	coworker, companion
contra-	Against	contradict, contrary
de-	negation or reversal	deflate, deodorant
extra-	outside, beyond	extraterrestrial, extracurricular
in-, im-, il-, ir-	Not	impossible, irregular
inter-	Between	international, intervene
intra-	Within	intramural, intranet
mis-	Wrongly	mistake, misunderstand
mono-	One	monolith, monopoly
non-	Not	nonpartisan, nonsense
pre-	Before	preview, prediction
re-	Again	review, renew
semi-	Half	semicircle, semicolon
sub-	Under	subway, submarine
super-	Above	superhuman, superintendent
trans-	across, beyond, through	trans-Siberian, transform
un-	Not	unwelcome, unfriendly

While the addition of a prefix alters the meaning of the base word, the addition of a **suffix** may also affect a word's part of speech. For example, adding a suffix can change the noun *material* into the verb *materialize* and back to a noun again in *materialization*.

Suffix	Part of Speech	Meaning	Example
-able, -ible	adjective	having the ability to	honorable, flexible
-acy, -cy	noun	state or quality	intimacy, dependency
-al, -ical	adjective	having the quality of	historical, tribal
-en	verb	to cause to become	strengthen, embolden
-er, -ier	adjective	comparative	happier, longer
-est, -iest	adjective	superlative	sunniest, hottest
-ess	noun	female	waitress, actress
-ful	adjective	full of, characterized by	beautiful, thankful
-fy, -ify	verb	to cause, to come to be	liquefy, intensify
-ism	noun	doctrine, belief, action	Communism, Buddhism
-ive, -ative, -itive	adjective	having the quality of	creative, innovative
-ize	verb	to convert into, to subject to	Americanize, dramatize
-less	adjective	without, missing	emotionless, hopeless
-ly	adverb	in the manner of	quickly, energetically
-ness	noun	quality or state	goodness, darkness
-ous, -ious, -eous	adjective	having the quality of	spontaneous, pious
-ship	noun	status or condition	partnership, ownership
-tion	noun	action or state	renovation, promotion
-y	adjective	characterized by	smoky, dreamy

Through knowledge of prefixes and suffixes, a student's vocabulary can be instantly expanded with an understanding of **etymology**—the origin of words. This, in turn, can be used to add sentence structure variety to academic writing.

Meaning of Words in Context

There will be many occasions in one's reading career in which an unknown word or a word with multiple meanings will pop up. There are ways of determining what these words or phrases mean that do not require the use of the dictionary, which is especially helpful during a test where one may not be available. Even outside of the exam, knowing how to derive an understanding of a word via context clues will be a critical skill in the real world. The context is the circumstances in which a story or a passage is happening and can usually be found in the series of words directly before or directly after the word or phrase in question. The clues are the words that hint towards the meaning of the unknown word or phrase.

There may be questions that ask about the meaning of a particular word or phrase within a passage. There are a couple ways to approach these kinds of questions:

- Define the word or phrase in a way that is easy to comprehend (using context clues).
- Try out each answer choice in place of the word.

To demonstrate, here's an example from *Alice in Wonderland*:

> Alice was beginning to get very tired of sitting by her sister on the bank, and of having nothing to do: once or twice she peeped into the book her sister was reading, but it had no pictures or conversations in it, "and what is the use of a book," thought Alice, "without pictures or conversations?"

Q: As it is used in the selection, the word peeped means:

Using the first technique, before looking at the answers, define the word *peeped* using context clues and then find the matching answer. Then, analyze the entire passage in order to determine the meaning, not just the surrounding words.

To begin, imagine a blank where the word should be and put a synonym or definition there: "once or twice she ______ into the book her sister was reading." The context clue here is the book. It may be tempting to put *read* where the blank is, but notice the preposition word, *into*. One does not read *into* a book, one simply reads a book, and since reading a book requires that it is seen with a pair of eyes, then *look* would make the most sense to put into the blank: "once or twice she looked into the book her sister was reading."

Once an easy-to-understand word or synonym has been supplanted, readers should check to make sure it makes sense with the rest of the passage. What happened after she looked into the book? She thought to herself how a book without pictures or conversations is useless. This situation in its entirety makes sense.

Now check the answer choices for a match:

a. To make a high-pitched cry
b. To smack
c. To look curiously
d. To pout

Since the word was already defined, Choice *C* is the best option.

Using the second technique, replace the figurative blank with each of the answer choices and determine which one is the most appropriate. Remember to look further into the passage to clarify that they work, because they could still make sense out of context.

a. Once or twice, she made a high pitched cry into the book her sister was reading
b. Once or twice, she smacked into the book her sister was reading
c. Once or twice, she looked curiously into the book her sister was reading
d. Once or twice, she pouted into the book her sister was reading

For Choice *A*, it does not make much sense in any context for a person to cry into a book, unless maybe something terrible has happened in the story. Given that afterward Alice thinks to herself how useless a book without pictures is, this option does not make sense within context.

For Choice *B*, smacking a book someone is reading may make sense if the rest of the passage indicates a reason for doing so. If Alice was angry or her sister had shoved it in her face, then maybe smacking the book would make sense within context. However, since whatever she does with the book causes her to think, "what is the use of a book without pictures or conversations?" then answer Choice *B* is not an appropriate answer. Answer Choice *C* fits well within context, given her subsequent thoughts on the matter. Answer Choice *D* does not make sense in context or grammatically, as people do not pout into things.

This is a simple example to illustrate the techniques outlined above. There may, however, be a question in which all of the definitions are correct and also make sense out of context, in which the appropriate context clues will really need to be honed in on in order to determine the correct answer. For example, here is another passage from *Alice in Wonderland*:

> ... but when the Rabbit actually took a watch out of its waistcoat pocket, and looked at it, and then hurried on, Alice started to her feet, for it flashed across her mind that she had never before seen a rabbit with either a waistcoat-pocket or a watch to take out of it, and burning with curiosity, she ran across the field after it, and was just in time to see it pop down a large rabbit-hole under the hedge.

Q: As it is used in the passage, the word *started* means _____.

a. to turn on
b. to begin
c. to move quickly
d. to be surprised

All of these words qualify as a definition of *start*, but using context clues, the correct answer can be identified using one of the two techniques above. It's easy to see that one does not turn on, begin, or be surprised to one's feet. The selection also states that she "ran across the field after it," indicating that she was in a hurry. Therefore, to move quickly would make the most sense in this context.

The same strategies can be applied to vocabulary that may be completely unfamiliar. In this case, focus on the words before or after the unknown word in order to determine its definition. Take this sentence, for example:

> Sam was such a miser that he forced Andrew to pay him twelve cents for the candy, even though he had a large inheritance and he knew his friend was poor.

Unlike with assertion questions, for vocabulary questions, it may be necessary to apply some critical thinking skills when something isn't explicitly stated within the passage. Think about the implications of the passage, or what the text is trying to say. With this example, it is important to realize that it is considered unusually stingy for a person to demand so little money from someone instead of just letting their friend have the candy, especially if this person is already wealthy. Hence, a miser is a greedy or stingy individual.

Questions about complex vocabulary may not be explicitly asked, but this is a useful skill to know. If there is an unfamiliar word while reading a passage and its definition goes unknown, it is possible to miss out on a critical message that could inhibit the ability to appropriately answer the questions. Practicing this technique in daily life will sharpen this ability to derive meanings from context clues with ease.

Analyzing Nuances of Word Meaning and Figures of Speech

Many words contain two levels of meaning: connotation and denotation. A word's **denotation** is its most literal meaning—the definition that can readily be found in the dictionary. A word's **connotation** includes all of its emotional and cultural associations.

In literary writing, authors rely heavily on connotative meaning to create mood and characterization. The following are two descriptions of a rainstorm:

- The rain slammed against the windowpane, and the wind howled through the fireplace. A pair of hulking oaks next to the house cast eerie shadows as their branches trembled in the wind.
- The rain pattered against the windowpane, and the wind whistled through the fireplace. A pair of stately oaks next to the house cast curious shadows as their branches swayed in the wind.

The first description paints a creepy picture for readers with strongly emotional words like *slammed*, connoting force and violence. *Howled* connotes pain or wildness, and *eerie* and *trembled* connote fear. Overall, the connotative language in this description serves to inspire fear and anxiety.

However, as can be seen in the second description, swapping out a few key words for those with different connotations completely changes the feeling of the passage. *Slammed* is replaced with the more cheerful *pattered*, and *hulking* has been swapped out for *stately*. Both words imply something large, but *hulking* is more intimidating whereas *stately* is more respectable. *Curious* and *swayed* seem more playful than the language used in the earlier description. Although both descriptions represent roughly the same situation, the nuances of the emotional language used throughout the passages create a very different sense for readers.

Selective choice of connotative language can also be extremely impactful in other forms of writing, such as editorials or persuasive texts. Through connotative language, writers reveal their biases and opinions while trying to inspire feelings and actions in readers:

- Parents won't stop complaining about standardized tests.
- Parents continue to raise concerns about standardized tests.

Readers should be able to identify the nuance in meaning between these two sentences. The first one carries a more negative feeling, implying that parents are being bothersome or whiny. Readers of the second sentence, though, might come away with the feeling that parents are concerned and involved in their children's education. Again, the aggregate of even subtle cues can combine to give a specific emotional impression to readers, so from an early age, students should be aware of how language can be used to influence readers' opinions.

Another form of non-literal expression can be found in **figures of speech**. As with connotative language, figures of speech tend to be shared within a cultural group and may be difficult to pick up on for learners outside of that group. In some cases, a figure of speech may be based on the literal denotation of the words it contains, but in other cases, a figure of speech is far removed from its literal meaning. A case in point is **irony**, where what is said is the exact opposite of what is meant:

> The new tax plan is poorly planned, based on faulty economic data, and unable to address the financial struggles of middle-class families. Yet legislators remain committed to passing this brilliant proposal.

When the writer refers to the proposal as brilliant, the opposite is implied—the plan is "faulty" and "poorly planned." By using irony, the writer means that the proposal is anything but brilliant by using the word in a non-literal sense.

Another figure of speech is **hyperbole**—extreme exaggeration or overstatement. Statements like "I love you to the moon and back" or "Let's be friends for a million years" utilize hyperbole to convey a greater depth of emotion, without literally committing oneself to space travel or a life of immortality.

Figures of speech may sometimes use one word in place of another. **Synecdoche**, for example, uses a part of something to refer to its whole. The expression "Don't hurt a hair on her head!" implies protecting more than just an individual hair, but rather her entire body. "The art teacher is training a class of Picassos" uses Picasso, one individual notable artist, to stand in for the entire category of talented artists. Another figure of speech using word replacement is **metonymy**, where a word is replaced with something closely associated to it. For example, news reports may use the word *Washington* to refer to the American government or *the crown* to refer to the British monarch.

Transitional Words and Phrases

There are approximately 200 transitional words and phrases that are commonly used in the English language. Below are lists of common transition words and phrases used throughout transitions:

Time

- after
- before
- during
- in the middle

Example about to be Given

- for example
- in fact
- for instance

Compare

- likewise
- also

Contrast

- however
- yet
- but

Addition

- and
- also
- furthermore
- moreover

Logical Relationships

- if
- then
- therefore
- as a result
- since

Steps in a Process

- first
- second
- last

Transitional words and phrases are important writing devices because they connect sentences and paragraphs. Transitional words and phrases present logical order to writing and provide more coherent meaning to readers.

Transition words can be categorized based on the relationships they create between ideas:

- General order: signaling elaboration of an idea to emphasize a point—e.g., *for example, for instance, to demonstrate, including, such as, in other words, that is, in fact, also, furthermore, likewise, and, truly, so, surely, certainly, obviously, doubtless*

- Chronological order: referencing the time frame in which the main event or idea occurs—e.g., *before, after, first, while, soon, shortly thereafter, meanwhile*

- Numerical order/order of importance: indicating that related ideas, supporting details, or events will be described in a sequence, possibly in order of importance—e.g., *first, second, also, finally, another, in addition, equally important, less importantly, most significantly, the main reason, last but not least*

- Spatial order: referring to the space and location of something or where things are located in relation to each other—e.g., *inside, outside, above, below, within, close, under, over, far, next to, adjacent to*

- Cause and effect order: signaling a causal relationship between events or ideas—e.g., *thus, therefore, since, resulted in, for this reason, as a result, consequently, hence, for, so*

- Compare and contrast order: identifying the similarities and differences between two or more objects, ideas, or lines of thought—e.g., *like, as, similarly, equally, just as, unlike, however, but, although, conversely, on the other hand, on the contrary*

- Summary order: indicating that a particular idea is coming to a close—e.g., *in conclusion, to sum up, in other words, ultimately, above all*

Author's Use of Evidence to Support Claims

Authors utilize a wide range of techniques to tell a story or communicate information. Readers should be familiar with the most common of these techniques. Techniques of writing are also commonly known as rhetorical devices; these are different ways of using evidence to support claims.

In nonfiction writing, authors employ argumentative techniques to present their opinion to readers in the most convincing way. Persuasive writing usually includes at least one type of appeal: an appeal to logic (logos), emotion (pathos), or credibility and trustworthiness (ethos). When a writer appeals to logic, they are asking readers to agree with them based on research, evidence, and an established line of reasoning. An author's argument might also appeal to readers' emotions, perhaps by including personal stories and anecdotes (a short narrative of a specific event). A final type of appeal, appeal to authority, asks the reader to agree with the author's argument on the basis of their expertise or credentials. Consider three different approaches to arguing the same opinion:

Logic (Logos)

Below is an example of an appeal to logic. The author uses evidence to disprove the logic of the school's rule (the rule was supposed to reduce discipline problems, but the number of problems has not been reduced; therefore, the rule is not working) and call for its repeal.

> Our school should abolish its current ban on campus cell phone use. The ban was adopted last year as an attempt to reduce class disruptions and help students focus more on their lessons. However, since the rule was enacted, there has been no change in the number of disciplinary problems in class. Therefore, the rule is ineffective and should be done away with.

Emotion (Pathos)

An author's argument might also appeal to readers' emotions, perhaps by including personal stories and anecdotes.

The next example presents an appeal to emotion. By sharing the personal anecdote of one student and speaking about emotional topics like family relationships, the author invokes the reader's empathy in asking them to reconsider the school rule.

> Our school should abolish its current ban on campus cell phone use. If students aren't able to use their phones during the school day, many of them feel isolated from their loved ones. For example, last semester, one student's grandmother had a heart attack in the morning. However, because he couldn't use his cell phone, the student didn't know about his grandmother's condition until the end of the day—when she had already passed away, and it was too late to say goodbye. By preventing students from contacting their friends and family, our school is placing undue stress and anxiety on students.

Credibility (Ethos)

Finally, an appeal to authority includes a statement from a relevant expert. In this case, the author uses a doctor in the field of education to support the argument. All three examples begin from the same opinion—the school's phone ban needs to change—but rely on different argumentative styles to persuade the reader.

> Our school should abolish its current ban on campus cell phone use. According to Dr. Bartholomew Everett, a leading educational expert, "Research studies show that cell phone usage has no real impact on student attentiveness. Rather, phones provide a valuable technological resource for learning. Schools need to learn how to integrate this new technology into their curriculum." Rather than banning phones altogether, our school should follow the advice of experts and allow students to use phones as part of their learning.

How an Author's Word Choice Shapes Meaning, Style, and Tone

Authors choose their words carefully in order to artfully depict meaning, style, and tone, which is most commonly inferred through the use of adjectives and verbs. The **tone** is the predominant emotion present in the text and represents the attitude or feelings that an author has towards a character or event.

To review, an adjective is a word used to describe something, and usually precedes the noun, a person, place, or object. A verb is a word describing an action. For example, the sentence "The scary woodpecker ate the spider" includes the adjective "scary," the noun "woodpecker," and the verb "ate." Reading this sentence may rouse some negative feelings, as the word "scary" carries a negative charge. The **charge** is the emotional connotation that can be derived from the adjectives and verbs and is either positive or negative. Recognizing the charge of a particular sentence or passage is an effective way to understand the meaning and tone the author is trying to convey.

Many authors have conflicting charges within the same text, but a definitive tone can be inferred by understanding the meaning of the charges relative to each other. It's important to recognize key conjunctions, or words that link sentences or clauses together. There are several types and subtypes of conjunctions. Three are most important for reading comprehension:

- **Cumulative conjunctions** add one statement to another.
    - Examples: and, both, also, as well as, not only
    - e.g. The juice is sweet *and* sour.
- **Adversative conjunctions** are used to contrast two clauses.
    - Examples: but, while, still, yet, nevertheless
    - e.g. She was tired, *but* she was happy.
- **Alternative conjunctions** express two alternatives.
    - Examples: or, either, neither, nor, else, otherwise
    - e.g. He must eat, *or* he will die.

Identifying the meaning and tone of a text can be accomplished with the following steps:

- Identify the adjectives and verbs.
- Recognize any important conjunctions.
- Label the adjectives and verbs as positive or negative.
- Understand what the charge means about the text.

To demonstrate these steps, examine the following passage from the classic children's poem, "The Sheep":

> Lazy sheep, pray tell me why
>
> In the pleasant fields you lie,
>
> Eating grass, and daisies white,
>
> From the morning till the night?
>
> Everything can something do,
>
> But what kind of use are you?

–Taylor, Jane and Ann. "The Sheep."

This selection is a good example of conflicting charges that work together to express an overall tone. Following the first two steps, identify the adjectives, verbs, and conjunctions within the passage. For this example, the adjectives are <u>underlined</u>, the verbs are in **bold**, and the conjunctions *italicized*:

> <u>Lazy</u> sheep, pray **tell** me why
>
> In the <u>pleasant</u> fields you **lie**,
>
> **Eating** grass, and daisies <u>white,</u>
>
> From the morning till the night?
>
> Everything can something do,
>
> *But* what kind of use are you?

For step three, read the passage and judge whether feelings of positivity or negativity arose. Then assign a charge to each of the words that were outlined. This can be done in a table format, or simply by writing a + or – next to the word.

The word <u>lazy</u> carries a negative connotation; it usually denotes somebody unwilling to work. To **tell** someone something has an exclusively neutral connotation, as it depends on what's being told, which has not yet been revealed at this point, so a charge can be assigned later. The word <u>pleasant</u> is an inherently positive word. To **lie** could be positive or negative depending on the context, but as the subject (the sheep) is lying in a pleasant field, then this is a positive experience. **Eating** is also generally positive.

After labeling the charges for each word, it might be inferred that the tone of this poem is happy and maybe even admiring or innocuously envious. However, notice the adversative conjunction, "but" and what follows. The author has listed all the pleasant things this sheep gets to do all day, but the tone changes when the author asks, "What kind of use are you?" Asking someone to prove their value is a rather hurtful thing to do, as it implies that the person asking the question doesn't believe the subject has any value, so this could be listed under negative charges. Referring back to the verb **tell**, after reading the whole passage, it can be deduced that the author is asking the sheep to tell what use the sheep is, so this has a negative charge.

+	−
• Pleasant • Lie in fields • From morning to night	• Lazy • Tell me • What kind of use are you

Upon examining the charges, it might seem like there's an even amount of positive and negative emotion in this selection, and that's where the conjunction "but" becomes crucial to identifying the tone. The conjunction "but" indicates there's a contrasting view to the pleasantness of the sheep's daily life, and this view is that the sheep is lazy and useless, which is also indicated by the first line, "lazy sheep, pray tell me why."

It might be helpful to look at questions pertaining to tone. For this selection, consider the following question:

The author of the poem regards the sheep with a feeling of what?

a. Respect
b. Disgust
c. Apprehension
d. Intrigue

Considering the author views the sheep as lazy with nothing to offer, Choice *A* appears to reflect the opposite of what the author is feeling.

Choice *B* seems to mirror the author's feelings towards the sheep, as laziness is considered a disreputable trait, and people (or personified animals, in this case) with unfavorable traits might be viewed with disgust.

Choice *C* doesn't make sense within context, as laziness isn't usually feared.

Choice *D* is tricky, as it may be tempting to argue that the author is intrigued with the sheep because they ask, "pray tell me why." This is another out-of-scope answer choice as it doesn't *quite* describe the feelings the author experiences and there's also a much better fit in Choice *B*.

The Purpose of a Passage

When it comes to an author's writing, readers should always identify a position or stance. No matter how objective a text may seem, readers should assume the author has preconceived beliefs. One can reduce the likelihood of accepting an invalid argument by looking for multiple articles on the topic, including those with varying opinions. If several opinions point in the same direction and are backed by reputable peer-reviewed sources, it's more likely the author has a valid argument. Positions that run contrary to widely held beliefs and existing data should invite scrutiny. There are exceptions to the rule, so be a careful consumer of information.

Though themes, symbols, and motifs are buried deep within the text and can sometimes be difficult to infer, an author's purpose is usually obvious from the beginning. No matter the genre or format, all authors are writing to persuade, inform, entertain, or express feelings. Often, these purposes are blended, with one dominating the rest. It's useful to learn to recognize the author's intent.

Persuasive writing is used to persuade or convince readers of something. It often contains two elements: the argument and the counterargument. The argument takes a stance on an issue, while the counterargument pokes holes in the opposition's stance. Authors rely on logic, emotion, and writer credibility to persuade readers to agree with them. If readers are opposed to the stance before reading, they are unlikely to adopt that stance. However, those who are undecided or committed to the same stance are more likely to agree with the author.

Informative writing tries to teach or inform. Workplace manuals, instructor lessons, statistical reports, and cookbooks are examples of informative texts. Informative writing is usually based on facts and is often void of emotion and persuasion. Informative texts generally contain statistics, charts, and graphs. Though most informative texts lack a persuasive agenda, readers still must examine the text carefully to determine whether one exists within a given passage.

Stories or narratives are designed to entertain. When you go to the movies, you often want to escape for a few hours, not necessarily to think critically. Entertaining writing is designed to delight and engage the reader. However, sometimes this type of writing can be woven into more serious materials, such as persuasive or informative writing to hook the reader before transitioning into a more scholarly discussion.

Emotional writing works to evoke the reader's feelings, such as anger, euphoria, or sadness. The connection between reader and author is an attempt to cause the reader to share the author's intended emotion or tone. Sometimes in order to make a piece more poignant, the author simply wants readers to feel the same emotions that the author has felt. Other times, the author attempts to persuade or manipulate the reader into adopting his stance. While it's okay to sympathize with the author, be aware of the individual's underlying intent.

The various writing styles are usually blended, with one purpose dominating the rest. A persuasive text, for example, might begin with a humorous tale to make readers more receptive to the persuasive message, or a recipe in a cookbook designed to inform might be preceded by an entertaining anecdote that makes the recipes more appealing.

Counterarguments

If an author presents a differing opinion or a counterargument in order to refute it, the reader should consider how and why the information is being presented. It is meant to strengthen the original argument and shouldn't be confused with the author's intended conclusion, but it should also be considered in the reader's final evaluation.

Authors can also use bias if they ignore the opposing viewpoint or present their side in an unbalanced way. A strong argument considers the opposition and finds a way to refute it. Critical readers should look for an unfair or one-sided presentation of the argument and be skeptical, as a bias may be present. Even if this bias is unintentional, if it exists in the writing, the reader should be wary of the validity of the argument. Readers should also look for the use of stereotypes, which refer to specific groups. Stereotypes are often negative connotations about a person or place and should always be avoided.

When a critical reader finds stereotypes in a piece of writing, they should be critical of the argument, and consider the validity of anything the author presents. Stereotypes reveal a flaw in the writer's thinking and may suggest a lack of knowledge or understanding about the subject.

Rhetoric

The IELTS™ Reading section will test a reader's ability to identify an author's use of rhetoric within text passages. Rhetoric is the use of positional or persuasive language to convey one or more central ideas. The idea behind the use of rhetoric is to convince the reader of something. Its use is meant to persuade or motivate the reader. An author may choose to appeal to their audience through logic, emotion, the use of ideology, or by conveying that the central idea is timely, and thus, important to the reader. There are a variety of rhetorical techniques an author can use to achieve this goal.

An author may choose to use traditional elements of style to persuade the reader. They may also use a story's setting, mood, characters, or a central conflict to build emotion in the reader. Similarly, an author may choose to use specific techniques such as alliteration, irony, metaphor, simile, hyperbole, allegory, imagery, onomatopoeia, and personification to persuasively illustrate one or more central ideas they wish the reader to adopt. In order to be successful in a standardized reading comprehension test situation, a reader needs to be well acquainted in recognizing rhetoric and rhetorical devices.

Identifying Rhetorical Devices

If a writer feels strongly about a subject, or has a passion for it, strong words and phrases can be chosen. Think of the types of rhetoric (or language) our politicians use. Each word, phrase, and idea is carefully crafted to elicit a response. Hopefully, that response is one of agreement to a certain point of view, especially among voters. Authors use the same types of language to achieve the same results. For example, the word "bad" has a certain connotation, but the words "horrid," "repugnant," and "abhorrent" paint a far better picture for the reader. They're more precise. They're interesting to read and they should all illicit stronger feelings in the reader than the word "bad." An author generally uses other devices beyond mere word choice to persuade, convince, entertain, or otherwise engage a reader.

Rhetorical devices are those elements an author utilizes in painting sensory, and hopefully persuasive ideas to which a reader can relate. They are numerable. Test takers will likely encounter one or more standardized test questions addressing various rhetorical devices. This study guide will address the more common types: alliteration, irony, metaphor, simile, hyperbole, allegory, imagery, onomatopoeia, and personification, providing examples of each.

Alliteration is a device that uses repetitive beginning sounds in words to appeal to the reader. Classic tongue twisters are a great example of alliteration. *She sells sea shells down by the sea shore* is an extreme example of alliteration. Authors will use alliterative devices to capture a reader's attention. It's interesting to note that marketing also utilizes alliteration in the same way. A reader will likely remember products that have the brand name and item starting with the same letter. Similarly, many songs, poems, and catchy phrases use this device. It's memorable. Use of alliteration draws a reader's attention to ideas that an author wants to highlight.

Irony is a device that authors use when pitting two contrasting items or ideas against each other in order to create an effect. It's frequently used when an author wants to employ humor or convey a sarcastic tone. Additionally, it's often used in fictional works to build tension between characters or between a particular character and the reader. An author may use **verbal irony** (sarcasm), **situational**

irony (where actions or events have the opposite effect than what's expected), and **dramatic irony** (where the reader knows something a character does not). Examples of irony include:

- **Dramatic Irony**: An author describing the presence of a hidden killer in a murder mystery, unbeknownst to the characters but known to the reader.

- **Situational Irony**: An author relating the tale of a fire captain who loses her home in a fire.

- **Verbal Irony**: This is where an author or character says one thing but means another. For example, telling a police officer "Thanks a lot" after receiving a ticket.

Metaphor is a device that uses a figure of speech to paint a visual picture of something that is not literally applicable. Authors relate strong images to readers, and evoke similar strong feelings using metaphors. Most often, authors will mention one thing in comparison to another more familiar to the reader. It's important to note that metaphors do not use the comparative words "like" or "as." At times, metaphors encompass common phrases such as clichés. At other times, authors may use mixed metaphors in making identification between two dissimilar things.

Examples of metaphors include:

- An author describing a character's anger as *a flaming sheet of fire.*
- An author relating a politician as having been a folding chair under close questioning.
- A novel's character telling another character to *take a flying hike.*
- Shakespeare's assertion that *all the world's a stage.*

Simile is a device that compares two dissimilar things using the words "like" and "as." When using similes, an author tries to catch a reader's attention and use comparison of unlike items to make a point. Similes are commonly used and often develop into figures of speech and catch phrases. Examples of similes include:

- An author describing a character as having a complexion like a faded lily.

- An investigative journalist describing his interview subject as being like cold steel and with a demeanor hard as ice.

- An author asserting the current political arena is just like a three-ring circus and as dry as day old bread.

Similes and metaphors can be confusing. When utilizing simile, an author will state one thing is like another. A metaphor states one thing is another. An example of the difference would be if an author states a character is *just like a fierce tiger and twice as angry,* as opposed to stating the character *is a fierce tiger and twice as angry.*

Hyperbole is simply an exaggeration that is not taken literally. A potential test taker will have heard or employed hyperbole in daily speech, as it is a common device we all use. Authors will use hyperbole to draw a reader's eye toward important points and to illicit strong emotional and relatable responses. Examples of hyperbole include:

- An author describing a character as being as big as a house and twice the circumference of a city block.

- An author stating the city's water problem as being old as the hills and more expensive than a king's ransom in spent tax dollars.

- A journalist stating the mayoral candidate died of embarrassment when her tax records were made public.

Allegories are stories or poems with hidden meanings, usually a political or moral one. Authors will frequently use allegory when leading the reader to a conclusion. Allegories are similar to parables, symbols, and analogies. Often, an author will employ the use of allegory to make political, historical, moral, or social observations. As an example, Jonathan Swift's work *Gulliver's Travels into Several Remote Nations of the World* is an allegory in and of itself. The work is a political allegory of England during Jonathan Swift's lifetime. Set in the travel journal style plot of a giant amongst smaller people, and a smaller Gulliver amongst the larger, it is a commentary on Swift's political stance of existing issues of his age. Many fictional works are entire allegories in and of themselves. George Orwell's *Animal Farm* is a story of animals that conquer man and form their own farm society with swine at the top; however, it is not a literal story in any sense. It's Orwell's political allegory of Russian society during and after the Communist revolution of 1917.

Other examples of allegory in popular culture include:

- Aesop's fable "The Tortoise and the Hare," which teaches readers that being steady is more important than being fast and impulsive.

- The popular *Hunger Games* by Suzanne Collins that teaches readers that media can numb society to what is truly real and important.

- Dr. Seuss's *Yertle the Turtle* which is a warning against totalitarianism and, at the time it was written, against the despotic rule of Adolf Hitler.

Imagery is a rhetorical device that an author employs when they use visual or descriptive language to evoke a reader's emotion. Use of imagery as a rhetorical device is broader in scope than this study guide addresses, but in general, the function of imagery is to create a vibrant scene in the reader's imagination and, in turn, tease the reader's ability to identify through strong emotion and sensory experience. In the simplest of terms, imagery, as a rhetoric device, beautifies literature. An example of poetic imagery is below:

> Pain has an element of blank
>
> It cannot recollect
>
> When it began, or if there were
>
> A day when it was not.
>
> It has no future but itself,
>
> Its infinite realms contain

Its past, enlightened to perceive

New periods of pain.

In the above poem, Emily Dickinson uses strong imagery. Pain is equivalent to an "element of blank" or of nothingness. Pain cannot recollect a beginning or end, as if it was a person (see **personification** below). Dickinson appeals to the reader's sense of a painful experience by discussing the unlikelihood that discomfort sees a future but does visualize a past and present. She simply indicates that pain, through the use of imagery, is cyclical and never ending. Dickenson's theme is one of painful depression, and it is through the use of imagery that she conveys this to her readers.

Onomatopoeia is the author's use of words that create sound. Words like *pop* and *sizzle* are examples of onomatopoeia. When an author wants to draw a reader's attention in an auditory sense, they will use onomatopoeia. An author may also use onomatopoeia to create sounds as interjection or commentary.

Examples include:

- An author describing a cat's vocalization as the kitten's chirrup echoed throughout the empty cabin.
- A description of a campfire as crackling and whining against its burning green wood.
- An author relating the sound of a car accident as *metallic screeching against crunching asphalt.*
- A description of an animal roadblock as being *a symphonic melody of groans, baas, and moans.*

Personification is a rhetorical device that an author uses to attribute human qualities to inanimate objects or animals. Once again, this device is useful when an author wants the reader to strongly relate to an idea. As in the example of George Orwell's *Animal Farm*, many of the animals are given the human abilities to speak, reason, apply logic, and otherwise interact as humans do. This helps the reader see how easily it is for any society to segregate into the haves and the have-nots through the manipulation of power. Personification is a device that enables the reader to empathize through human experience.

Examples of personification include:

- An author describing the wind as *whispering through the trees.*

- A description of a stone wall as being a hardened, unmovable creature made of cement and brick.

- An author attributing a city building as having slit eyes and an unapproachable, foreboding façade.

- An author describing spring as a beautiful bride, blooming in white, ready for summer's matrimony.

When identifying rhetorical devices, look for words and phrases that capture one's attention. Make note of the author's use of comparison between the inanimate and the animate. Consider words that make the reader feel sounds and envision imagery. Pay attention to the rhythm of fluid sentences and to the use of words that evoke emotion. The ability to identify rhetorical devices is another step in achieving successful reading comprehension and in being able to correctly answer standardized questions related to those devices.

Writing

The IELTS™ Writing section lasts 60 minutes and contains two tasks, both of which must be completed. On the Academic Test, the first task asks test takers to use a formal style of writing to explain or summarize a provided diagram, graph, table, or chart pertaining to data, the stages of a process, or the mechanics of an object or an event. It is expected that test takers write at least 150 words in about 20 minutes and that they describe the visual in their own words. In the second task, test takers are given a point of view or problem and must write a formal essay of 250 words in response. To do so, they are given about 40 minutes. Answers must be recorded on the answer sheet and must use complete sentences. Answers that are shorter than the stated lengths will be penalized. Longer responses are permitted so long as they are completed within the timeframe and remain on topic; points are deducted for answers that deviate from the question or topic.

On the General Training test, the first task asks test takers to write a personal or formal letter explaining a certain situation or requesting clarification or information. The topics for the letter writing task are everyday ones such as a letter to an employer justifying the request for a raise, one to a landlord to complain about issues with the maintenance department, or a letter to the local newspaper about an upcoming event in the planning stages. The instructions will have bullet points to inform test takers about the specific information they must include in the letter.

Test takers can expect to make some sort of complaint, express an opinion or desire, explain a situation in detail, provide suggestions, and/or ask for or give factual information in the letter writing task. Another important consideration in the planning and writing stages is the style of writing that the writer will use to communicate their message. This will depend on the particular assignment they are given: who their audience is, how well they are supposed to know the recipient, and the purpose for the letter. For example, a more formal style should be employed when writing to a manager, whereas a personal or informal style is more appropriate when writing to an aunt or friend.

Like the Academic Test, for the second task, test takers are given a point of view or problem and must write an essay in response, but it can be more personal in style and the topics are more general interest like the pros and cons of intergenerational households, whether children should get "screen time" (television, tablets, etc.), if sugary beverages should be taxed, solutions to landfill and trash problems, and how to enforce traffic laws like seatbelt use and no texting while driving.

Both tasks on both tests require test takers to carefully and fully read all provided instructions with the assignment to ensure that all relevant points are covered. Examiners are looking for responses to not only be of sufficient length (150 words for Task 1 and 250 for Task 2), but that writers stay on topic, organize ideas clearly and coherently, support their argument or opinion with facts and examples, and can communicate their ideas in a logical order, using a range of vocabulary and sentence structures with complex ideas, compelling writing, and a command of the English language. It should be noted that the response for Task 2 is expected to demonstrate more advanced grammar and vocabulary, more abstract ideas, and employ strong evidence and justification of ideas. Resultantly, Task 2 carries twice as much weight in scoring as Task 1 for the test taker's overall Writing Section score.

Written responses are evaluated on the following criteria:

- Task achievement/response: The strength and adherence to the assignment instructions, the degree to which one explains their thoughts or opinions, the ability to appropriately structure the written response to meet the objectives in a logical and cohesive manner, and the writer's skill in generating and expressing complex ideas and remaining on topic.
- Coherence and cohesion: The overall clarity, cohesion, logical organization, sequencing, and linking of ideas and language for fluid and sensible readability.
- Lexical resource: The breadth, precision, and accuracy of word choice and vocabulary used for the given assignment conditions
- Grammatical range and accuracy: The breadth, precision, and accuracy of grammatical choices and sentence structures used for the given assignment conditions

The two sections below are called "Writing the Essay" and "Conventions of Standard English." The first section is designed to help you structure your essay and employ prewriting strategies that will help you brainstorm and begin writing the essay. The second section is common mistakes used in the English language. It also contains a section about American English spelling conventions. The IELTS™ accepts either British or American spelling. The information in this section should also inform the spelling of responses to the other sections of the exam. Lastly, there is information about interpreting graphs, which contains helpful tips for the first task on the Academic Test.

Writing the Essay

Brainstorming

One of the most important steps in writing an essay is prewriting. Before drafting an essay, it's helpful to think about the topic for a moment or two, in order to gain a more solid understanding of the task. Then, spending about five minutes jotting down the immediate ideas that could work for the essay is recommended. It is a way to get some words on the page and offer a reference for ideas when drafting. Scratch paper is provided for writers to use any prewriting techniques such as webbing, free writing, or listing. The goal is to get ideas out of the mind and onto the page.

Considering Opposing Viewpoints

In the planning stage, it's important to consider all aspects of the topic, including different viewpoints on the subject. There are more than two ways to look at a topic, and a strong argument considers those opposing viewpoints. Considering opposing viewpoints can help writers present a fair, balanced, and informed essay that shows consideration for all readers. This approach can also strengthen an argument by recognizing and potentially refuting opposing viewpoint(s).

Drawing from personal experience may help to support ideas. For example, if the goal for writing is a personal narrative, then the story should come from the writer's own life. Many writers find it helpful to draw from personal experience, even in an essay that is not strictly narrative. Personal anecdotes or short stories can help to illustrate a point in other types of essays as well.

Moving from Brainstorming to Planning

Once the ideas are on the page, it's time to turn them into a solid plan for the essay. The best ideas from the brainstorming results can then be developed into a more formal outline. An outline typically has one main point (the thesis) and at least three sub-points that support the main point.

Here's an example:

Main Idea

- Point #1
- Point #2
- Point #3

Of course, there will be details under each point, but this approach is the best for dealing with timed writing.

Staying on Track

Basing the essay on the outline aids in both organization and coherence. The goal is to ensure that there is enough time to develop each sub-point in the essay, roughly spending an equal amount of time on each idea. Keeping an eye on the time will help. If there are fifteen minutes left to draft the essay, then it makes sense to spend about 5 minutes on each of the ideas. Staying on task is critical to success and timing out the parts of the essay can help writers avoid feeling overwhelmed.

Parts of the Essay

The **introduction** has to do a few important things:

- Establish the **topic** of the essay in original wording (i.e., not just repeating the prompt)
- Clarify the significance/importance of the topic or purpose for writing (not too many details, a brief overview)
- Offer a **thesis statement** that identifies the writer's own viewpoint on the topic (typically one to two brief sentences as a clear, concise explanation of the main point on the topic)

Body paragraphs reflect the ideas developed in the outline. Three to four points is probably sufficient for a short essay, and they should include the following:

- A **topic sentence** that identifies the sub-point (e.g., a reason why, a way how, a cause or effect)
- A detailed **explanation** of the point, explaining why the writer thinks this point is valid
- Illustrative **examples**, such as personal examples or real-world examples, that support and validate the point (i.e., "prove" the point)
- A **concluding sentence** that connects the examples, reasoning, and analysis to the point being made

The **conclusion**, or final paragraph, should be brief and should reiterate the focus, clarifying why the discussion is significant or important. It is important to avoid adding specific details or new ideas to this paragraph. The purpose of the conclusion is to sum up what has been said to bring the discussion to a close.

Don't Panic!

Writing an essay can be overwhelming, and performance panic is a natural response. The outline serves as a basis for the writing and helps writers keep focused. Getting stuck can also happen, and it's helpful to remember that brainstorming can be done at any time during the writing process. Following the steps of the writing process is the best defense against writer's block.

Timed essays can be particularly stressful, but assessors are trained to recognize the necessary planning and thinking for these timed efforts. Using the plan above and sticking to it helps with time management. Timing each part of the process helps writers stay on track. Sometimes writers try to cover too much in their essays. If time seems to be running out, this is an opportunity to determine whether all of the ideas in the outline are necessary. Three body paragraphs are sufficient, and more than that is probably too much to cover in a short essay.

More isn't always *better* in writing. A strong essay will be clear and concise. It will avoid unnecessary or repetitive details. It is better to have a concise, five-paragraph essay that makes a clear point, than a ten-paragraph essay that doesn't. The goal is to write one to two pages of quality writing. Paragraphs should also reflect balance; if the introduction goes to the bottom of the first page, the writing may be going off-track or be repetitive. It's best to fall into the one to two-page range, but a complete, well-developed essay is the ultimate goal.

The Final Steps

Leaving a few minutes at the end to revise and proofread offers an opportunity for writers to polish things up. Putting one's self in the reader's shoes and focusing on what the essay actually says helps writers identify problems—it's a movement from the mindset of writer to the mindset of editor. The goal is to have a clean, clear copy of the essay. The following areas should be considered when proofreading:

- Sentence fragments
- Awkward sentence structure
- Run-on sentences
- Incorrect word choice
- Grammatical agreement errors
- Spelling errors
- Punctuation errors
- Capitalization errors

The Short Overview

The essay may seem challenging, but following these steps can help writers focus:

- Take one to two minutes to think about the topic.
- Generate some ideas through brainstorming (three to four minutes).
- Organize ideas into a brief outline, selecting just three to four main points to cover in the essay (eventually the body paragraphs).
- Develop essay in parts:
- Introduction paragraph, with intro to topic and main points
- Viewpoint on the subject at the end of the introduction
- Body paragraphs, based on outline

- Each paragraph: makes a main point, explains the viewpoint, uses examples to support the point
- Brief conclusion highlighting the main points and closing
- Read over the essay (last five minutes).
- Look for any obvious errors, making sure that the writing makes sense.

Parts of Speech

Nouns

A **common noun** is a word that identifies any of a class of people, places, or things. Examples include numbers, objects, animals, feelings, concepts, qualities, and actions. *A, an,* or *the* usually precedes the common noun. These parts of speech are called *articles*. Here are some examples of sentences using nouns preceded by articles.

> *A* building is under construction.
>
> *The* girl would like to move to *the* city.

A **proper noun** (also called a **proper name**) is used for the specific name of an individual person, place, or organization. The first letter in a proper noun is capitalized. "My name is *Mary*." "I work for *Walmart*."

Nouns sometimes serve as adjectives (which themselves describe nouns), such as "hockey player" and "state government."

Pronouns

A word used in place of a noun is known as a **pronoun**. Pronouns are words like *I, mine, hers,* and *us*.

Pronouns can be split into different classifications (as shown below) which make them easier to learn; however, it's not important to memorize the classifications.

- **Personal pronouns:** refer to people
- **First person pronouns:** we, I, our, mine
- **Second person pronouns:** you, yours
- **Third person pronouns**: he, she, they, them, it
- **Possessive pronouns:** demonstrate ownership (mine, his, hers, its, ours, theirs, yours)
- **Interrogative pronouns:** ask questions (what, which, who, whom, whose)
- **Relative pronouns:** include the five interrogative pronouns and others that are relative (whoever, whomever, that, when, where)
- **Demonstrative pronouns:** replace something specific (this, that, those, these)

- **Reciprocal pronouns:** indicate something was done or given in return (each other, one another)
- **Indefinite pronouns:** have a nonspecific status (anybody, whoever, someone, everybody, somebody)

Indefinite pronouns such as *anybody, whoever, someone, everybody,* and *somebody* command a singular verb form, but others such as *all, none,* and *some* could require a singular or plural verb form.

Antecedents

An **antecedent** is the noun to which a pronoun refers; it needs to be written or spoken before the pronoun is used. For many pronouns, antecedents are imperative for clarity. In particular, a lot of the personal, possessive, and demonstrative pronouns need antecedents. Otherwise, it would be unclear who or what someone is referring to when they use a pronoun like *he* or *this*.

Pronoun reference means that the pronoun should refer clearly to one, clear, unmistakable noun (the antecedent).

Pronoun-antecedent agreement refers to the need for the antecedent and the corresponding pronoun to agree in gender, person, and number. Here are some examples:

> The *kidneys* (plural antecedent) are part of the urinary system. *They* (plural pronoun) serve several roles.
>
> The kidneys are part of the *urinary system* (singular antecedent). *It* (singular pronoun) is also known as the renal system.

Pronoun Cases

The **subjective pronouns** —*I, you, he/she/it, we, they,* and *who*—are the subjects of the sentence.

> Example: *They* have a new house.

The **objective pronouns**—*me, you* (*singular*), *him/her, us, them,* and *whom*—are used when something is being done for or given to someone; they are objects of the action.

> Example: The teacher has an apple for *us*.

The **possessive pronouns**—*mine, my, your, yours, his, hers, its, their, theirs, our,* and *ours*—are used to denote that something (or someone) belongs to someone (or something).

> Example: It's *their* chocolate cake.
>
> Even Better Example: It's *my* chocolate cake!

One of the greatest challenges and worst abuses of pronouns concerns *who* and *whom*. Just knowing the following rule can eliminate confusion. *Who* is a subjective-case pronoun used only as a subject or subject complement. *Whom* is only objective-case and, therefore, the object of the verb or preposition.

> *Who* is going to the concert?
>
> You are going to the concert with *whom*?

Hint: When using *who* or *whom*, think of whether someone would say *he* or *him*. If the answer is *he*, use *who*. If the answer is *him*, use *whom*. This trick is easy to remember because *he* and *who* both end in vowels, and *him* and *whom* both end in the letter *M*.

Many possessive pronouns sound like contractions. For example, many people get *it's* and *its* confused. The word *it's* is the contraction for *it is*. The word *its* without an apostrophe is the possessive form of *it*.

I love that wooden desk. It's beautiful. (contraction)

I love that wooden desk. Its glossy finish is beautiful. (possessive)

If you are not sure which version to use, replace *it's/its* with *it is* and see if that sounds correct. If so, use the contraction (*it's*). That trick also works for *who's/whose*, *you're/your*, and *they're/their*.

Adjectives

"The *extraordinary* brain is the *main* organ of the central nervous system." The adjective *extraordinary* describes the brain in a way that causes one to realize it is more exceptional than some of the other organs while the adjective *main* defines the brain's importance in its system.

An **adjective** is a word or phrase that names an attribute that describes or clarifies a noun or pronoun. This helps the reader visualize and understand the characteristics—size, shape, age, color, origin, etc.—of a person, place, or thing that otherwise might not be known. Adjectives breathe life, color, and depth into the subjects they define. Life would be *drab* and *colorless* without adjectives!

Adjectives often precede the nouns they describe.

She drove her <u>new</u> car.

However, adjectives can also come later in the sentence.

Her car is <u>new</u>.

Adjectives using the prefix *a*– can only be used after a verb.

Correct: The dog was alive until the car ran up on the curb and hit him.

Incorrect: The alive dog was hit by a car that ran up on the curb.

Other examples of this rule include *awake, ablaze, ajar, alike,* and *asleep*.

Other adjectives used after verbs concern states of health.

The girl was finally *well* after a long bout of pneumonia.

The boy was *fine* after the accident.

An adjective phrase is not a bunch of adjectives strung together, but a group of words that describes a noun or pronoun and, thus, functions as an adjective. Very happy is an adjective phrase; so are way too hungry and passionate about traveling.

Possessives

In grammar, **possessive nouns** and **possessive pronouns** show ownership.

Singular nouns are generally made possessive with an apostrophe and an *s* (*'s*).

> My *uncle's* new car is silver.
>
> The *dog's* bowl is empty.
>
> *James's* ties are becoming outdated.

Plural nouns ending in *s* are generally made possessive by just adding an apostrophe ('):

> The pistachio nuts' saltiness is added during roasting. (The saltiness of pistachio nuts is added during roasting.)
>
> The students' achievement tests are difficult. (The achievement tests of the students are difficult.)

If the plural noun does not end in an *s* such as *women,* then it is made possessive by adding an *apostrophe s* (*'s*)*—women's.*

Possessive pronouns can be first person (*mine*), second person (*yours*), or third person (*theirs*).

Indefinite possessive pronouns such as *nobody* or *someone* become possessive by adding an *apostrophe s* to become *nobody's* or *someone's.*

Verbs

A verb is the part of speech that describes an action, state of being, or occurrence.

A verb forms the main part of a predicate of a sentence. This means that the verb explains what the noun (which will be discussed shortly) is doing. A simple example is *time flies*. The verb *flies* explains what the action of the noun, *time*, is doing. This example is a *main* verb.

Helping (auxiliary) verbs are words like *have, do, be, can, may, should, must,* and *will.* "I *should* go to the store." Helping verbs assist main verbs in expressing tense, ability, possibility, permission, or obligation.

Particles are minor function words like *not, in, out, up,* or *down* that become part of the verb itself. "I might *not.*"

Participles are words formed from verbs that are often used to modify a noun, noun phrase, verb, or verb phrase.

> The *running* teenager collided with the cyclist.

Participles can also create compound verb forms.

> He is *speaking.*

Verbs have five basic forms: the **base** form, the ***-s*** form, the ***-ing*** form, the **past** form, and the **past participle** form.

The past forms are either **regular** (*love/loved; hate/hated*) or **irregular** because they don't end by adding the common past tense suffix "-ed" (*go/went; fall/fell; set/set*).

Adverbs

Adverbs have more functions than adjectives because they modify or qualify verbs, adjectives, or other adverbs as well as word groups that express a relation of place, time, circumstance, or cause. Therefore, adverbs answer any of the following questions: *How, when, where, why, in what way, how often, how much, in what condition,* and/or *to what degree. How good looking is he? He is <u>very</u> handsome.*

Here are some examples of adverbs for different situations:

- how: quickly
- when: daily
- where: there
- in what way: easily
- how often: often
- how much: much
- in what condition: badly
- what degree: hardly

As one can see, for some reason, many adverbs end in *-ly.*

Adverbs do things like emphasize (*really, simply,* and *so*), amplify (*heartily, completely,* and *positively*), and tone down (*almost, somewhat,* and *mildly*).

Adverbs also come in phrases.

> The dog ran as <u>though his life depended on it.</u>

Prepositions

Prepositions are connecting words and, while there are only about 150 of them, they are used more often than any other individual groups of words. They describe relationships between other words. They are placed before a noun or pronoun, forming a phrase that modifies another word in the sentence. **Prepositional phrases** begin with a preposition and end with a noun or pronoun, the **object of the preposition.** *A pristine lake is <u>near the store</u> and <u>behind the bank</u>.*

Some commonly used prepositions are *about, after, anti, around, as, at, behind, beside, by, for, from, in, into, of, off, on, to,* and *with.*

Complex prepositions, which also come before a noun or pronoun, consist of two or three words such as *according to, in regards to,* and *because of.*

Interjections

Interjections are words used to express emotion. Examples include *wow, ouch*, and *hooray*. Interjections are often separate from sentences; in those cases, the interjection is directly followed by an exclamation point. In other cases, the interjection is included in a sentence and followed by a comma. The punctuation plays a big role in the intensity of the emotion that the interjection is expressing. Using a comma or semicolon indicates less excitement than using an exclamation mark.

Conjunctions

Conjunctions are vital words that connect words, phrases, thoughts, and ideas. Conjunctions show relationships between components. There are two types:

Coordinating conjunctions are the primary class of conjunctions placed between words, phrases, clauses, and sentences that are of equal grammatical rank; the coordinating conjunctions are *for, and, nor, but, or, yet,* and *so*. A useful memorization trick is to remember that all the first letters of these conjunctions collectively spell the word fanboys.

> I need to go shopping, *but* I must be careful to leave enough money in the bank.
>
> She wore a black, red, *and* white shirt.

Subordinating conjunctions are the secondary class of conjunctions. They connect two unequal parts, one **main** (or **independent**) and the other **subordinate** (or **dependent**). I must go to the store *even though* I do not have enough money in the bank.

> *Because* I read the review, I do not want to go to the movie.

Notice that the presence of subordinating conjunctions makes clauses dependent. *I read the review* is an independent clause, but *because* makes the clause dependent. Thus, it needs an independent clause to complete the sentence.

Sentences

First, let's review the basic elements of sentences.

A **sentence** is a set of words that make up a grammatical unit. The words must have certain elements and be spoken or written in a specific order to constitute a complete sentence that makes sense.

1. A sentence must have a **subject** (a noun or noun phrase). The subject tells whom or what the sentence is addressing (i.e., what it is about).

2. A sentence must have an **action** or **state of being** (*a* verb). To reiterate: A verb forms the main part of the predicate of a sentence. This means that it explains what the noun is doing.

3. A sentence must convey a complete thought.

When examining writing, be mindful of grammar, structure, spelling, and patterns. Sentences can come in varying sizes and shapes; so, the point of grammatical correctness is not to stamp out creativity or diversity in writing. Rather, grammatical correctness ensures that writing will be enjoyable and clear. One of the most common methods for catching errors is to mouth the words as you read them. Many typos are fixed automatically by our brain, but mouthing the words often circumvents this instinct and helps one read what's actually on the page. Often, grammar errors are caught not by memorization of grammar rules but by the training of one's mind to know whether something *sounds* right or not.

Types of Sentences

There isn't an overabundance of absolutes in grammar, but here is one: every sentence in the English language falls into one of four categories.

- Declarative: a simple statement that ends with a period

    The price of milk per gallon is the same as the price of gasoline.

- Imperative: a command, instruction, or request that ends with a period

    Buy milk when you stop to fill up your car with gas.

- Interrogative: a question that ends with a question mark

    Will you buy the milk?

- Exclamatory: a statement or command that expresses emotions like anger, urgency, or surprise and ends with an exclamation mark

    Buy the milk now!

Declarative sentences are the most common type, probably because they are comprised of the most general content, without any of the bells and whistles that the other three types contain. They are, simply, declarations or statements of any degree of seriousness, importance, or information.

Imperative sentences often seem to be missing a subject. The subject is there, though; it is just not visible or audible because it is *implied*. Look at the imperative example sentence.

Buy the milk when you fill up your car with gas.

You is the implied subject, the one to whom the command is issued. This is sometimes called *the understood you* because it is understood that *you* is the subject of the sentence.

Interrogative sentences—those that ask questions—are defined as such from the idea of the word *interrogation*, the action of questions being asked of suspects by investigators. Although that is serious business, interrogative sentences apply to all kinds of questions.

To exclaim is at the root of **exclamatory sentences**. These are made with strong emotions behind them. The only technical difference between a declarative or imperative sentence and an exclamatory one is the exclamation mark at the end. The example declarative and imperative sentences can both become an exclamatory one simply by putting an exclamation mark at the end of the sentences.

The price of milk per gallon is the same as the price of gasoline!
Buy milk when you stop to fill up your car with gas!

After all, someone might be really excited by the price of gas or milk, or they could be mad at the person that will be buying the milk! However, as stated before, exclamation marks in abundance defeat their own purpose! After a while, they begin to cause fatigue! When used only for their intended purpose, they can have their expected and desired effect.

Independent and Dependent Clauses

Independent and dependent clauses are strings of words that contain both a subject and a verb. An **independent clause** *can* stand alone as complete thought, but a **dependent clause** *cannot*. A dependent clause relies on other words to be a complete sentence.

Independent clause: The keys are on the counter.
Dependent clause: If the keys are on the counter

Notice that both clauses have a subject (*keys*) and a verb (*are*). The independent clause expresses a complete thought, but the word *if* at the beginning of the dependent clause makes it *dependent* on other words to be a complete thought.

Independent clause: If the keys are on the counter, please give them to me.

This presents a complete sentence since it includes at least one verb and one subject and is a complete thought. In this case, the independent clause has two subjects (*keys* & an implied *you*) and two verbs (*are* & *give*).

Independent clause: I went to the store.
Dependent clause: Because we are out of milk,

Complete Sentence: Because we are out of milk, I went to the store.
Complete Sentence: I went to the store because we are out of milk.

Sentence Structures

A **simple sentence** has one independent clause.

I am going to win.

A **compound sentence** has two independent clauses. A conjunction—*for, and, nor, but, or, yet, so*—links them together. Note that each of the independent clauses has a subject and a verb.

I am going to win, but the odds are against me.

A **complex sentence** has one independent clause and one or more dependent clauses.

I am going to win, even though I don't deserve it.

Even though I don't deserve it is a dependent clause. It does not stand on its own. Some conjunctions that link an independent and a dependent clause are *although, because, before, after, that, when, which*, and *while*.

A **compound-complex sentence** has at least three clauses, two of which are independent and at least one that is a dependent clause.

While trying to dance, I tripped over my partner's feet, but I regained my balance quickly.

The dependent clause is *While trying to dance*.

Run-Ons and Fragments

Run-Ons

A common mistake in writing is the run-on sentence. A **run-on** is created when two or more independent clauses are joined without the use of a conjunction, a semicolon, a colon, or a dash. We don't want to use commas where periods belong. Here is an example of a run-on sentence:

> Making wedding cakes can take many hours I am very impatient, I want to see them completed right away.

There are a variety of ways to correct a run-on sentence. The method you choose will depend on the context of the sentence and how it fits with neighboring sentences:

> Making wedding cakes can take many hours. I am very impatient. I want to see them completed right away. (Use periods to create more than one sentence.)
>
> Making wedding cakes can take many hours; I am very impatient—I want to see them completed right away. (Correct the sentence using a semicolon, colon, or dash.)
>
> Making wedding cakes can take many hours, and I am very impatient and want to see them completed right away. (Correct the sentence using coordinating conjunctions.)
>
> I am very impatient because I would rather see completed wedding cakes right away than wait for it to take many hours. (Correct the sentence by revising.)

Fragments

Remember that a complete sentence must have both a subject and a verb. Complete sentences consist of at least one independent clause. Incomplete sentences are called **sentence fragments**. A sentence fragment is a common error in writing. Sentence fragments can be independent clauses that start with subordinating words, such as *but, as, so that,* or *because,* or they could simply be missing a subject or verb.

A fragment error can be corrected by adding the fragment to a nearby sentence or by adding or removing words to make it an independent clause. For example:

> Dogs are my favorite animals. Because cats are too lazy. (Incorrect; the word because creates a sentence fragment)
>
> Dogs are my favorite animals because cats are too lazy. (Correct; this is a dependent clause.)
>
> Dogs are my favorite animals. Cats are too lazy. (Correct; this is a simple sentence.)

Subject and Predicate

Every complete sentence can be divided into two parts: the subject and the predicate.

Subjects: Subjects are needed in sentences to tell the reader who or what the sentence describes. Subjects can be simple or complete, and they can be direct or indirect. There can also be compound subjects.

Simple subjects are the noun or pronouns the sentence describes, without modifiers. The simple subject can come before or after the verb in the sentence:

The big brown dog is the calmest one.

Complete subjects are the subject together with all of its describing words or modifiers.

The big brown dog is the calmest one. (The complete subject is big brown dog.)

Direct subjects are subjects that appear in the text of the sentence, as in the example above. **Indirect subjects** are implied. The subject is "you," but the word *you* does not appear.

Indirect subjects are usually in imperative sentences that issue a command or order:

Feed the short skinny dog first. (The understood you is the subject.)

Watch out—he's really hungry! (The sentence warns you to watch out.)

Compound subjects occur when two or more nouns join together to form a plural subject.

Carson and Emily make a great couple.

Predicates: Once we have identified the subject of the sentence, the rest of the sentence becomes the predicate. Predicates are formed by the verb, the direct object, and all words related to it.

We went to see the Cirque du' Soleil performance.

The gigantic green character was funnier than all the rest.

Direct objects are the nouns in the sentence that are receiving the action. Sentences don't necessarily need objects. Sentences only need a subject and a verb.

The clown brought the acrobat the hula-hoop. (What is being brought? the hula-hoop)

Then he gave the trick pony a soapy bath. (What is being given? a soapy bath)

Indirect objects are words that tell us to or for whom or what the action is being done. For there to be an indirect object, there first must always be a direct object.

The clown brought the acrobat the hula-hoop. (Who is getting the direct object? the acrobat)

Then he gave the trick pony a soapy bath. (What is getting the bath? the trick pony)

Phrases

A **phrase** is a group of words that go together but do not include both a subject and a verb. They are used to add information, explain something, or make the sentence easier for the reader to understand. Unlike clauses, phrases can never stand alone as their own sentence. They do not form complete thoughts. There are noun phrases, prepositional phrases, verbal phrases, appositive phrases, and absolute phrases. Here are some examples of phrases:

I know all the shortest routes.

Before the sequel, we wanted to watch the first movie. (introductory phrase)

The jumpers have hot cocoa to drink right away.

Subject-Verb Agreement

The subject of a sentence and its verb must agree. The cornerstone rule of subject-verb agreement is that subject and verb must agree in number. Whether the subject is singular or plural, the verb must follow suit.

Incorrect: The houses is new.

Correct: The houses are new.

Also Correct: The house is new.

In other words, a singular subject requires a singular verb; a plural subject requires a plural verb.

The words or phrases that come between the subject and verb do not alter this rule.

Incorrect: The houses built of brick is new.

Correct: The houses built of brick are new.

Incorrect: The houses with the sturdy porches is new.

Correct: The houses with the sturdy porches are new.

The subject will always follow the verb when a sentence begins with *here* or *there.* Identify these with care.

Incorrect: Here *is* the *houses* with sturdy porches.

Correct: Here *are* the *houses* with sturdy porches.

The subject in the sentences above is not *here*, it is *houses*. Remember, *here* and *there* are never subjects. Be careful that contractions such as *here's* or *there're* do not cause confusion!

Two subjects joined by *and* require a plural verb form, except when the two combine to make one thing:

Incorrect: Garrett and Jonathan is over there.

Correct: Garrett and Jonathan are over there.

Incorrect: Spaghetti and meatballs are a delicious meal!

Correct: Spaghetti and meatballs is a delicious meal!

In the example above, *spaghetti and meatballs* is a compound noun. However, *Garrett and Jonathan* is not a compound noun.

Two singular subjects joined by *or, either/or,* or *neither/nor* call for a singular verb form.

Incorrect: Butter or syrup are acceptable.

Correct: Butter or syrup is acceptable.

Plural subjects joined by *or, either/or*, or *neither/nor* are, indeed, plural.

The chairs or the boxes are being moved next.

If one subject is singular and the other is plural, the verb should agree with the closest noun.

Correct: The chair or the boxes are being moved next.

Correct: The chairs or the box is being moved next.

Some plurals of money, distance, and time call for a singular verb.

Incorrect: Three dollars *are* enough to buy that.

Correct: Three dollars *is* enough to buy that.

For words declaring degrees of quantity such as *many of, some of,* or *most of,* let the noun that follows *of* be the guide:

Incorrect: Many of the books is in the shelf.

Correct: Many of the books are in the shelf.

Incorrect: Most of the pie *are* on the table.

Correct: Most of the pie *is* on the table.

For indefinite pronouns like anybody or everybody, use singular verbs.

Everybody *is* going to the store.

However, the pronouns *few, many, several, all, some,* and *both* have their own rules and use plural forms.

Some *are* ready.

Some nouns like *crowd* and *congress* are called *collective nouns* and they require a singular verb form.

Congress *is* in session.

The news *is* over.

Books and movie titles, though, including plural nouns such as *Great Expectations*, also require a singular verb. Remember that only the subject affects the verb. While writing tricky subject-verb arrangements, say them aloud. Listen to them. Once the rules have been learned, one's ear will become sensitive to them, making it easier to pick out what's right and what's wrong.

Dangling and Misplaced Modifiers

A **modifier** is a word or phrase meant to describe or clarify another word in the sentence. When a sentence has a modifier but is missing the word it describes or clarifies, it's an error called a **dangling modifier**. We can fix the sentence by revising to include the word that is being modified. Consider the following examples with the modifier underlined:

> Incorrect: <u>Having walked five miles</u>, this bench will be the place to rest. (This implies that the bench walked the miles, not the person.)
>
> Correct: <u>Having walked five miles</u>, Matt will rest on this bench. (*Having walked five miles* correctly modifies *Matt*, who did the walking.)
>
> Incorrect: <u>Since midnight</u>, my dreams have been pleasant and comforting. (The adverb clause *since midnight* cannot modify the noun *dreams*.)
>
> Correct: <u>Since midnight</u>, I have had pleasant and comforting dreams. (*Since midnight* modifies the verb have had, telling us when the dreams occurred.)

Sometimes the modifier is not located close enough to the word it modifies for the sentence to be clearly understood. In this case, we call the error a **misplaced modifier**. Here is an example with the modifier underlined.

> Incorrect: We gave the hot cocoa to the children <u>that was filled with marshmallows</u>. (This sentence implies that the children are what are filled with marshmallows.)
>
> Correct: We gave the hot cocoa <u>that was filled with marshmallows</u> to the children. (The cocoa is filled with marshmallows. The modifier is near the word it modifies.)

Parallel Structure in a Sentence

Parallel structure, also known as **parallelism**, refers to using the same grammatical form within a sentence. This is important in lists and for other components of sentences.

> Incorrect: At the recital, the boys and girls were dancing, singing, and played musical instruments.
> Correct: At the recital, the boys and girls were dancing, singing, and playing musical instruments.

Notice that in the second example, *played* is not in the same verb tense as the other verbs, nor is it compatible with the helping verb *were*. To test for parallel structure in lists, try reading each item as if it were the only item in the list.

> The boys and girls were dancing.
> The boys and girls were singing.
> The boys and girls were played musical instruments.

Suddenly, the error in the sentence becomes very clear. Here's another example:

> Incorrect: After the accident, I informed the police *that Mrs. Holmes backed* into my car, *that Mrs. Holmes got out* of her car to look at the damage, and *she was driving* off without leaving a note.

Correct: After the accident, I informed the police *that Mrs. Holmes backed* into my car, *that Mrs. Holmes got out* of her car to look at the damage, and *that Mrs. Holmes drove off* without leaving a note.

Correct: After the accident, I informed the police that Mrs. Holmes *backed* into my car, *got out* of her car to look at the damage, and *drove off* without leaving a note.

Note that there are two ways to fix the nonparallel structure of the first sentence. The key to parallelism is consistent structure.

Punctuation

Commas

A **comma** (,) is the punctuation mark that signifies a pause—breath—between parts of a sentence. It denotes a break of flow. As with so many aspects of writing structure, authors will benefit by memorizing all of the different ways in which commas can be used so as not to abuse them.

In a complex sentence—one that contains a subordinate (dependent) clause or clauses—the use of a comma is dictated by where the subordinate clause is located. If the subordinate clause is located before the main clause, a comma is needed between the two clauses.

Because I don't have enough money, I will not order steak.

Generally, if the subordinate clause is placed after the main clause, no punctuation is needed.

I did well on my exam because I studied two hours the night before.

Notice how the last clause is dependent because it requires the earlier independent clauses to make sense.

Use a comma on both sides of an interrupting phrase.

I will pay for the ice cream, *chocolate and vanilla*, and then will eat it all myself.

The words forming the phrase in italics are nonessential (extra) information. To determine if a phrase is nonessential, try reading the sentence without the phrase and see if it's still coherent.

A comma is not necessary in this next sentence because no interruption—nonessential or extra information—has occurred. Read sentences aloud when uncertain.

I will pay for his chocolate and vanilla ice cream and then will eat it all myself.

If the nonessential phrase comes at the beginning of a sentence, a comma should only go at the end of the phrase. If the phrase comes at the end of a sentence, a comma should only go at the beginning of the phrase.

Other types of interruptions include the following:

- interjections: Oh no, I am not going.
- abbreviations: Barry Potter, M.D., specializes in heart disorders.
- direct addresses: Yes, Claudia, I am tired and going to bed.

- parenthetical phrases: His wife, lovely as she was, was not helpful.
- transitional phrases: Also, it is not possible.

The second comma in the following sentence is called an Oxford comma.

> I will pay for ice cream, syrup, and pop.

It is a comma used after the second-to-last item in a series of three or more items. It comes before the word *or* or *and*. Not everyone uses the Oxford comma; it is optional, but many believe it is needed. The comma functions as a tool to reduce confusion in writing. So, if omitting the Oxford comma would cause confusion, then it's best to include it.

Commas are used in math to mark the place of thousands in numerals, breaking them up so they are easier to read. Other uses for commas are in dates (*March 19, 2016*), letter greetings (*Dear Sally,*), and in between cities and states (*Louisville, KY*).

Apostrophes

This punctuation mark, the apostrophe ('), is a versatile little mark. It has a few different functions:

- Quotes: Apostrophes are used when a second quote is needed within a quote.

- In my letter to my friend, I wrote, "The girl had to get a new purse, and guess what Mary did? She said, 'I'd like to go with you to the store.' I knew Mary would buy it for her."

- Contractions: Another use for an apostrophe in the quote above is a contraction. *I'd* is used for *I would.*

  The basic rule for making *contractions* is one area of spelling that is pretty straightforward: combine the two words by inserting an apostrophe (') in the space where a letter is omitted. For example, to combine *you* and *are*, drop the *a* and put the apostrophe in its place: *you're.*

  > he + is = he's
  >
  > you + all = y'all (informal but often misspelled)

- Possession: An apostrophe followed by the letter *s* shows possession (*Mary's* purse). If the possessive word is plural, the apostrophe generally just follows the word.

- The trees' leaves are all over the ground.

Ellipses

An **ellipsis** (...) is used to show that there is more to the quoted text than is necessary for the current discussion. Writers use them in place of words, lines, phrases, list content, or paragraphs that might just as easily have been omitted from a passage of writing. This can be done to save space or to focus only on the specifically relevant material.

> Exercise is good for some unexpected reasons. Watkins writes, "Exercise has many benefits such as...reducing cancer risk."

In the example above, the ellipsis takes the place of the other benefits of exercise that are more expected.

The ellipsis may also be used to show a pause in sentence flow.

> "I'm wondering...how this could happen," Dylan said in a soft voice.

Semicolons

The **semicolon** (;) might be described as a heavy-handed comma. Take a look at these two examples:

> I will pay for the ice cream, but I will not pay for the steak.
> I will pay for the ice cream; I will not pay for the steak.

What's the difference? The first example has a comma and a conjunction separating the two independent clauses. The second example does not have a conjunction, but there are two independent clauses in the sentence, so something more than a comma is required. In this case, a semicolon is used.

Two independent clauses can only be joined in a sentence by either a comma and conjunction or a semicolon. If one of those tools is not used, the sentence will be a run-on. Remember that while the clauses are independent, they need to be closely related in order to be contained in one sentence.

Another use for the semicolon is to separate items in a list when the items themselves require commas.

> The family lived in Phoenix, Arizona; Oklahoma City, Oklahoma; and Raleigh, North Carolina.

Colons

Colons (:) have many miscellaneous functions. Colons can be used to precede further information or a list. In these cases, a colon should only follow an independent clause.

> Humans take in sensory information through five basic senses: sight, hearing, smell, touch, and taste.

The meal includes the following components:

- Caesar salad
- spaghetti
- garlic bread
- cake

Colons can also be used to introduce an appositive.

> The family got what they needed: a reliable vehicle.

While a comma is more common, a colon can also precede a formal quotation.

> He said to the crowd: "Let's begin!"

The colon is used after the greeting in a formal letter.

> Dear Sir:
> To Whom It May Concern:

In the writing of time, the colon separates the minutes from the hour (*4:45 p.m.*). The colon can also be used to indicate a ratio between two numbers (*50:1*).

Hyphens

The **hyphen** (-) is a little hash mark that can be used to join words to show that they are linked.

Hyphens can connect two words that work together as a single adjective (a compound adjective).

> honey-covered biscuits

Some words always require hyphens even if not serving as an adjective.

> merry-go-round

Hyphens always go after certain prefixes like *anti-* & *all-*.

Hyphens should also be used when the absence of the hyphen would cause a strange vowel combination (*semi-engineer*) or confusion. For example, *re-collect* should be used to describe something being gathered twice rather than being written as *recollect*, which means to remember.

Parentheses and Dashes

Parentheses are half-round brackets that look like this: *( )*. They set off a word, phrase, or sentence that is an afterthought, explanation, or side note relevant to the surrounding text but not essential. A pair of commas is often used to set off this sort of information, but parentheses are generally used for information that would not fit well within a sentence or that the writer deems not important enough to be structurally part of the sentence.

> The picture of the heart (see above) shows the major parts you should memorize.
> Mount Everest is one of three mountains in the world that are over 28,000 feet high (K2 and Kanchenjunga are the other two).

See how the sentences above are complete without the parenthetical statements? In the first example, *see above* would not have fit well within the flow of the sentence. The second parenthetical statement could have been a separate sentence, but the writer deemed the information not pertinent to the topic.

The **em-dash** (—) is a mark longer than a hyphen used as a punctuation mark in sentences and to set apart a relevant thought. Even after plucking out the line separated by the dash marks, the sentence will be intact and make sense.

> Looking out the airplane window at the landmarks—Lake Clarke, Thompson Community College, and the bridge—she couldn't help but feel excited to be home.

The dashes use is similar to that of parentheses or a pair of commas. So, what's the difference? Many believe that using dashes makes the clause within them stand out while using parentheses is subtler. It's advised to not use dashes when commas could be used instead.

Quotation Marks

Quotation marks ("") are used in a number of ways. Here are some instances where *quotation marks* should be used:

- To indicate a quote that was taken from somewhere else, either from a verbal or written source
- Dialogue for characters in narratives. When characters speak, the first word should always be capitalized, and the punctuation goes inside the quotes. For example:

  Janie said, "The tree fell on my car during the hurricane."

- Around titles of songs, short stories, essays, and chapters in books
- To emphasize a certain word
- To refer to a word as the word itself

Capitalization

Here's a non-exhaustive list of things that should be capitalized:

- The first word of every sentence
- The first word of every line of poetry
- The first letter of proper nouns (World War II)
- Holidays (Valentine's Day)
- The days of the week and months of the year (Tuesday, March)
- The first word, last word, and all major words in the titles of books, movies, songs, and other creative works (In the novel, *To Kill a Mockingbird*, note that *a* is lowercase since it's not a major word, but *to* is capitalized since it's the first word of the title.)
- Titles when preceding a proper noun (President Roberto Gonzales, Aunt Judy)

When simply using a word such as president or secretary, though, the word is not capitalized.

> Officers of the new business must include a *president* and *treasurer*.

Seasons—spring, fall, etc.—are not capitalized.

North, *south*, *east*, and *west* are capitalized when referring to regions but are not when being used for directions. In general, if it's preceded by *the* it should be capitalized.

> I'm from the South.
> I drove south.

Various Homonyms

That/Which

The pronouns that and which are both used to refer to nouns—but they are not interchangeable. The rule is to use the word that in essential clauses and phrases that help convey the meaning of the sentence. Use the word *which* in nonessential (less important) clauses. Typically, *which* clauses are enclosed in commas.

The morning that I fell asleep in class caused me a lot of trouble.

This morning's coffee, which had too much creamer, woke me up.

Who/Whom

We use the pronouns *who* and *whom* to refer to people. We always use who when it is the subject of the sentence or clause. Whom is always the object of a verb or preposition.

Who hit the baseball for the home run? (subject)

The baseball fell into the glove of whom? (object of the preposition of)

The umpire called whom "out"? (object of the verb called)

To/Too/Two

to: a preposition or infinitive (*to walk, to run, walk to the store, run to the tree*)
too: means also, as well, or very (*She likes cookies, too.; I ate too much.*)
two: a number (*I have two cookies. She walked to the store two times.*)

There/Their/They're

there: an adjective, adverb, or pronoun used to start a sentence or indicate place (*There are four vintage cars over there.*)
their: a possessive pronoun used to indicate belonging (*Their car is the blue and white one.*)
they're: a contraction of the words "they are" (*They're going to enter the vintage car show.*)

Your/You're

your: a possessive pronoun (*Your artwork is terrific.*)
you're: a contraction of the words "you are" (*You're a terrific artist.*)

Its/It's

its: a possessive pronoun (*The elephant had its trunk in the water.*)
it's: a contraction of the words "it is" (*It's an impressive animal.*)

Affect/Effect

affect: as a verb means "to influence" (*How will the earthquake affect your home?*); as a noun means "emotion or mood" (*Her affect was somber.*)
effect: as a verb means "to bring about" (*She will effect a change through philanthropy.*); as a noun means "a result of" (*The effect of the earthquake was devastating.*)

Other mix-ups: Other pairs of words cause mix-ups but are not necessarily homonyms. Here are a few of those:

Bring/Take

bring: when the action is coming toward (*Bring me the money.*)
take: when the action is going away from (*Take her the money.*)

Can/May

can: means "able to" (*The child can ride a bike.*)

may: asks permission (*The child asked if he may ride his bike*.)

Than/Then

than: a conjunction used for comparison (*I like tacos better than pizza.*)
then: an adverb telling when something happened (*I ate and then slept.*)

Disinterested/Uninterested

disinterested: used to mean "neutral" (*The jury remains disinterested during the trial.*)
uninterested: used to mean "bored" (*I was uninterested during the lecture*.)

Percent/Percentage

percent: used when there is a number involved (*Five percent of us like tacos.*)
percentage: used when there is no number (*That is a low percentage.*)

Fewer/Less

fewer: used for things you can count (*He has fewer playing cards.*)
less: used for things you cannot count, as well as time (*He has less talent. You have less than a minute*.)

Farther/Further

farther: used when discussing distance (*His paper airplane flew farther than mine*.)
further: used to mean "more" (*He needed further information*.)

Lend/Loan

lend: a verb used for borrowing (*Lend me your lawn mower. He will lend it to me*.)
loan: a noun used for something borrowed (*She applied for a student loan*.)

Note

Some people have problems with these:

- regardless/irregardless
- a lot/alot

Irregardless and *alot* are always incorrect. Don't use them.

Speaking

The IELTS™ Speaking Section assesses the test taker's ability to communicate effectively in English. This section lasts 11–14 minutes and consists of an oral interview between the test taker and an exam administrator and is recorded. The three parts to this test section are as follows:

- **Introduction and interview**: This section lasts 4–5 minutes and consists of general introductions between the test taker and the examiner. It will include basic questions about familiar life topics such as hobbies, family, studies, and home life. The questions are taken from a script to ensure equivalence in expectations for candidates.

- **Individual long turn**: Test takers will be handed a card that prompts them to talk about a specific topic, gives specific aspects that must be addressed, and instructs test takers to elaborate and more fully explain at least one of their points. This section lasts 3–4 minutes: one minute for preparation after reading the card, a one- to two-minute oral response, and then the examiner will ask the test taker one or two questions relating to the same topic. It should be noted that test takers are stopped after two minutes of talking, even if they have not addressed all of their points or the assignment's tasks, so test takers are encouraged to practice effective time management skills and use the one-minute preparation time to structure their speech and consider the time requirements.

  It is recommended that test takers jot down notes or a basic outline during the preparation period. Talking much less than 60–90 seconds will likely result in an incomplete answer and may detract from one's score. Some of the most effective and successful long turns result from the test takers drawing upon their own life experiences. The speech should be coherent, well-organized, grammatically correct, and compelling.

- **Discussion**: This section lasts 4–5 minutes and consists of more of a back-and-forth conversation between the test takers and examiner. The same topic addressed in Part 2 will be discussed, but this time, in more depth. The examiner is looking for evidence of the test taker's ability to analyze different viewpoints on issues and express and justify their opinion.

For all three tasks, examiners are evaluating test takers on the following four criteria:

- **Fluency and coherence**: The skill and ease with which the test taker talks with a steady, natural, and fluid rate, connecting ideas and words in a coherent and continuous manner. Test takers should structure their thoughts, points, and arguments in a logical sequence with appropriate use of cohesive devices like conjunctions, connecting words, and pronouns to link words, phrases, sentences, and topics.

- **Lexical resource**: The breadth and precision of vocabulary used and the effectiveness of word choice to accurately and exactly convey intended meaning.

- **Grammatical range and accuracy:** The number and effect of grammatical errors, the length, complexity, and variety of the sentence structures delivered in the oral responses, the appropriate use of clauses, parts of speech, and language.

- **Pronunciation**: The proper pronunciation of the language used to answer the questions.

While this section can sound daunting, the good news is that the Speaking section of the IELTS™ is the easiest one to prepare for because the opportunities to practice are endless. Candidates should take advantage of every opportunity to practice their English-speaking skills, not only to optimize their test performance, but also because they will be frequently conversing in English in diverse situations long after passing the exam. Nearly every situation presents a valid opportunity to practice—driving the car, walking the dog, commuting to work, visiting a friend, doing errands, etc.

In addition to capitalizing on every chance to practice speaking, there are some other helpful strategies that successful test takers employ for this section.

Practice, but Don't Memorize

As mentioned, it's impossible to over-practice and the more speaking time a test taker has under their belt, the better. However, memorizing responses, particularly for the first two tasks (which tend to pose only a handful of possible questions), is not recommended. For one thing, scorers are looking for a natural speaking style that feels conversational and relaxed. Rehearsing and memorizing a predetermined response will likely lower one's delivery score even if the content is good. It is better to sound authentic and organic in the delivery of the answer, even if it means slightly less content is delivered in the allotted time. On that note, for the long turn, it's wise to practice speaking for two minutes to build confidence and time management skills for that task.

Listen and Read the Question Carefully

It's easy to jump to an answer when nervous, but successful test takers make sure to pay careful attention to the specific question posed in the task and ensure that their response addresses the exact points desired. For example, the first task usually asks general questions such as what do you enjoy doing in your spare time, what is your family like, or what are your favorite places to visit? Test takers who are overly rehearsed may begin to hear a familiar prompt and then assume they know what the question is asking and prepare to deliver their memorized response. However, this hastiness can lead to mistakes; oftentimes, there are slight changes in the wording of the questions such that the exact question test administrators are looking for is different than that assumed. Instead of what do you enjoy doing on your spare time, the question may be more specific and ask, what do you enjoy doing by yourself in your spare time? If a test taker did not listen carefully or jumped to a prepared answer about enjoying basketball with their team or shopping with friends, points would be deducted for inappropriate content for the intended answer.

Organize

Test takers should take advantage of the 15–30 seconds provided to reflect on the question and organize their thoughts before they have to deliver their response. Many people find it helpful to write down a couple of bullet points that they plan to highlight in their answer. These should be just a word or short phrase, rather than a whole sentence, so as to save time and sound organic and natural in the response. Reading fully composed sentences tends to sound overly rehearsed and may affect one's delivery score.

Speak Clearly and Simply

Many test takers feel anxious or self-conscious about delivering their responses with as little influence of an accent as possible. The good news is that the IELTS™ does not expect candidates to speak with any sort of "English" accent, and scores are not influenced by the responder's accent one way or another as long as pronunciation is adequate. What is important is that the response is clear, audible, and comprehensible. After all, if scorers cannot hear or understand the recorded answer, they cannot award it with high marks. Test takers should speak as fluidly as possible, without rushing or interjecting long pauses or words of varying volumes.

As much as possible, words should be enunciated with all syllables present and emphasizing those necessary for proper pronunciation. The more even and rhythmic the spoken answer, the better. One more point to note is that many test takers imagine that adding fancy vocabulary words will bolster their score. While demonstrating a rich vocabulary and strong command of English grammar and language skills is important, it is more important to ensure that words are used properly and that sentence structure and intended meaning are on point. If test takers are not confident in the meaning or proper usage of a word, it is better to use a seemingly simpler word whose meaning they are sure of.

Make Speech Flow

As mentioned, answers should flow as naturally and fluidly as possible. With that said, short pauses should be interjected at the end of each sentence or where commas would be used in written text to help listeners understand the thoughts and the organization of the response. Rushing into each subsequent sentence without an adequate pause tends to make answers sound confusing. To connect thoughts together and create a logical flow to the response, test takers should demonstrate command of the use of conjunctions and employ effective connecting words and phrases such as: *because, due to, for example, after this, if...then,* and *however*.

Structure the Answer

Although spoken language is often not as formal as written communication, answers should still be organized, with well-developed thoughts presented in a logical order. Successful test takers generate their ideas and plan their delivery during the reflection time prior to recording their responses. It is wise to start the answer by stating the topic thought (like a topic sentence in a written essay) and then expand or describe that thought in the subsequent sentences. Adding a concluding sentence that ties back to the beginning thought gives the listener clarity and pulls all the details together into a comprehensive and intelligent answer.

Tell a Story

The most memorable conversations are those that include a captivating story. Speakers should try to make responses engaging and personal, when appropriate. This may not only make for a more enjoyable listen for scorers, but may also improve one's score by garnering more delivery points.

Be Confident

Everyone has important things to say. Test takers should not worry about saying something "stupid" or "boring." They should speak from the heart and be confident in their command of English as well as their comprehension of the posed question. There is no need to rush when delivering the response; there is plenty of time in 45 seconds to get out a complete answer. On that note, if there is extra time at the end of the allotted recording time, it is generally recommended to simply end the response when the question has been fully answered rather than fill every last second with speaking. It is unnecessary to speak aimlessly at the end, as this can reduce one's content score if the answer starts deviating from what was asked. Test takers should just pace themselves, stay relaxed, and speak with authority.

IELTS Practice Test #1

Listening

Directions: The Listening section measures your ability to understand conversations and lectures in English. In this test, you will listen to several pieces of content and answer questions after each one. The questions typically ask about the main idea and supporting details. Some questions ask about a speaker's purpose or attitude. Answer the questions based on what is stated or implied by the speakers.

Listen to all of these passages by going to testprepbooks.com/bonus/ielts or by scanning the QR code below:

SCAN ME

Note that on the actual test, you may take notes while you listen and use your notes to help you answer the questions. Your notes will not be scored.

For your convenience, the transcripts of all of the audio passages are provided after the answer explanations. However, on the actual test, no such transcripts will be provided.

Passage #1: Conversation

Questions 1–3: Complete the sentences below: Write NO MORE THAN TWO WORDS for each answer.

1. Greg is looking for help with ________________.

2. Greg lost his ID at the ____________________.

3. The female student studies in the ___________ of the library.

4. How does a student replace their campus ID according to Deborah? Mark all that apply.
   a. Go to the library by the encyclopedias
   b. Go to the administration building
   c. Fill out a form and show a picture ID
   d. Pay a replacement fee
   e. Bring a piece of mail with a home address

5. Read the following statement from the conversation, and then answer the question:
   (Male student) I haven't really gotten into a study rhythm yet this semester. That may be part of my problem. I guess I study in my room, when my roommate and I aren't playing video games, that is.

What does the male student mean when he says he has not really gotten into "a study rhythm yet"?
   a. He has not yet studied with music.
   b. He needs to study with video games.
   c. He has not yet established a study routine or habit.

6. Why does the female student say: "Well, hey, I've got to run to Economics class now"?
   a. She is preparing to end the conversation
   b. She enjoys running for the school's track team
   c. She is trying to change the topic of conversation

Questions 7-10. Fill out the following diagram by choosing items from the provided box. Write the letter of your choice for each line in questions 7-10.

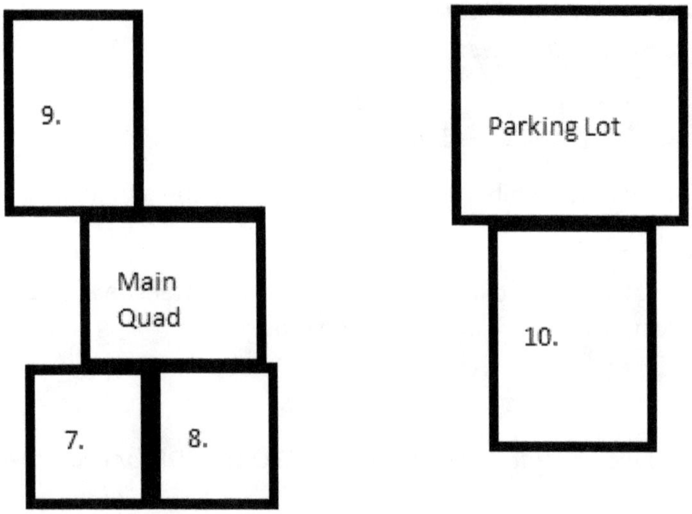

A. Computer lab
B. Library
C. Dormitory
D. Baseball field
E. Administration building
F. Science center
G. Dining hall
H. Auditorium

7. ______

8. ______

9. ______

10. ______

Passage #2: Monologue

Questions 11–14: Complete the summary below using NO MORE THAN ONE WORD per space.

- Basement
- First floor
- Second floor
- Third floor
- Fourth floor
- Does not exist

Community members are encouraged to sign up for the center's 11. _____________ to stay informed of the programs and special offers. Members are encouraged to 12. ______________ new members and doing so will enter them into a 13. _________ program. "Arts bucks" will be accrued and can be 14. _________________ for credits.

Questions 15–20: Match the given room or offering to the floor in which it is located. Write the letter of the answer choice in the blank provided.

15. Snack café ______

16. Instrument lending library ______

17. Stained glass class ______

18. Photography studio ______

19. Theater rehearsals ______

20. Band practices ______

Passage #3: Conversation

21. What is the main problem the student is having?
   a. She does not know which classes to register for
   b. She needs to get a job on campus
   c. Her bill is higher than she predicted

22. Which of the following are ways that students can receive financial assistance with their school bills? Select all that apply.
   a. Scholarships
   b. Loans
   c. Work-study
   d. Tuition

23. Why is the student's scholarship pending?
   a. The financial aid office has not received the student's FAFSA yet.
   b. The student did not pass all of their classes the previous semester.
   c. The financial aid office made a mistake with the student's account.

24. Based on the conversation, which job is the student most likely to apply for?
   a. A job at the financial aid office
   b. A job at the computer lab
   c. A job at the sports center
   d. A job at the librar

Questions 25–30. The financial aid officer explains to the student what she needs to do to fill out her FASFA, apply for a work-study, and fix the hold on her account. In what order does he list the steps? Not all answer choices will be utilized.

25	
26	
27	
28	
29	
30	

A. Register for classes
B. Apply for a campus job
C. Wait for financial aid package evaluation
D. Pay balance on the account
E. Register to fill out the FAFSA
F. Input prior year's tax information
G. Ask for tuition reduction

Passage #4: Lecture

31. What was the main topic addressed in the lecture?
    a. The contributions of various historical astronomers to our understanding of modern astronomy
    b. The importance of the telescope in our understanding of the Universe
    c. The history of how the Universe and Solar System formed billions of years ago

32. What does the professor imply about the scientists discussed in the lecture?
    a. That only their accurate discoveries or proposals were important to our understanding
    b. That they made a lot of mistakes in their discoveries
    c. That their contributions, even when inaccurate, helped shape our current understanding

33. Read the following sentences about Brahe and then answer the question.

    (Female Professor) He thought the Earth was not moving and that the Sun and Moon revolved around the stationary planet, so we know now that this part was off-base but he's still a key player in our progression of knowledge.

What does the professor imply about Brahe in this sentence?
    a. That his ideas were wrong and not important in the discussion of astronomy
    b. That other scientists and other humans continued to evolve from his DNA
    c. That he is important in any discussion of the history of astronomy, even if some of his ideas were incorrect

34. Fill in the following sentence using ONE word only.

The information in the lecture was organized in ____________________ order.

Questions 35–40: Match the astronomical contribution to the astronomer who is credited with the advancement. Write the letter of the corresponding astronomer for your answer.

35. He proposed the three laws of motion. ______

36. He said the Sun was a star. ______

37. He invented the telescope. ______

38. He lay the foundation for scientific thought and experimentation. ______

39. He developed the idea that Earth, and the other planets, rotate around the Sun. ______

40. He made astronomical tools to help with mapping the "heavens" and the Solar System. ______

A. Galileo

B. Brahe

C. Copernicus

D. Newton

E. Keppler

Academic Test Reading

Passage #1: Anatomy and Physiology

The following passage about the circulatory system would be found in an introductory anatomy and physiology textbook. Read the passage and then answer the associated questions.

(A) The circulatory system is a network of organs and tubes that transports blood, hormones, nutrients, oxygen, and other gases to cells and tissues throughout the body. It is also known as the cardiovascular system. The major components of the circulatory system include blood vessels, blood, and the heart.

(B) In the circulatory system, blood vessels are responsible for transporting blood throughout the body. The blood vessels, in order of decreasing size as blood moves away from the heart, are arteries, arterioles, and capillaries. Towards the heart, from smallest to largest, are capillaries, venules, and veins.

Arteries carry blood from the heart to the rest of the body. Veins carry blood from the body to the heart. Capillaries connect arteries to veins and form networks that exchange materials between the blood and the cells.

In general, arteries are stronger and thicker than veins, as they withstand high pressures exerted by the blood as the heart pumps it through the body. Arteries control blood flow through either *vasoconstriction* (narrowing of the blood vessel's diameter) or *vasodilation* (widening of the blood vessel's diameter). The blood in veins is under much lower pressures, so veins have valves to prevent the backflow of blood.

Most of the exchanges between the blood and tissues take place via the capillaries. There are three types of capillaries: continuous, fenestrated, and sinusoidal.

Continuous capillaries are made up of epithelial cells tightly connected together. As a result, they limit the types of materials that pass into and out of the blood. Continuous capillaries are the most common type of capillary. *Fenestrated capillaries* have openings that allow materials to be freely exchanged between the blood and tissues. They are commonly found in the digestive, endocrine, and urinary systems. *Sinusoidal capillaries* have larger openings and allow proteins and blood cells through. They are found primarily in the liver, bone marrow, and spleen.

(C) Blood is vital to the human body. It is a liquid connective tissue that serves as a transport system for supplying cells with nutrients and carrying away their wastes. The average adult human has five to six quarts of blood circulating through their body. Approximately 55% of blood is *plasma* (the fluid portion), and the remaining 45% is composed of solid cells and cell parts. There are three major types of blood cells: red blood cells, white blood cells, and platelets. Red blood cells transport oxygen throughout the body. They contain a protein called *hemoglobin* that allows them to carry oxygen. The iron in the hemoglobin gives the cells and the blood their red colors. White blood cells are responsible for fighting infectious diseases and maintaining the immune system. There are five types of white blood cells: neutrophils, lymphocytes, eosinophils, monocytes, and basophils. Platelets are cell fragments which play a central role in the blood clotting process.

All blood cells in adults are produced in the bone marrow—red blood cells from red marrow and white blood cells from yellow marrow.

(D) The heart is a two-part, muscular pump that forcefully pushes blood throughout the human body. The human heart, also called the *myocardium*, has four chambers—two upper atria and two lower ventricles, a pair on the left and a pair on the right. Anatomically, *left* and *right* correspond to the sides of the body that the patient themselves would refer to as left and right.

Four valves help to section off the chambers from one another. Between the right atrium and ventricle, the three flaps of the tricuspid valve keep blood from backflowing from the ventricle to the atrium, similar to how the two flaps of the mitral valve work between the left atrium and ventricle. As these two valves lie between an atrium and a ventricle, they are referred to as *atrioventricular* (AV) valves. The other two valves are *semilunar* (SL) and control blood flow into the two great arteries leaving the ventricles. The pulmonary valve connects the right ventricle to the pulmonary artery, while the aortic valve connects the left ventricle to the aorta.

Blood enters the (1) right atrium. When the right atrium contracts, blood passes through the (2) tricuspid valve into the (3) right ventricle. After filling, the right ventricle contracts, and the tricuspid valve closes, pushing blood through the (4) pulmonary semilunar valve into the (5) pulmonary arteries. These arteries, unlike all other arteries in the body, carry deoxygenated blood to the lungs, where blood travels through the (6) alveolar capillaries. Here, oxygen is absorbed, and carbon dioxide is removed.

The newly-oxygenated blood is carried by the (7) pulmonary veins back to the (8) left atrium. Contraction of the left atrium moves blood through the (9) bicuspid valve into the (10) left ventricle (the largest heart chamber). When the bicuspid valve closes and the left ventricle contracts, blood is forced into the (11) aortic valve through the aorta and passed on to systemic circulation.

(E) One complete sequence of cardiac activity is referred to as a cardiac cycle. The cardiac cycle represents the relaxation and contraction of the heart and can be divided into two phases: *diastole* and *systole*.

Diastole is the phase during which the heart relaxes and fills with blood. During this phase, it becomes possible to measure the diastolic blood pressure (DBP), which is the bottom number of a blood pressure reading. Systole is the phase during which the heart contracts and discharges blood. It creates the systolic blood pressure (SBP), which is the top number of a blood pressure reading. The heart's electrical conduction system coordinates the cardiac cycle.

(F) The mechanical contraction of the heart is controlled by an electrical conduction system. The conduction system has numerous components that are responsible for the transmission of the electrical impulse that causes the contraction and recovery of the atria and ventricles. The *sinoatrial (SA) node*, considered to be the intrinsic pacemaker, normally is the initiator of rhythmic electrical impulses. It consists of a small amount of specialized muscle tissue and is located in the upper wall of the right atrium. Internodal pathways conduct the electrical impulse between the SA node and *AV node*, which is the location where the electrical impulse is slightly delayed before it passes into the ventricles. The *AV bundle*, which is divided into left and right bundle branches, conducts the electrical impulse to both ventricles. The bundle branches are further divided into *Purkinje fibers*, which transmit the impulse throughout the ventricles.

(G) The autonomic nervous system (ANS) is responsible for the rhythmicity and conduction properties of the myocardium. The atria have both sympathetic and parasympathetic fibers, while the ventricles have mostly sympathetic fibers. Sympathetic fibers increase the speed at which the SA node depolarizes, resulting in a faster heart rate. Parasympathetic fibers decrease the speed of SA node depolarization, which decreases the heart rate. The normal range for a resting heart rate is 60-100 beats/minute. *Bradycardia* is an abnormally slow heart (less than 60 beats/minute), and *tachycardia* is an abnormally fast heart rate (greater than 100 beats/minute).

(H) An *electrocardiogram* (ECG or EKG) graphically represents the heart's electrical changes (recorded by electrodes on the skin) during the cardiac cycle. The cardiac cycle consists of several waves that represent depolarization and repolarization of the atria and ventricles. The first wave is the *P-wave*. This corresponds to atrial depolarization, which causes the contraction of the atria and the movement of blood down to the ventricles. The depolarization of the ventricles during the *QRS complex* (QRS complex consists of the *Q-wave*, *R-wave*, and *S-wave*) results in ventricular contraction, which produces the force to circulate blood through the pulmonary and peripheral blood vessels. The *T-wave* corresponds to ventricular repolarization, which can be thought of as the recovery from depolarization. The atria also repolarize, but on an EKG this activity is masked by the larger QRS complex, which occurs simultaneously.

(I) Five major blood vessels manage blood flow to and from the heart: the superior and inferior venae cavae, the aorta, the pulmonary artery, and the pulmonary vein.

The superior vena cava is a large vein that drains blood from the head and upper body. The inferior vena cava is a large vein that drains blood from the lower body. The aorta is the largest artery in the human body and carries blood from the heart to body tissues. The pulmonary arteries carry blood from the heart to the lungs. The pulmonary veins transport blood from the lungs to the heart.

In the human body, there are two types of circulation: pulmonary circulation and systemic circulation. Pulmonary circulation supplies blood to the lungs. Deoxygenated blood enters the right atrium of the heart and is routed through the tricuspid valve into the right ventricle. Deoxygenated blood then travels from the right ventricle of the heart through the pulmonary valve and into the pulmonary arteries. The pulmonary arteries carry the deoxygenated blood to the lungs. In the lungs, oxygen is absorbed, and carbon dioxide is released. The pulmonary veins carry oxygenated blood to the left atrium of the heart.

Systemic circulation supplies blood to all other parts of the body, except the lungs. Oxygenated blood flows from the left atrium of the heart through the mitral, or bicuspid, valve into the left ventricle of the heart. Oxygenated blood is then routed from the left ventricle of the heart through the aortic valve and into the aorta. The aorta delivers blood to the systemic arteries, which supply the body tissues. In the tissues, oxygen and nutrients are exchanged for carbon dioxide and other wastes. The deoxygenated blood, along with carbon dioxide and wastes, enter the systemic veins, where they are returned to the right atrium of the heart via the superior and inferior vena cava.

Questions 1-6: The sample passage has nine sections, A-I. Choose the correct heading for the sections requested below from the list of headings provided.

i. Types of Circulation
ii. The Myocardium
iii. The Circulatory System
iv. Measuring the Electrical Activity of the Heart
v. The Electrical Conduction System
vi. The Arteries
vii. Regulation of the Electrical Activity of the Heart
viii. The Heartbeat
ix. The Cardiac Cycle
x. Blood
xi. Blood Vessels

Write the correct number i-xi in the space provided.

1. Section B ____

2. Section C ____

3. Section D ____

4. Section E ____

5. Section F ____

6. Section H ____

Questions 7-11: Label the parts of the heart on the diagram below using words from the adjacent box. Write your answers in the spaces provided.

Right Atrium
Myocardium
Right Ventricle
Septum
Left Ventricle
Aorta
Tricuspid Valve
Left Atrium
Mitral Valve
Semilunar Valve

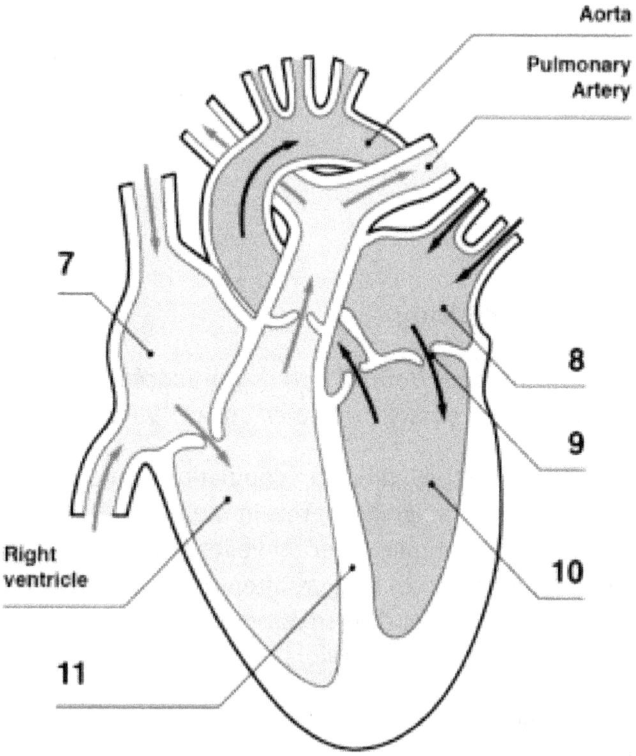

7. ____________________

8. ____________________

9. ____________________

10. ____________________

11. ____________________

12. Which of the following reflects the correct blood flow pathway (heart-valve-vessel)?
    a. Right atrium, left atrium, right ventricle, mitral valve, left ventricle, aorta
    b. Right atrium, tricuspid valve, right ventricle, left atrium, left ventricle, aorta
    c. Right atrium, right ventricle, left atrium, tricuspid valve, left ventricle, aorta
    d. Right atrium, right ventricle, pulmonary circulation, left atrium, mitral valve, left ventricle, aorta

13. Why do arteries have valves?
    a. They have valves to maintain high blood pressure so that capillaries diffuse nutrients properly.
    b. Their valves are designed to prevent backflow due to their low blood pressure.
    c. They have valves due to a leftover evolutionary trait that, like the appendix, is useless.
    d. They do not have valves, but veins do have valves.

14. What area of the heart is responsible for initiating rhythmic electrical impulses?
   a. Purkinje fibers
   b. Atrioventricular (AV) bundle
   c. Sinoatrial (SA) node
   d. Atrioventricular (AV) node

15. When reading an electrocardiogram, ventricular repolarization is associated with which graphical component?
   a. QRS complex
   b. P-wave
   c. T-wave
   d. PR segment

Passage #2: Sociology

The following passage is from an introductory sociology textbook, discussing the demographic structure of a society. Read the passage and then answer the questions that follow.

Demography, or the study of human populations, involves a variety of closely related stimuli. First, economic factors play a significant role in the movement of people, as do climate, natural disasters, or internal unrest. For example, in recent years, millions of immigrants from the war-torn country of Syria have sought refuge far from danger, often risking their lives to cross the Mediterranean Sea. Although people move and settle for diverse reasons, sociologists have identified some consistencies in movement and settlement behaviors.

First, people tend to live near reliable sources of food and water, which is why the first human civilizations sprung up in river valleys like the Indus River Valley in India, the Nile River Valley in Egypt, and the Yellow River Valley in China. Second, extreme temperatures tend to push people away, which is why the high latitudinal regions near the North and South Poles have such few inhabitants. Third, the vast majority of people tend to live in the Northern Hemisphere, due to the simple fact that more land lies in that part of the Earth. In keeping with these factors, human populations tend to be greater where human necessities are easily accessible, or at least are more readily available. In other words, such areas have a greater chance of having a higher population density than places without such characteristics.

Demographic patterns on Earth are not always stagnant. In contrast, people move and will continue to move as both push and pull factors fluctuate over time. For example, in the 1940s, thousands of Europeans fled their homelands due to the impact of the Second World War. Today, thousands of migrants arrive on European shores each month due to conflicts in the Levant and difficult economic conditions in Northern Africa. Furthermore, as previously discussed, people tend to migrate to places with a greater economic benefit for themselves and their families. As a result, developed nations, such as the United States, Germany, Canada, and Australia, have a net gain of migrants, while developing nations, such as Somalia, Zambia, and Cambodia, tend to see thousands of their citizens seek better lives elsewhere.

There are several key variables which contribute to changes in human population and its composition worldwide, including religion, economic opportunity, social unrest, and cost of living. These factors can show up in myriad ways; as revealed in the following examples, religion and religious conflict can play multifaceted roles in where people choose to live. Take the nation of Israel: the country won its independence in 1948 and has since attracted thousands of people of Jewish descent from all over the world, all the while, remaining embroiled in violent conflict with Palestinian residents and driving them from the land. Additionally, the United States has long attracted people from all over the world, due to the promise of religious freedom inherent in its Constitution. Finally, Saudi Arabia does not tolerate the practice of non-Muslim religions, resulting in a decidedly uniform religious composition.

Such factors can influence human migration, or the movement of people from one country to another. Migration is governed by two primary causes: *push factors*, which are reasons causing someone to leave an area, and *pull factors*, which are factors luring someone to a particular place. These two factors often work in concert with one another. For example, the United States of America has experienced significant *internal migration* from industrial states in the Northeast (such as New York, New Jersey, Connecticut) to southern and western states (such as Florida, Texas, Arizona). This massive migration, which continues into the present day, is in part due to high rents in the northeast, frigid winters, and a lack of adequate retirement housing, all of which are push factors. These push factors lead to migration to the *Sunbelt*, a term used by geographers to describe states with warm climates and less intense winters.

In addition to internal migrations within nations or regions, migration also takes place between countries, continents, and other regions. The United States has long been the world's leading nation in regard to *immigration*, the process of having people crossing into a nation's boundaries to settle permanently. Conversely, developing nations that suffer from high levels of poverty, pollution, warfare, and other violence all have significant push factors, which cause people to leave and move elsewhere. Push factors commonly lead to *emigration*, the process by which people in a particular area leave in order to seek a better life in a different location.

Patterns of migration are generally economically motivated. For example, the United States underwent a significant population shift from 1916-1930 due to its entrance into the First World War. Because of the war, thousands of factories opened and needed workers to produce munitions for the war effort. Answering the call of opportunity, thousands of African Americans, who had lived on farms since the cessation of the Civil War, packed up their belongings and moved to cities like Detroit, Los Angeles, Milwaukee, and Cleveland. This mass internal migration, which historians termed the *Great Migration*, is an excellent example of how economic forces work to stimulate human migration, thus drastically altering a nation's demographic patterns.

Demographic shifts—apparent changes in the size, distribution, composition, and growth of a population—inevitably catalyze social changes as micro- and macro-communities expand, disperse, shift, and contract. Demographic shifts influence human beings to respond in different ways. Demographic shifts can be the root of war, immigration, genocide, famine, and panic. However, they also can be the root of harmony, peace, stability, and social justice. Demography and sociology are so integrally linked that it is hard to disassociate the two fields.

In sociology, there are two major theories of demographic change: the Malthusian theory and the demographic transition theory. Created by English economist Thomas Malthus (1766-1834), Malthusian theory argues that if births and population increases burgeon in an unchecked fashion, then a national, regional, or global community will outstrip its food supply. According to Malthus, who presented his argument in a book entitled *An Essay on the Principle of Population* (1789), food supplies increase arithmetically or linearly (1, 2, 3, 4, etc.) while populations increase geometrically (2, 4, 8, 16, etc.). Inheritors of Malthusian theory, frequently referred to as the New Malthusians, later developed the exponential growth curve, which states that population growth tends to double at near-equal intervals.

Detractors of Malthusian theory, traditionally called Anti-Malthusians, gravitate toward demographic transition theory. Demographic transition refers to a three-stage historical process of population growth: 1) high birth rates/high death rates, 2) high birth rates/low death rates, 3) low birth rates/low death rates. Some inheritors of this theory add a fourth stage: 4) deaths outnumber births.

The availability of resources affects the human population. Humans require basic resources, like food and water, for survival as well as additional resources for healthy lifestyles. Therefore, access to these resources helps determine the survival rate of humans. For much of human existence, economies have had limited abilities to extract resources from the natural world, which restricted the growth rate of populations. However, the development of new technologies, combined with increasing demand for certain products, has now pushed resource use to a much higher level. On the one hand, this led to higher living standards that ensured that fewer people would die. However, this has also brought mass population growth. Admittedly, countries with higher standards of living often have lower birthrates. Even so, the increasing exploitation of resources has sharply increased the world's population to unsustainable levels. The rising population leads, in turn, to a greater demand for resources that cannot be met. This creates poverty, reduced living conditions, and higher death rates. As a result, economics can significantly influence local and world population levels.

Technology is also intricately related to population, resources, and economics. The role of demand within economies has incentivized people to innovate new technologies that enable societies to have a higher quality of life and greater access to resources. Entrepreneurs expand technologies by finding ways to create new products for the market. The Industrial Revolution, in particular, illustrates the relationship between economics and technology because, during it, the ambitions of businessmen led to new infrastructure that enabled more efficient and sophisticated use of resources. Many of these inventions reduced the amount of work necessary for individuals and allowed the development of leisure activities, which, in turn, created new economic markets. However, economic systems can also limit the growth of technology. In the case of monopolies, a lack of alternative suppliers for a product reduces the incentive to meet and exceed consumer expectations. Moreover, as demonstrated by the effects of economics on resources, technology's increasing ability to extract resources can lead to their depletion and create significant issues.

A population's size may grow or decline, depending on fluctuating birth rates, death rates, immigration, and emigration. The *birth rate* is defined as the total number of live births per 1,000 individuals in a defined population in a year. The *death rate*, or *mortality rate*, is defined as the total number of deaths per 1,000 individuals in a defined population in a year. *Immigration* refers to a person or organism coming from another population to the one currently being examined, and *emigration* refers to a person or organism leaving that population to settle elsewhere. Because these are the chief factors affecting a population's size, they can be used to determine the rate of its growth.

Other variables such as food availability, adequate shelter, and water supply can also affect population. These resources are finite and help determine the carrying capacity of a particular geographic area. *Carrying capacity* is defined as the maximum number of individuals that can be sustained indefinitely in a particular habitat. As a particular human population grows, other factors such as government, education, economics, healthcare, and cultural values will also begin to influence the population.

At specific points in time, certain countries may experience population growth while others experience its decline. Population growth, especially if left unchecked, can be troubling when a community grows to a point that exceeds carrying capacity. Levels of emigration may rise as individuals leave in search of more favorable conditions, and the resulting population decline can diminish pools of individuals available for labor and reproduction. Ultimately, rising levels of immigration will be needed to relieve the stress on the population.

The Demographic Transition Model (DTM) explains changes in two key areas, birth rate and death rate, and their effects on the total population of a country as it undergoes economic and industrial development. This model was introduced by American demographer Warren Thompson in 1929. Again, birth rate is defined as the number of live births per 1,000 individuals in a population over the course of an entire year, while death rate is defined as the total number of deaths per 1,000 individuals in a population within the same time frame.

As a general rule, a country will progress through four stages as it undergoes economic and industrial development. Very few countries are in stage 1 of the model. Most developing countries are grouped in stage 2 or 3 of the model, while most industrialized countries are categorized in stage 3 or 4 of the model. The first stage of the DTM is termed the High Stationary phase and is characterized by both a high birth and a high death rate. These conditions combine to produce a constant, relatively low total population. High birth rates may be accounted for by factors such as poor family planning, high infant and child death rates, and child labor requirements for farming and manufacturing. High death rates may be accounted for by factors such as famine, poor sanitation, poor healthcare, and disease epidemics. Before the Industrial Revolution, most of the world's countries were categorized as stage 1. Today, only the least economically developed countries are classified as this stage. The second stage is called the Early Expanding stage and is characterized by a high birth rate and a rapidly decreasing death rate.

These conditions converge to produce a rapid increase in the total population. Rapidly decreasing death rates may be explained by falling infant and child death rates, improved sanitation, healthcare advancements, and better nutrition. Today, the African countries of Ethiopia, Kenya, and Egypt are examples of countries classified as this stage. The Late Expanding stage, the third stage of the DTM, is distinguished by a decreasing birth rate along with a continuously but less rapidly falling death rate. These conditions combine to produce a persistent increase in total population that occurs at a slower rate than seen in stage 2. Child welfare laws, peoples' desire for smaller families, and the changing role of women in the workplace may contribute to falling birth rates in a stage 3 population. Current examples of countries grouped in this stage include Brazil, South Korea, and India. Lastly, in the fourth stage, the Low Stationary phase, a population experiences both a low birth and death rate. In this stage, the combined factors have a stabilizing effect on total population. Current examples of countries classified as this stage include the United States, Canada, and Great Britain.

16. All EXCEPT which of the following are true of an area with an extremely high population density?
    a. Competition for resources is intense.
    b. Greater strain on public services exists.
    c. More people live in rural areas.
    d. More people live in urban areas.

17. Which of the following could be considered a pull factor for a particular area?
    a. High rates of unemployment
    b. Low GDP
    c. Educational opportunity
    d. High crime rates

Questions 18-23: Match each statement with the stage of the Demographic Transition Model in which it occurs or is TRUE. Write the corresponding letter of the stage on the spaces provided. You may use each letter more than once or not at all.

18. Characterized by both a low birth rate and death rate ____

19. The factors of this stage interact in such a way as to have a stabilizing effect on the total population ____

20. Characterized by a high birth rate and a rapidly decreasing death rate ____

21. There is a constant, relatively low population ____

22. In current times, the least common or likely stage for a country ____

23. Examples of countries in this stage include Ethiopia and Egypt ____

A. Stage 1
B. Stage 2
C. Stage 3
D. Stage 4

24. Reread the following sentences:

> Demographic patterns on Earth are not always stagnant. In contrast, people move and will continue to move as both push and pull factors fluctuate over time.

The word *stagnant* most nearly means:

a. Predictable
b. Changing
c. Stationary
d. Putrid

Questions 25-28: Complete the following table using the letters that correspond to the correct information. You may use each letter more than once or not at all.

Pull Factor	25.
Push Factor	26.
Immigration	27.
Emigration	28.

A. Moving to the United States from Finland
B. Religious freedom
C. Cost of living
D. Poor economic conditions
E. Leaving Ireland for Scotland

Passage #3: History

The following passage about the origins of the American Revolution and founding of the United States would be found in an introductory history textbook. Read the passage and then answer the questions that follow.

The French colonies in Canada threatened the British settlements. France and Britain had been enemies for centuries and religious differences reinforced their hostility; the British were Protestant, and the French were mostly Catholic. Far fewer colonists had settled in "New France," but they often clashed with the British, especially over the lucrative fur trade. Both the British and French sought to dominate the trade of beaver pelts, which were used to make hats in Europe. The British and French fought a series of colonial wars between 1689 and 1748 that failed to resolve the struggle for dominance in North America.

Eventually, the contest culminated in the French and Indian War (also known as the Seven Years' War), which ended in 1763. The French initially enjoyed the upper hand because they were able to persuade more Native American tribes to support them, since the Native Americans felt the French were less likely to encroach on their territory than the land-hungry British. The Native Americans launched devastating raids along the British colonial frontier. However, the British eventually emerged victorious after blockading the French colonies in Canada, which prevented the French from bringing in reinforcements or from resupplying their Native American allies with gunpowder and ammunition. Native American raids subsided, and the French eventually surrendered almost all of their colonial possessions in North America. Some historians consider this war the first global conflict because some of its battles were also fought in Europe, Asia, and Africa.

The French defeat radically altered the balance of power in North America. Previously, Native Americans had been able to play the French and British against each other, but now they were without many of their French allies. The French and Indian War also set the stage for the American Revolution. Although triumphant, the British monarchy had spent an enormous amount of money to secure victory, and the war doubled the national debt. In order to pay off the debt, King George III began imposing taxes upon the North American colonies, which eventually led to revolution.

Since 1651, the British crown had tried to control trade within its empire, thereby fostering tension and discontent in the North American colonies. That year, the monarchy introduced the Navigation Acts, which prevented the North American colonies from trading directly with other European powers—all goods had to be shipped to Britain first. This was an attempt to keep wealth within the British Empire and to prevent other empires profiting from their colonies. This was an example of mercantilism—an economic policy that formed the foundation of Britain's empire. Mercantilism called for government regulation in the form of tariffs, a tax on imports from other countries. This raised prices on foreign goods, encouraged British imperial subjects to purchase goods made in Britain or the colonies, and, ultimately, enriched the British Empire by reducing imports and maximizing exports.

The Molasses Act in 1731 was another outgrowth of mercantilism. This law imposed a higher tax on molasses that colonists purchased from the Dutch, French, or Spanish colonies. The tax was unpopular with the colonists, and British imperial officials eventually decided not to enforce it because the law threatened to disrupt the pattern of triangular trade that had emerged in the Atlantic world. First, ships from Britain's North American colonies carried rum to Africa where it was traded for slaves and gold. Then, the ships took the slaves to French and Spanish colonies in the Caribbean and exchanged them for sugar or molasses. In the last part of the triangular trade system, merchants sailed back to North America where the sugar and molasses was used to make rum, and the cycle could start over again.

In addition to economic ties, many other types of connections linked the colonies with their originating empire across the Atlantic Ocean. Most colonists shared a common language, common religion, and common culture with the British. However, communications between the colonies and Britain were slow because it took months for a ship to cross the Atlantic and return with a response. Therefore, as the colonies grew in population, they began to develop local institutions and a separate sense of identity. For example, it became common for ministers to receive their education at seminaries in North America rather than those in Britain. Newspapers began to focus on printing more local news. Perhaps most importantly, the colonies began to exercise more control over their own political affairs. Colonies began to form their own political assemblies and elected landowners to represent local districts. The British government retained control over international issues, such as war and trade, but the colonists controlled domestic affairs.

Following the end of the French and Indian War in 1763, a number of political acts by the British monarchy led to more discontent among the colonies. First, in the Proclamation of 1763, the king declared that the colonists could not settle west of the Appalachian Mountains. The declaration frustrated many colonists because they had expected this territory to be open for expansion after the French were defeated.

Additionally, taxes were imposed in an effort to help reduce the debt Britain amassed during the French and Indian War. In 1764, Parliament passed the Sugar Act, which reduced the tax on molasses but also strengthened customs enforcement powers. Some colonists protested by organizing boycotts on British goods. One year later, in 1765, Parliament passed the Quartering Act, which required colonists to provide housing and food to British troops. This law was also very unpopular and led to protests in the North American colonies.

The Stamp Act of 1765 required the colonists to pay a tax on legal documents, newspapers, magazines, and other printed materials. Colonial assemblies protested the tax and petitioned the British government to repeal it. Merchants also organized boycotts and established correspondence committees in order to share resistance information between colonies. Eventually, Parliament repealed the Stamp Act but simultaneously reaffirmed the Crown's right to tax the colonies.

In 1767, Parliament introduced the Townshend Acts, which imposed a tax on goods the colonies imported from Britain, such as tea, lead, paint, glass, and paper. The colonies protested again and, in some cases, assaulted British imperial officials. The British government responded by sending additional troops to North America to restore order. However, the arrival of troops in Boston only led to more tension that eventually culminated in the Boston Massacre of 1770, during which five colonists were killed and eight were wounded. Except for the duty on tea, all of the Townshend Act taxes were repealed after the Boston Massacre.

Parliament passed the Tea Act in 1773 and, although it actually reduced the price of tea, it was another unpopular piece of legislation. The Tea Act made the British East India Company the sole legal seller of tea in the colonies in North America and allowed the Company to ship its products directly to the colonies without stopping in England and paying import taxes, effectively cutting out colonial merchants and stirring more Anglo-American anger and resentment. This resulted in the Boston Tea Party of 1773, an incident in which colonial tea merchants disguised themselves as Indians before storming several British ships anchored in Boston harbor. Once aboard, the disguised colonists dumped more than 300 chests of tea into the water.

Because the British government could not identify the perpetrators, Parliament passed a series of laws that punished the entire colony of Massachusetts. These acts were known as the Coercive or Intolerable Acts. The first law closed the Port of Boston until the tea had been paid for (an estimated $1.7 million in today's currency). The second act curtailed the authority of Massachusetts' colonial government. Instead of being elected by colonists, most government officials would be appointed by the king. In addition, the act restricted town meetings, the basic form of government in Massachusetts, and limited most villages to one meeting per year. This act angered colonists throughout the thirteen colonies because they feared their rights could be stripped as well. The third act allowed British soldiers to be tried in Britain if they were accused of a crime, and the fourth act once again required colonists to provide food and shelter to British soldiers.

Colonists responded by forming the First Continental Congress in 1774, and all the colonies except for Georgia sent delegates. The delegates sought a compromise with the British government instead of launching an armed revolt; therefore, they sent a petition to King George III affirming their loyalty but demanding the repeal of the Intolerable Acts. The delegates organized a boycott on trade with Britain until their demands were met.

The colonists began to form militias and gathered weapons and ammunition. The first battle of the revolution began at Lexington and Concord in April 1775 when British troops tried to seize a supply of gunpowder and were confronted by about eighty *minutemen*, a term used to refer to members of the colonial militia. A brief skirmish left eight colonists dead and ten wounded. Colonial reinforcements poured in and harassed the British forces as they retreated to Boston, and soon laid siege to the city. Although the battle did not result in many casualties, it marked the beginning of war.

Colonists built fortifications on Bunker Hill outside of Boston and British troops attacked the position in June 1775. The colonists initially inflicted heavy casualties on the British, killing a number of officers. However, the defenders eventually ran out of ammunition, and British troops captured Bunker Hill on their third assault. Although it concluded in defeat for the colonists, the Battle of Bunker Hill demonstrated that the inexperienced colonial troops could hold their own against the disciplined and professional British army.

Following the battle, the Second Continental Congress, which had convened in Philadelphia in May 1775, formalized the colonial army and appointed George Washington as commander-in-chief. The delegates were still reluctant to repudiate their allegiance to King George III and did not do so until they issued the Declaration of Independence on July 4, 1776. Drawn from the ideas of the Enlightenment, the document declared that the colonists had "the right to life, liberty, and the pursuit of happiness" and stated that the colonists were compelled to seek autonomy from Britain because King George III had violated these rights.

For a time, the British army maintained the upper hand, defeating colonial forces in a number of engagements. The Americans did not achieve a victory until the Battle of Trenton in December 1776, during which Washington famously crossed the Delaware River on Christmas Day and launched a surprise attack against a garrison of Hessians, German auxiliary troops hired by the British to fight on their behalf. Washington's army captured more than 1,000 soldiers and suffered minimal casualties. The victory at Trenton bolstered American morale and showed that they could defeat professional European soldiers.

The Battle of Saratoga in New York in the fall of 1777 was another important turning point in the American War for Independence during which American troops surrounded and captured more than 6,000 British soldiers. This victory convinced the French king to support the revolutionaries by sending troops, money, weapons, and ships to the Americans. French officers who fought alongside the Patriots brought back many ideas with them that eventually sparked a revolution in France in 1789.

French support was key in the last major battle of the revolution at Yorktown, Virginia in 1781. American troops laid siege to General Cornwallis's British forces at Yorktown. Meanwhile, a French fleet defeated a British naval squadron sent to relieve Cornwallis. French and American troops began attacking the British fortifications in Yorktown; thereafter, a sustained artillery bombardment by American guns eventually forced Cornwallis to surrender. This ended the Revolutionary War, and, in 1783, the British signed the Treaty of Paris in which they recognized the United States as an independent country, officially ceding all territory east of the Mississippi River to the burgeoning nation. However, British troops continued to occupy several forts in the Great Lakes region.

Tens of thousands of colonists who remained loyal to the British Empire, a group known as loyalists, had joined militias to fight against the patriots. After the war, many of them fled for Canada or Britain, but many chose to remain in the United States. Many Native American tribes had sided with the British as well in an attempt to curb western expansion; accordingly, no Native American leaders signed the Treaty of Paris. They refused to cede their territories, which led to further conflict as the new American nation began to expand westward.

Questions 29-40: Fill out the provided flow chart with important events leading up to and involving the American Revolution in chronological order. Write the letter of the correct answer from the answer bank in the numbered box. Each letter will be used exactly ONE time.

A. Boston Tea Party	B. First Continental Congress
C. French and Indian War Ends	D. Battle of Trenton
E. The Sugar Act	F. Declaration of Independence
G. Townshend Acts	H. The Stamp Act
I. Boston Massacre	J. Treaty of Paris
K. Battle at Lexington and Concord	L. Battle of Saratoga

Molasses Act

↓

29.

↓

30.

↓

31.

↓

32.

↓

33.

↓

34.

↓

35.

↓

36.

↓

37.

↓

38.

↓

39.

↓

40.

General Training Reading

Section #1

The following train timetable should be used for questions 1-5.

Departs	From	To	Arrives	Duration	Changes
8:41	Whitestone Platform 1	Paddington Platform 3	9:56	1h 15m	1
8:58	Whitestone Platform 1	Greensboro Platform 1	9:56	58m	0
9:07	Whitestone Platform 3	Paddington Platform 2	10:31	1h 24m	1
9:19	Whitestone Platform 1	Paddington Platform 4	10:23	1h 4m	0
9:56	Whitestone Platform 3	Greensboro Platform 1	11:23	1h 27m	2

Question 1-5: Fill in the blanks using the table above. Write NO MORE THAN the words or numbers that fill a SINGLE box from the train table.

1. The fastest train that goes to Paddington departs at _______________.

2. A rider who wants to arrive in Paddington on Platform 2 should catch the train from ____________.

3. The train ride that is 1hr 24min departs at _________________.

4. If someone needs to arrive in Paddington by 10:00, he or she should take the train that leaves at _________________.

5. The train that leaves at 9:07 has ______________ change(s).

The following listing was posted in the "Rooms and Shares Available" section of an online community marketplace. Read the listing and then answer the questions that follow.

Suite of rooms available for rent in downtown Easthampton - $700/month

We have a large house, and we aren't using much of the space. It would be perfect for a student or someone seeking summer housing. We are open to continuing the arrangement beyond the summer, but if you just want to do summer, that works too.

About us: We are a mid-20's married couple with a sweet dog. One of us is a full-time student who commutes every day, and the other is a working professional. We both have extremely long days, so we aren't home much.

The house: located in the center of town right on the bus line, close to the library, YMCA, grocery store, etc. We have a good sized fenced-in yard and a garden with raspberries and several vegetables, as long as the weather cooperates!

Your space in the house: Upstairs in the house, half of the rooms close off completely in their own wing; this is your space. There are three rooms: a large room (16x16) that you could turn into a living room, an office or smaller bedroom (10x12), and the master bedroom (20x10). You would use the bathroom and kitchen downstairs (there is a toilet but no shower upstairs). We have laundry facilities in the basement that you can use in the evenings. We have a deck and a nice big yard, and we are on a quiet street, even though it is right in the center of town.

Please ask if you have any questions, would like to see pictures, or want to come over and take a look. All we ask is that whoever is interested does not smoke and is respectful of our fairly quiet house. If you have a car, there is plenty of parking right in our driveway.

Rent is $700 a month and includes all utilities, except Internet and cable; these are an additional $40 a month if you want to join our package. To move in, you need first month's rent, a $500 security deposit, and the names and numbers of two references we can call on your behalf.

Questions 6-16: The following table is a checklist made by a potential tenant to take notes as she searches listings. Complete the table using the information in the ad. Write 'YES' if the information is given in the ad and permitted or present in the rental, 'NO' if it is given in the ad but not permitted or present, and 'NO MENTION' if the information is not present in the ad.

6. Total cost to move in less than $1200	
7. Laundry use	
8. Number of pets allowed	
9. At least 3 rooms available	
10. Any prohibited activities	
11. Home gym	
12. Current tenants are all professionals	
13. Garden with strawberries	
14. Looking for female tenants only	
15. Close to the shopping center	
16. Monthly rent with Internet less than $720	

Section #2

Read the following cover letter and then answer the questions that follow.

To Whom It May Concern:

I'm writing in regard to the Writer/Producer position at Shadow Heat. I graduated with my MA degree in English at the University of Texas in May 2016, where I taught technical writing and writing arguments for my fellowship. My years taking and teaching English courses have enabled me to develop strong writing skills, which I believe will contribute greatly to the position in question.

Although a work in progress, my website, linked below, features technical writing, graphic design, blog writing, and creative writing samples. My passion for writing that connects with a specific audience is demonstrated by my various publications as well as my degrees that focus heavily on academic and creative writing.

I'm highly motivated, bringing energy and creativity into my work. My nine years of experience in higher education enables me to adapt to changing ideals and trends while also maintaining personal values. I would love to write for your company and hope you'll consider me for this position. I look forward to hearing from you!

Thanks!

17. What type of writing is this passage?
    a. A how-to document on teaching
    b. A consumer email to a corporation
    c. A letter of interest for a job
    d. A memo concerning employees in the workplace

18. Which of the following is correct?
    a. The writer of the letter is a writer/producer at Shadow Heat.
    b. The writer of the letter has a master's degree in English.
    c. The writer of the letter has ten years' experience in higher education.
    d. The writer of the letter is applying to be a website designer.

19. The writer of the letter has experience with which of the following? Select all that apply.
    a. Working at Shadow Heat
    b. Blog writing
    c. Technical writing
    d. Teaching graphic design
    e. Publishing writing
    f. Changing trends

20. Which of the following people would most likely be the intended recipient of the letter?
    a. A job candidate looking for work as a writer
    b. A job candidate looking for a job at Shadow Heat
    c. An employee at Shadow Heat
    d. The hiring manager at Shadow Heat

21. Which additional piece of information from the letter writer would be most useful for the recipient of the letter?
    a. A resume
    b. A professional headshot
    c. A job description for the desired position
    d. Shadow Heat's business card

Read the following job description and then answer the questions that follow.

University of Greenwich
Alumni Relations and Development Office
Prospect Research Assistant - Job Description

Job Description: The Prospect Research Assistant position provides data support to the University by receiving, reviewing, researching, and entering data into the University's fundraising database in accordance with established procedures. There are also opportunities to work at events, including Alumni Weekend and Commencement, and to assist with general office duties.

Duties & Responsibilities:

- Updates fundraising database with information compiled from Prospect Research products.
- Enters constituent data by following data policies and procedures.
- Maintains high level of accuracy, consistency, and integrity of data, and ensures information is input into database in a timely manner.
- Researches and updates donor records in response to information received through the Research Request box and social media vehicles.
- Reviews news alerts for alumni-related updates and suggests recommendations of alumni to be featured in University publications and social media.
- Proofreads research documents.
- Assists in basic research as required.
- Contributes to a team effort and performs other duties as needed, such as compiling, copying, filing, and sorting.
- Performs other duties as assigned.

Desired Qualifications: We are seeking someone with strong skills in attention to detail, confidentiality, thoroughness, data entry, organization, and information analysis. The candidate should possess the ability to work independently and be professional, positive, results-driven, and trustworthy.

The candidate must be available to work 4-8 hours per week within the hours of 9:00am-5:00pm Monday through Friday. We are happy to offer a flexible work schedule around a student's class schedule.

The candidate must be able to travel to 24 Willow Street; however, please note that an on-campus shuttle service is available to and from our office if needed.

22. This sample would most likely be composed by which of the following people?
    a. A job candidate
    b. A research assistant
    c. A manager at the University of Greenwich
    d. A fundraiser

Questions 23-27: Complete the following sentences using NO MORE THAN 3 words.

23. Job candidates without cars can reach the office by way of the ______________________.

24. The employee will update donor records in response to information received through social media outlets and the __________________________.

25. The employee may assist at events like Alumni Weekend and ______________________.

26. The university maintains a ________________________ database.

27. The job schedule can be worked around a ______________________.

Section #3

The next thirteen questions are based on the following passage:

Smoking is Terrible

Smoking tobacco products is terribly destructive. A single cigarette contains over 4,000 chemicals, including 43 known carcinogens and 400 deadly toxins. Some of the most dangerous ingredients include tar, carbon monoxide, formaldehyde, ammonia, arsenic, and DDT. Smoking can cause numerous types of cancer, including throat, mouth, nasal cavity, esophagus, stomach, pancreas, kidney, bladder, and cervical.

Cigarettes contain a drug called nicotine, one of the most addictive substances known. Addiction is defined as a compulsion to seek a substance despite negative consequences. According to the National Institute on Drug Abuse, nearly 35 million smokers expressed a desire to quit smoking in 2015; however, more than 85 percent of those addicts will not achieve their goal. Almost all smokers regret picking up that first cigarette. You would be wise to learn from their mistake if you have not yet started smoking.

According to the US Department of Health and Human Services, 16 million people in the United States presently suffer from a smoking-related condition, and nearly nine million suffer from a serious smoking-related illness. According to the Centers for Disease Control and Prevention (CDC), tobacco products cause nearly six million deaths per year. This number is projected to rise to over eight million deaths by 2030. Smokers, on average, die ten years earlier than their nonsmoking peers.

In the United States, local, state, and federal governments typically tax tobacco products, which leads to high prices. Nicotine addicts sometimes pay more for a pack of cigarettes than for a few gallons of gas. Additionally, smokers tend to stink. The smell of smoke is all-consuming and creates a pervasive nastiness. Smokers also risk staining their teeth and fingers with yellow residue from the tar.

Smoking is deadly, expensive, and socially unappealing. Clearly, smoking is not worth the risks.

28. Which of the following statements most accurately summarizes the passage?
    a. Tobacco is less healthy than many alternatives.
    b. Tobacco is deadly, expensive, and socially unappealing, and smokers would be much better off kicking the addiction.
    c. In the United States, local, state, and federal governments typically tax tobacco products, which leads to high prices.
    d. Tobacco shortens smokers' lives by ten years and kills more than six million people per year.

29. The author would be most likely to agree with which of the following statements?
    a. Smokers should only quit cold turkey and avoid all nicotine cessation devices.
    b. Other substances are more addictive than tobacco.
    c. Smokers should quit for whatever reason that gets them to stop smoking.
    d. People who want to continue smoking should advocate for a reduction in tobacco product taxes.

30. Which of the following represents an opinion statement on the part of the author?
    a. According to the Centers for Disease Control and Prevention (CDC), tobacco products cause nearly six million deaths per year.
    b. Nicotine addicts sometimes pay more for a pack of cigarettes than for a few gallons of gas.
    c. They also risk staining their teeth and fingers with yellow residue from the tar.
    d. Additionally, smokers tend to stink. The smell of smoke is all-consuming and creates a pervasive nastiness.

31. Which of the following represents data presented by the author?
    a. Additionally, smokers tend to stink. The smell of smoke is all-consuming and creates a pervasive nastiness.
    b. Smoking is deadly, expensive, and socially unappealing.
    c According to the Centers for Disease Control and Prevention (CDC), tobacco products cause nearly six million deaths per year.
    d. Nicotine addicts sometimes pay more for a pack of cigarettes than for a few gallons of gas.

Questions 32-40: Complete the following summary using NO MORE THAN 1 WORD per answer.

Nicotine is a/an 32. ____________substance found in 33. ______________. Throat, mouth, and esophagus are among the many types of 34. __________ that smoking can cause. Nearly six million deaths annually are caused by 35. ____________ products. Smoking can shorten one's 36. ____________. In the United States, tobacco products are taxed by the 37. ___________, state, and federal governments, which leads to 38. __________ prices. Smoking can also stain 39. __________ and fingers with yellow 40. ____________ from the tar.

First Essay

Academic Test

Prepare a response of at least 150 words on the topic below. You should spend approximately 20 minutes on this task.

The graph below shows the percentage of calories from fast food among adults aged 20 and over, by age, race, and ethnicity in the United States from 2007–2010. Ethnicity for each age category is represented from left to right corresponding with the order at the top of the graph.

Summarize the main information presented in the graph and make any relevant comparisons.

Percentage of calories from fast food among adults aged 20 and over, by age, race, and ethnicity: United States, 2007–2010

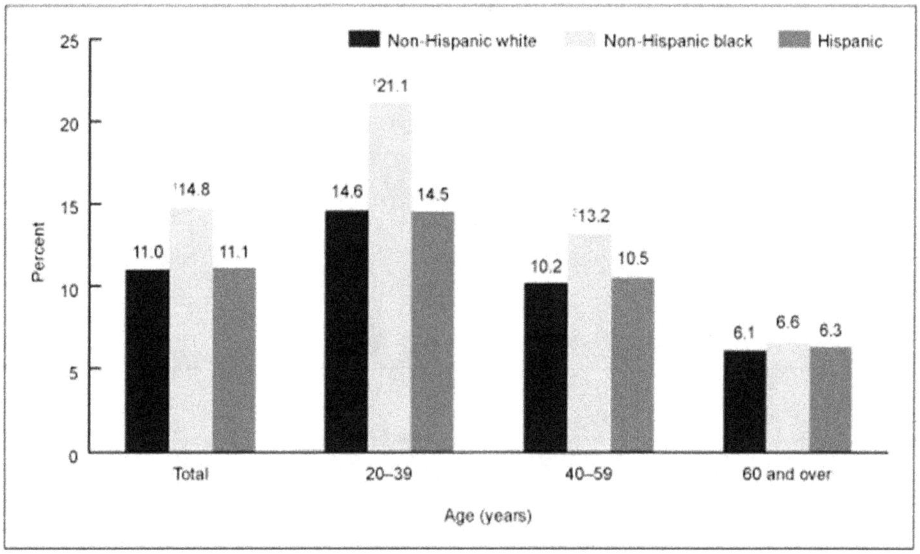

[1]Statistically different from non-Hispanic white and Hispanic adults ($p < 0.05$).
[2]Statistically different from non-Hispanic white adults ($p < 0.05$).
NOTE: Total estimates are age adjusted to the 2000 projected U.S. standard population using three age groups: 20–39, 40–59, and 60 and over.
SOURCE: National Health and Nutrition Examination Survey, 2007–2010.

The following pages are provided for writing your essay.

General Training Exam

Prepare a response of at least 150 words on the topic below. You should spend approximately 20 minutes on this task.

You have lived in an apartment complex for two years. The manager recently sent letters to all tenants saying that monthly rental fees are increasing by $150 with all lease renewals to cover recent maintenance work and property upgrades. You disagree with this decision.

Prepare a letter to the building manager. In your letter, cover the following:

- Briefly paraphrase the situation
- Explain specifically why you disagree with the rental increase
- Suggest alternative solutions

The following pages are provided for writing your essay.

Second Essay

Academic Test

Prepare an essay of at least 250 words on the topic below. You should spend approximately 40 minutes on this task.

A recent analysis revealed that physical inactivity is responsible for over 5 million deaths annually worldwide, which is similar to the death toll of tobacco smoking. The World Health Organization estimates that physical inactivity is the fourth leading cause of death globally, which is lower than hypertension and tobacco smoking, similar to obesity, and higher than dietary patterns and hyperglycemia. Most inactivity-related deaths occur in low- and middle-income countries, so this is not just a concern in high-income countries. Some consider physical inactivity to be a global pandemic. Physical inactivity also is the fourth underlying cause of death in the United States, with an estimated 200,000 deaths per year. These are about half the deaths attributable to tobacco smoking but twice the deaths attributable to alcohol use and low intake of fruits and vegetables.

Write an essay discussing the harm associated with physical inactivity and modern factors that impact physical activity levels. Make sure to define physical activity in your answer.

The following pages are provided for writing your essay.

General Training Exam

Prepare an essay of at least 250 words on the topic below. You should spend approximately 40 minutes on this task.

Some people feel that sharing their lives on social media sites such as Facebook, Instagram, and Snapchat is fine. They share every aspect of their lives, including pictures of themselves and their families, what they ate for lunch, who they are dating, and when they are going on vacation. They even say that if it's not on social media, it didn't happen. Other people believe that sharing so much personal information is an invasion of privacy and could prove dangerous. They think sharing personal pictures and details invites predators, cyberbullying, and identity theft.

Write an essay to someone who is considering whether to participate in social media. Take a side on the issue and argue whether or not he/she should join a social media network. Use specific examples to support your argument.

The following pages are provided for writing your essay.

Speaking

Task #1 (4-5 minutes)

Let's talk about where you are from.

- Describe your favorite places in your city, town, or campus and explain why you like them.
- Do you think it's a good or bad place to live and why?
- What types of industries or jobs are popular in your town?

Now let's talk about your education and career plans.

- What would you like to study in university and why?
- What are your career goals and how will your studies help you reach these goals?
- What sorts of jobs have you had before?
- Do you prefer working or attending school? Why?

Task #2 (3-4 minutes)

Prompt card:

Some people think it's better to set realistic goals that they are confident they can achieve, while others argue it's better to set ambitious goals that one may fail to achieve.

What is your opinion? Explain why.

Preparation Time: 1 minute
Response Time: 1-2 minutes

Rounding off questions:

Do you engage in any goal setting practices? Why or why not?

Task #3 (4-5 minutes)

Let's discuss financial goals:

- What are the benefits and potential pitfalls of setting money-related goals?
- What do you think are the most important budgeting tools or practices for young people?.
- Imagine you are a high school counselor. What financial guidance would you give to a graduating student considering taking out loans for college?

Now let's talk about education and career goals:

- A student is offered a prestigious internship that would delay their graduation by a year. Would you advise accepting the internship or graduating on time?
- What are the benefits and drawbacks of each possibility?
- What factors should students consider when choosing a career?

Answer Explanations #1

Listening

1. Biology (material): At the beginning of the conversation, listeners should recall that the male student, Greg, was asking the female student, Deborah, how she did on the biology exam. Deborah informs Greg that she did well, earning a 96, while Greg responds that he only got a 69. He says, "This stuff isn't making sense to me." *Stuff,* in this case, refers to the biology class material.

2. Basketball game: Greg says, "I lost my ID at the basketball game last weekend. Do you know where I can get a new one?"

3. Reference section: The female student says, "I'm usually at the library around 4:00pm. I sit in the back by the reference section. Do you know where the encyclopedias are?"

4. B, C, D: Deborah says that a student must go to the administration building with their student ID or another form of picture ID, pay a $15 replacement fee, and fill out a form. She mentions the encyclopedia section in the library in an earlier part of the conversation, referring to where she studies.

5. C: When Greg says that he has not really gotten into "a study rhythm yet" he means that he has not yet established a study routine or habit.

6. A: Deborah says, "Well, I've got to run to Economics class now," to signal that she is preparing to end the conversation. This is a common phrase used in casual conversation to convey that one person needs to leave and move on to the next thing and that he or she wants to end the conversation. She may not literally need to "run" to class, but she is wrapping up the conversation.

7. B: Library

8. E: Administration building

9. G: Dining hall

10. C: Dormitory

11. Newsletter

12. Refer

13. Rewards

14. Redeemed

15. D

16. C

17. F

18. F

19. D

20. C

21. C: The student is having an issue with her bill. It is higher than she predicted. She starts the conversation by saying, "Hi. Is this the right place to ask about a problem with my bill?" Then she later says, "So, I received my bill for the semester, and it says I owe $18,000. I thought I had a scholarship so there's no way I can pay this bill."

22. A, B, C: The financial aid officer says, "If you qualify for additional financial aid, we can set up a package for you. Some students get additional scholarships based on financial need, or there are loans, and work-study opportunities."

23. A: The financial aid officer tells the student, "Well, it looks like you have a scholarship that is pending...It has not been applied because we are waiting on your financial aid application. Did you fill out the FAFSA? We need a current copy of that on file."

24. B: The student is most likely to apply for a job at the computer lab. Listeners can select this response based on the student's comment: "Back home, I worked as a computer programmer at my mom's software company."

25. E: Register to fill out the FAFSA

26. F: Input prior year's tax information

27. C: Wait for financial aid package evaluation

28. B: Apply for a campus job

29. D: Pay balance on the account

30. A: Register for classes

31. A: This lecture is mainly focused on the contributions of various historical astronomers to our understanding of modern astronomy. While the telescope's importance is mentioned, Choice *B*, this is not the main topic of the lecture. Choice *C* is incorrect because the history of how the Universe and Solar System formed billions of years ago is not mentioned at all, while the history of advancements in astronomy is.

32. C: The professor implies that the contributions of the discussed scientists, even when inaccurate, helped shape our current understanding of astronomy. Perhaps the best evidence for this argument comes from when she is talking about Brahe's importance, even though some of his ideas were incorrect. "He thought the Earth was not moving and that the Sun and Moon revolved around the stationary planet, so we know now that this part was off-base, but he's still a key player in our evolution."

33. C: The selected statement implies that Brahe is important in any discussion of the history of astronomy, even if some of his ideas were incorrect. Choice *A* is incorrect because she said he *is* still important. Choice *B* is incorrect because "evolution" in this context isn't referring to human evolution or genetics, but the evolution or growth of our understanding of astronomy – how it is has changed over time.

34. Chronological: The professor structures the lecture in chronological order of the scientists' work. Although dates are not provided, listeners can answer this correctly based on what the professor says at the beginning of the lecture: "We are *continuing* our discussion today of the history of astronomers *from ancient times working up to the present day*. So, remember, we are talking about the key contributors that have helped build our understanding of astronomy today."

35. D

36. C

37. A

38. A

39. C

40. B

Academic Test Reading

1. xi

2. x

3. ii

4. ix

5. v

6. iv

7. Right Atrium

8. Left Atrium

9. Mitral Valve

10. Left Ventricle

11. Septum

12. D: Blood returning to the heart from the body enters the right atrium and then moves through the tricuspid valve into the right ventricle. After filling, the right ventricle contracts, and the tricuspid valve closes, pushing blood through the pulmonary semilunar valve into the pulmonary arteries for pulmonary circulation, after which it enters the left atrium. Contraction of the left atrium moves blood through the bicuspid valve into the left ventricle (the largest heart chamber). When the bicuspid valve closes and the left ventricle contracts, blood is forced into the aortic valve through the aorta and on to systemic circulation.

13. D: Veins have valves but arteries do not. Valves in veins are designed to prevent backflow, since they are the furthest blood vessels from the pumping action of the heart and steadily increase in volume (which decreases the available pressure). Capillaries diffuse nutrients properly because of their thin walls and high surface area and are not particularly dependent on positive pressure.

14. C: The sinoatrial (SA) node is the initiator of the rhythmic electrical impulses of the cardiac cycle. The SA node is located in the upper wall of the right atrium and contains a small locus of specialized muscle fibers that naturally generate action potentials.

15. C: On an EKG, the T-wave corresponds to the recovery of the ventricles from depolarization, which is also known as repolarization. On the reading, this occurs after the QRS complex — the graphical representation of ventricular depolarization and contraction.

16. C: Population density, which is the total number of people divided by the total land area, generally tends to be much higher in urban areas than rural ones. This is true due to the construction of high-rise apartment complexes, sewage and freshwater infrastructure, and complex transportation systems that allow for easy movement of food from nearby farms. Consequently, competition among citizens for resources is certainly higher in high-density areas, as are strains on infrastructure within urban centers.

17. C: Pull factors are reasons people immigrate to a particular area. Educational opportunities attract thousands of people on a global level and on a local level. For example, generally, areas with strong schools have higher property values due to the relative demand for housing in those districts. The same is true for nations with better educational opportunities. Unemployment, low GDP, and high crime rates may deter people from moving to a certain place and can be considered push factors.

18. D

19. D

20. B

21. A

22. A

23. B

24. C: The sentence states that demographic patterns are not always stagnant, and then contrasts the concept by saying that people move. Therefore, stagnant most nearly means stationary.

25. B

26. D

27. A

28. E

29. C: French and Indian War Ends, 1763

30. E: The Sugar Act, 1764

31. H: The Stamp Act, 1765

32. G: Townshend Acts, 1767

33. I: Boston Massacre, 1770

34. A: Boston Tea Party, 1773

35. B: First Continental Congress, 1774

36. K: Battle at Lexington and Concord, 1775

37. F: Declaration of Independence, July of 1776

38. D: Battle of Trenton, December of 1776

39. L: Battle of Saratoga, 1777

40. J: Treaty of Paris, 1783

General Training Reading

1. 9:19

2. Whitestone Platform 3

3. 9:07

4. 8:41

5. 1

6. No

7. Yes

8. No mention

9. Yes

10. Yes

11. No mention

12. No

13. No

14. No mention

15. No mention

16. No

17. C: This is a letter of interest or cover letter for a job position. It would likely accompany a resume and job application and be written by a job candidate interested in an available position. It does not explain the process or the "how-to" for anything, so Choice *A* is incorrect. Choices *B* and *D* are also incorrect because it is not written by a consumer of a product nor does it concern a workplace's employees.

18. B: The letter writer says: "I graduated with my MA degree in English at the University of Texas in May 2016, where I taught technical writing and writing arguments for my fellowship." MA is the abbreviation for Master of Arts, which is a master's degree. The other choices are inaccurate or not mentioned in the letter.

19. B, C: The letter writer is an experienced creative and technical writer with prior work in "technical writing, graphic design, blog writing, and creative writing." Choice *A* is incorrect because the person wants to work at Shadow Heat but does not yet have a position there, so he or she does not have experience working there. Choice *D* is incorrect because the writer has experience teaching English, not graphic design; he or she has experience with graphic design but did not mention teaching it. Choices *E* and *F* are also incorrect. Publishing writing is not a skill mentioned, and the writer doesn't have experience *changing* trends, but rather can adapt well to changes in trends, demonstrating flexibility.

20. D: This is a cover letter that would accompany a job application for a position at Shadow Heat. Therefore, it is written by an interested job candidate looking to become an employee at Shadow Heat and is intended for the employer or the hiring manager at Shadow Heat, which is Choice *D.* The other choices are ways to describe the letter writer.

21. A: A resume would support the letter writer's application, as he or she is a job candidate for an open position. A resume would detail his or her education background, career experience, and related skills as well as support the narrative presentation of this information in the letter. Choice *B,* a headshot, may accompany a resume or job application for some positions, but it is not particularly relevant for a writer, and therefore, is not the best choice. Choices *C* and *D* are pieces of information that the recipient of the letter (the employer), not the letter writer, may create or have.

22. C: The provided passage is a job description for a research assistant position in the University of Greenwich's Alumni Relations and Development Office. Therefore, the person who wrote the position would be the employer, or Choice *C,* a manager at the University, because he or she has the position to offer and is seeking a qualified candidate. All of the other choices are likely the intended audience for the job description or potential applicants for the position.

23. On-campus shuttle

24. Research Request Box

25. Commencement

26. Fundraising

27. Student's class schedule

28. B: The author is clearly opposed to tobacco use. He cites diseases and deaths associated with smoking. He points to the monetary expense and aesthetic costs. Choice *A* is wrong because alternatives to smoking are not even addressed in the passage. Choice *C* is wrong because it does not summarize the passage but rather is just a premise. Choice *D* is wrong because, while these statistics are a premise in the argument, they do not represent a summary of the piece. Choice *C* is the correct answer because it states the three critiques offered against tobacco and expresses the author's conclusion.

29. C: We are looking for something the author would agree with, so it will almost certainly be anti-smoking or an argument in favor of quitting smoking. Choice *A* is wrong because the author does not speak against means of cessation. Choice *B* is wrong because the author does not reference other substances, but does speak of how addictive nicotine, a drug in tobacco, is. Choice *D* is wrong because the author certainly would not encourage reducing taxes to encourage a reduction of smoking costs, thereby helping smokers to continue the habit. Choice *C* is correct because the author is definitely attempting to persuade smokers to quit smoking.

30. D: Here, we are looking for an opinion of the author rather than a fact or statistic. Choice *A* is wrong because quoting statistics from the Centers for Disease Control and Prevention is stating facts, not opinions. Choice *B* is wrong because it expresses the fact that cigarettes sometimes cost more than a few gallons of gas. It would be an opinion if the author said that cigarettes were not affordable. Choice *C* is incorrect because yellow stains are a known possible adverse effect of smoking. Choice *D* is correct as an opinion because smell is subjective. Some people might like the smell of smoke, they might not have working olfactory senses, and they might not find the smell of smoke akin to "pervasive nastiness," so this is the expression of an opinion. Thus, Choice *D* is the correct answer.

31. C: In this question, we are looking for data presented by the author to support their position. The only choice that includes data, or information supported by research, is Choice *C* because it includes the statistic provided by the Centers for Disease Control and Prevention. Choices *A* and *B* represent opinion statements. Choice *D* may be true, but it is not supported by data.

32. Addictive

33. Cigarettes

34. Cancers

35. Tobacco

36. Lifespan

37. Local

38. High

39. Teeth

40. Yellow

Speaking

Task #1

Examiner: Let's talk about where you are from. Describe your favorite places in your city, town, or campus and explain why you like them.

Test taker: I live in New York City and I love it here. There are a lot of interesting places and constant action around you to watch and engage with if you so choose. General Grant's tomb is situated next to Riverside Park and has beautiful views of the Hudson river and George Washington Bridge. The architecture of the tomb and the bridge are striking, and it is lovely walking along the pathways. There is an interesting museum dedicated to the history of General Grant and New York City there as well. I also love the Natural History Museum, which is on the west side of Central Park.

Although this museum attracts a lot of tourists, it does so rightfully because it has fascinating collections of rocks, minerals, and historic natural specimens as well as exhibits about animals, biomes, and the evolution of different cultures and societies. I saw a fantastic exhibit about the biodiversity and ecology of Cuba and an interesting planetarium show about the night sky. Besides the inherent wonder and intrigue of these places, I also enjoy these sites I have referenced because they are less well-known. This means they attract fewer tourists and are less crowded, while still embodying the energy and excitement of the city.

Examiner: Do you think it's a good or bad place to live and why?

Test taker: I think New York City is a great place to live because there is always so much going on that the opportunities are virtually endless. In my opinion, kids that grow up in the city are worldly and mature because they are exposed to all sorts of people of diverse backgrounds and also have to learn to be responsible and independent at a younger age. Riding the subway and navigating through various neighborhoods teaches kids to be alert and organized and instills good time management and judgment skills. In many cases, I think kids also learn more about themselves and their interests here because of the array of activities available to them.

Examiner: What types of industries or jobs are popular in your town?

Test taker: There are nearly as many popular industries here as there are people. There's a market for most jobs: business, finance, healthcare, fitness, fashion, architecture, science, and research; pretty much all industries offer viable career options. That's one of the many great benefits of living in such a large and thriving metropolis.

Examiner: Now let's talk about your education and career plans. What would you like to study in university and why?

Test taker: I would like to study business at university and also minor in marketing. In fact, I would like to get my MBA. I have always enjoyed entrepreneurship, and so I think business is a great field. It also seems like a degree with versatile career options, and there will always be a need for people with business acumen, so it gives me confidence in job security. I can say the same things about marketing, and I enjoy thinking about advertisements and what drives people's buying decisions.

Examiner: What are your career goals and how will your studies help you reach these goals?

Test taker: If my education plans work out, I see myself owning my own small financial consulting company with a handful of employees under my supervision. With my marketing and business education, I will be able to make an educated business plan, drive customers to use the services at my firm, and build a business that generates significant revenue in an ethical way. I also hope that, after a few years, my consulting firm will be thriving, so I can pay off my student loan debt and buy a nice house.

Examiner: What sorts of jobs have you had before?

Test taker: I have worked at my mom's real estate firm since I was in intermediate school. I mostly help with administrative tasks like calling clients, setting up showings, and organizing files. It is not particularly engaging work, but it is nice to see my mom and feel like I am helping her around the office. Also, because I have been assisting there for quite a few years at this point, I feel competent and comfortable there, which gives me confidence and makes me feel like I have a purpose. It's been rewarding to watch and play a part in the growth of the business over the past several years.

Examiner: Do you prefer working or attending school? Why?

Test taker: I actually prefer taking classes and attending school. I know this doesn't necessarily bode well for my future because we definitely work far more years of our life than we attend school. With that said, I've only ever had the administrative job at the real estate company. I anticipate enjoying my job more when I'm actually engaging in a vocation that I'm passionate about and running my own company.

Task #2

Examiner: Here is your prompt card. You have one minute to review it and then you have one to two minutes to respond. Don't worry about the need to keep time. I will alert you when the time is up.

Test taker: Okay.

Examiner: Okay. It is now time to begin speaking.

Test taker: I think it is better to set ambitious goals even if there is a chance of failure. When people set goals that are too easy, they are denying themselves the chance to really push themselves and grow. If someone doesn't set their sights high and just stays within their comfort zone, they'll never know what they can achieve, and they might limit their potential. If instead, they set a big, lofty goal, they may fall short and not fully achieve it, but they will likely still exceed where they would have landed with a low-level goal. For example, if an athlete wants to run a 5k race and get a fast time, setting a big goal that excites her will motivate her to train hard and stay disciplined. If she sets an easy goal that she is pretty confident she can achieve without putting in much work, she will probably not push herself as hard in workouts and might get a slower time.

Examiner: Thank you. Do you engage in any goal setting practices? Why or why not?

Test taker: I love setting goals and I use goal setting as a technique to keep me organized, motivated, and efficient with my time. I set short- and long-term goals in many facets of my life including my studies, career, physical health, and financial wellness. Over time, I have found that I achieve more and feel more prepared and poised for success when I dedicate time and thought toward setting goals.

Task #3

Examiner: Let's discuss financial goals. What are the benefits and pitfalls of setting money-related goals?

Test taker: I think setting financial goals can be really helpful for planning for the future. I can think of a few benefits. For example, setting financial goals can help people save for what is important to them, whether that's retirement, a house, or starting a family. Goals can be steppingstones to conquering daunting challenges, like paying off student loan debt. They can also help people prioritize the things that matter to them, which gives them more control and freedom in their lives. I can only think of a couple of pitfalls when it comes to financial goals. First, it can be difficult to set financial goals when resources are limited or nonexistent. In such cases, a financial goal can be something tangential to simple money management, like finding a new job or finding a way to break down socioeconomic barriers. Second, it is tempting for people to abandon financial goals when unexpected expenses or life events come up. To avoid this, people should set aside time to revisit their goals and course-correct if things have gotten off-track.

Examiner: What do you think are the most important budgeting tools or practices for young people?

Test taker: I think the most important money-related skill young people can learn is how to track spending. A lot of times, people grow up without having much real life experience handling their money, and thus they don't always know how to manage spending and saving. Many of my friends live paycheck to paycheck because they don't keep track of how they are using the money they earn. I think spend-tracking applications, or even Microsoft Excel, can help immensely with keeping a consistent eye on where the money goes. Similarly, I think it's important to use the tracking to develop a budget. That way, young people are able to plan spending before it happens. I usually divide my budget into categories, like food, housing, gas, utilities, and entertainment.

Examiner: Imagine you are a high school counselor. What financial guidance would you give to a graduating student considering taking out loans for college?

Test taker: I would tell the student to exhaust every option to pay for college before turning to loans. I would make sure to let them know about any scholarships, grants, or work-studies available. Only after considering these should they turn to loans. I would also try to inform the student about the differences between loan types (e.g. federal vs. private, subsidized vs. unsubsidized). The most important thing would be to make sure the graduating high school student has the information they need to make the right decisions for themselves.

Examiner: Now let's talk about education and career goals. A student is offered a prestigious internship that would delay their graduation by a year. Would you advise accepting the internship or graduating on time?

Test taker: Well, I think receiving an internship offer is big step professionally for a college student. It can provide experience and skills in the student's chosen field. It can be tough to graduate later than your peers, but ultimately I would advise the student to take the internship because it will pave the way for their future career.

Examiner: What are the benefits and drawbacks of each possibility?

Test taker: Accepting the internship could open professional doors for the student by giving them a chance to gain work experience, learn skills, make industry connections, and possibly earn money. The main drawback of accepting the internship is graduating late. Staying an extra semester can generate challenges with scholarships, financial aid, and course schedules. However, these challenges are usually solvable with a bit of planning. Graduating on time may eliminate these concerns and provide opportunities to deepen connections with college peers. Still, I think it's riskier to enter the job market without any career-related experience in a competitive economy.

Examiner: What factors should students consider when choosing a career?

Test taker: Students should consider their skills and interests when choosing a career path. Interests can reveal job possibilities that include topics, processes, or activities about which a student is passionate. For example, a student who has a keen interest in animals may consider jobs related to biology, zoology, or veterinary science. It is also important for students to take inventory of their unique skills, paying special attention to weaknesses as much as strengths. Awareness of their skillset can help a student avoid choosing a career that may be especially frustrating for them or find a career that gives them a chance to shine. Students should also make sure they have the time and financial resources to pursue the career that interests them.

Listening Transcripts #1

Passage #1: Conversation

(Narrator) Listen to the following conversation between two students and then answer the following questions.

(Male student) Hi Deborah! How did you do on the biology exam?

(Female student) Pretty well! I got a 96. How about you?

(Male student) Wow. I'm jealous. I got a 69. This stuff isn't making sense to me.

(Female student) Oh no, I'm sorry to hear that, Greg. I could help you study if you'd like. I usually go to the library after my classes for a couple hours. We could work together on the practice questions and tackle this week's assignment if you want.

(Male student) Actually, that would be great. Are you sure you don't mind?

(Female student) No, not at all. I have to go to my economics class right now, but I'm usually at the library around 4:00. I sit in the back by the reference section. Do you know where the encyclopedias are?

(Male student) Uh, to be honest, I've never been to the library here. I don't even know where on campus it is. Is it over by the dining hall on the main quad?

(Female student) Oh wow! You've never been?! Where you study? And yes, it's over next to the administration building on the main quad. It's directly across from the dining hall. And you need to make sure you have your college ID with you to get in.

(Male student) Yeah, I haven't really gotten into a study rhythm yet this semester. That may be part of my problem. I guess I study in my room, when my roommate and I aren't playing video games, that is. I lost my ID at the basketball game last weekend. Do you know where I can get a new one?

(Female student) Oh Greg! We need to get you organized. But yes, go to the administration building with another form of picture ID, and you'll need to pay a $15 replacement fee, and fill out a form.

(Male student) Does a driver's license work?

(Female student) Yes. Do you drive?

(Male student) Yes, I have a Honda Civic parked over by my dorm. I go off campus a lot to buy things at the grocery store or to go to the movies.

(Female student) That's awesome. I would love to get off campus once in a while and get a breath of "real-world" air, if you know what I mean.

(Male student) Yeah, absolutely. Hey, how about I take you with me when I go shopping tomorrow afternoon in exchange for you tutoring me with the biology stuff?

(Female student) Sounds perfect! Well, hey I've got to run to Economics class now. I'll see you at the library at 4:00. Let's just meet at the front steps and then we'll go in together and find somewhere to work.

(Male student) Thanks Deborah! I'll work on getting my ID and finding my biology book.

Passage #2: Monologue

(Narrator) Listen to the following welcome speech given to community members at the opening of a new arts center.

(Female Director) Welcome to the grand opening of the community arts center! We are thrilled that this idea we had in the works for years has finally come to fruition, thanks to the generous funding and support from our town's government, local businesses, and our community members such as yourselves. We truly feel like this center will be a wonderful asset to children and adults alike in our community. As part of our kick-off celebration, we would like to give a brief overview of some of the programs and services offered at the arts center in our first few months, and touch upon where we see ourselves growing over the next year. Please keep in mind that this is *your* center. We are open to feedback, suggestions, and concerns. We want this center to reflect the needs, personalities, interests, and passions of you: our community members.

So, let's see, the mission of our arts center is to promote and encourage creative expression and collaborative involvement in multidisciplinary arts for our community members. This is to be a safe environment to try your hand at new forms of art or polish your skills on things you may already be seasoned at. We offer classes in drawing, painting, sculpture, metal work, pottery, abstract art, music, dance, theater arts, jewelry making, and paper crafts. We plan to offer stained glass and photography in the coming months. We don't have studios set up for these yet. There are some courses that are offered exclusively to children or adults, but one unique aspect we are excited about are our blended classes of all ages and abilities. We think it will be an enriching experience to allow artists of all ages and stages to share the same workspace and classes. These blended classes are held during the weekend. In addition to formal classes that one must register for, there are "open studio" hours every day. For a nominal fee of $10 a month, members can come in and use materials and the studio space at their leisure.

We will take a full tour of the center today, but just to give you a general idea of the layout, we have all visual arts on the first floor. This includes our studios for painting, drawing, sculptures, and pottery. On the second floor, we have music. There is a large room with a piano. We have several soundproof studios for bands to jam together. These rooms are equipped with drum sets, amps, and microphones. We also have a lending library of instruments where patrons can rent instruments for the hour, day, or week. On the third floor, we have our performing arts center. There is an auditorium for plays and rehearsals, a dance studio with a beautiful floor, and a workshop space for making costumes, sets, and production-based stuff. We also have a library on the third floor with books and resources. There is also a snack café and a gift shop where food and art supplies can be purchased.

Lastly, we encourage everyone to sign up for our newsletter. You will receive briefings on the upcoming events and notices about everything going on at the center and be first in line to hear about special offers. Subscribers will also be entered into our rewards program. For every referral that person makes to a new member who signs up for a program, two "arts bucks" will be earned. These can be redeemed for credits for classes, snacks, rental fees, or items in the gift shop. Exciting! On that note, we will begin auditions and rehearsals for our first production, *The Wizard of Oz,* next Saturday! Any questions along the way can always be addressed to any of us here in blue shirts or by calling or emailing the center. Let's enjoy the delicious-looking cake, courtesy of Mylan's Bakery, and start collaborating, creating, and celebrating our artistic talents!

Passage #3: Conversation

(Narrator) Listen to the following conversation between a student and the school's financial aid officer.

(Female student) Hi. Is this the right place to ask about a problem with my bill?

(Male officer) Yes. This is the financial aid office so I can assist you with any tuition and billing questions.

(Female student) Great. So, I received my bill for the semester, and it says I owe $18,000. I thought I had a scholarship, so there's no way I can pay this bill. Plus, now there's a hold on my account, so I can't seem to register for classes, and I'm worried they are going to fill up.

(Male officer) Ok let's see. Do you have a copy of your bill with you?

(Female student) No. I left it in my dorm by accident.

(Male officer) No problem. Can I see your student ID? I can pull it up in our system.

(Female student) Yeah. Here it is. Don't mind the picture. I didn't know I was going to be photographed that day!

(Male officer) Oh, don't worry...you look nice! Ok. Let me just take a look here at your bill and see what's going on. Hmm...Yes, I see the tuition billed to your account is $8,500. Your meal plan and housing in the dorms is $7,000 this semester and there is a technology fee and other posted fees including your parking permit totaling $2,500. The total amount posted to your account is $18,000.

(Female student) Right. So, what about my scholarship?

(Male officer) Well, it looks like you have a scholarship that is pending in your account for the amount of tuition, the $8,500. It has not been applied because we are waiting on your financial aid application. Did you fill out the FAFSA? We need a current copy of that on file.

(Female student) No. I didn't know I needed to do that.

(Male officer) You'll definitely want to get that in as soon as possible. That way we can process your scholarship and also if you qualify for additional financial aid, we can set up a package for you. Some students get additional scholarships based on financial need, or there are loans and work-study opportunities.

(Female student) Oh, that sounds helpful. What is a work-study?

(Male officer) Work-study refers to campus-based jobs where your compensation comes directly off of your bill. There are a variety of available positions for students around campus like in the library, at the sports center, or even one of the administrative offices.

(Female student) Ok cool. Back home I worked as a computer programmer at my mom's software company.

(Male officer) So, what you need to do first is to fill out the FASFA on the website. You'll need to put in last year's tax information, so make sure you have that as well. Then, they will evaluate your financial aid package to determine what your needs are. If you want to do a work-study, you can apply for a campus job. Lastly, make sure you pay the remaining balance on your account so you can register for classes.

(Female student) Ok thanks. I better get going on this!

Passage #4: Lecture

(Narrator) Listen to part of a lecture from astronomy class and then answer the questions.

(Female Professor) We are continuing our discussion today of the history of astronomers from ancient times working up to the present day. So, remember, we are talking about the key contributors that have helped build our understanding of astronomy today. Let's pick up now with Nicolaus Copernicus. Copernicus, in many ways, can be thought of as the first in the modern astronomy scientists because he overturned the geocentric model of the solar system that had stood for over two thousand years, and instead, correctly (but shockingly at the time) suggested that the sun was the center of the solar system and the planets revolved around the sun. This was basically the birth of our present understanding of the solar system – the Heliocentric model.

Before we go on, I want to remind you about the geocentric model we talked about last class. Remember, the ancient Greeks believed in a geocentric model of the universe, such that the planets and stars rotated around the central, stationary Earth. But Copernicus recognized that the uh...that the moon rotated around the Earth and that the Earth is just one of several planets revolving around the Sun. He also noted that the Sun is a star, the closest star, and other stars are much further away, that Earth rotates around its axis every day in addition to its yearly revolution, and that closer planets have shorter "years." Pretty important discoveries, huh?

Then we have Tycho Brahe. Now, Brahe was instrumental in determining the positions of fixed stars, unaided by telescopes, which were not yet invented. He made astronomical tools to help with mapping and understanding the "heavens" and the Solar System. He thought the Earth was not moving and that the Sun and Moon revolved around the stationary planet, so we know now that this part was off-base, but he's still a key player in our evolution.

Johannes Kepler was interested in math and astronomy and felt that geometric figures influenced the universe. He built upon Copernicus' heliocentric model and you've probably heard of his three Laws of Planetary Motion. The first law states that planetary orbits are elliptical, not circular, and the Sun is at one of the foci and not the center. The second law says that the planetary speed is faster near the sun and slower when it is more distant. The third law is somewhat similar. This one states that um...that the larger the orbit of a planet, the slower its average velocity.

Next, we have Galileo Galilei. That's a fun name to say. Well, Galileo made many advancements to our thinking and to our ability to make further discoveries, like inventing the telescope. He used it to observe sunspots and discovered that the lunar surface, like Earth, had mountains and valleys. Let's see...he also noted that the Milky Way galaxy had separate stars, he discovered moons around Jupiter, and designed instruments such as a compass and this neat little calculating device. These discoveries helped prove the universe was dynamic and changing. Perhaps most importantly, he laid the foundations for scientific thought and process, the importance of logic and reason, and how to do experiments.

Lastly, we will discuss Sir Isaac Newton. Remember, Newton was the one that proposed the three laws of motion that I'm sure you've heard in physics class: an object in motion stays in motion and an object at rest stays at rest unless acted on by an external force, force equals mass times acceleration, and every action has an equal and opposite reaction. He also proposed the Universal Law of Gravitation, which states that gravity is a force and that every object in the Universe is attracted to every other object. The magnitude of this force is directly proportional to the product of the masses of the objects and inversely proportional to the square of the distances between them.

Practice Test #2

Listening

Directions: The Listening section measures your ability to understand conversations and lectures in English. In this test, you will listen to several pieces of content and answer questions after each one. The questions typically ask about the main idea and supporting details. Some questions ask about a speaker's purpose or attitude. Answer the questions based on what is stated or implied by the speakers.

Listen to all of these passages by going to testprepbooks.com/bonus/ielts or by scanning the QR code below:

SCAN ME

Note that on the actual test, you can take notes while you listen and use your notes to help you answer the questions. Your notes will not be scored.

For your convenience, the transcripts of all of the audio passages are provided after the answer explanations. However, on the actual test, no such transcripts will be provided.

Passage #1: Conversation

Questions 1–5: Complete the summary below using NO MORE THAN TWO WORDS per space.

The basketball fan says that hockey is mostly influenced by 1. ______. The hockey fan says the hockey team with the highest 2. ______ and 3. ______will be in a better position to win. The hockey player says a basketball team can easily score 4. _______ consecutive points within a few minutes in a game. The basketball player watches every 5. _______ during the season.

6. What point does the hockey fan doubt but not know enough about to dispute?
   a. Every basketball team has at least one talented player.
   b. Basketball teams can easily overcome massive deficits.
   c. Basketball games don't matter until the final few minutes of play.

7. Why does the hockey fan think only the last few minutes of a basketball game matter?
   a. Basketball teams can call timeouts and foul plays to generate more offensive possessions.
   b. All the talent in professional basketball is consolidated into a few teams.
   c. Basketball teams can score ten consecutive points within a few minutes of game time.

8. Why does the basketball fan think luck is so decisive in hockey?
   a. Icy conditions
   b. Lack of skill
   c. Defective equipment

9. The basketball fan concedes what point to the hockey fan?
   a. Some basketball teams are overpowering.
   b. Only the last few minutes of a basketball game matter.
   c. It is always obvious what team is going to win the championship at the start of the year.

10. What does the basketball fan mean when he says, "that sounds like a plan?"
   a. He's acknowledging that the hockey fan proposed something interesting.
   b. He's asking the hockey fan to watch a basketball game with him.
   c. He's agreeing to the hockey fan's proposal.

Passage #2: Court Case

11. What does this court case primarily address?
   a. General societal changes
   b. Evolution of freedom
   c. Transformation of marriage as an institution

12. Which one of the following best describes the role of parents under the traditional view of marriage?
   a. Parents played no role in the marriage process.
   b. Parents considered political, religious, and/or financial reasons for marriage, but they gave priority to their children's desires.
   c. Parents planned their children's marriages based on political, religious, and/or financial reasons.

13. What caused the institution of marriage to change?
   a. Parents realized they were harming their children.
   b. The law of coverture was declared unconstitutional.
   c. Women gained equal rights.

Questions 14–17: Complete the summary below using NO MORE THAN ONE WORD per space.

The institution of marriage has 14. _______, not 15. _______ over the years. The evolution of marriage is characteristic of a nation where new dimensions of 16. _______ become apparent to new 17. _______, often through perspectives beginning with pleas and protests.

18. Which of the following can be inferred from the judge's thoughts on marriage?
    a. The speaker believes the nation is strongest when it's male-dominated.
    b. The speaker believes the institution of marriage depends on the law of coverture.
    c. The speaker believes the public can influence the judicial process.

19. Read the following part of the lecture again. Then answer the question.
    (Judge) ...changed understandings of marriage are characteristic of a Nation where new dimensions of freedom become apparent to new generations...

What is an example of a "new dimension of freedom" that changed marriage?
    a. Women are no longer their husband's property.
    b. Coverture was passed as a law.
    c. Religious freedom was expanded to include marriage.

20. Read the following part of the lecture again. Then answer the question.
    (Judge) These and other developments in the institution of marriage over the past centuries were not mere superficial changes.

What does "not mere superficial changes" mean?
    a. Trivial changes
    b. Surface-level changes
    c. Significant changes

Passage #3: Speech

Questions 21–23: Complete the sentences below: Write NO MORE THAN ONE WORD for each answer.

21. John was brought up rich, but he is _____.

22. John is all out of breath when he walks up a _____.

23. John could not even crush a _____.

24. Which one of the following adjectives best describes John's emotional state?
    a. Confident
    b. Desperate
    c. Fulfilled

25. What did John study in school?
    a. Business
    b. Law
    c. Philosophy

26. John does NOT compare himself to which one of the following?
    a. A child
    b. A dog
    c. A fly

27. Read the following part of the monologue again. Then answer the question.

    (Speaker) I imagined that the treasure was all mine.

What is the "treasure"?
    a. Material wealth
    b. His mother
    c. Mariana's kindness

28. What can be inferred about John's father?
    a. He lost most of the family's money.
    b. He was a strong role model.
    c. He had a relationship with Mariana.

29. What does John want from Mariana?
    a. A loan
    b. A baby
    c. Her love

30. According to John, his mother hurt him professionally. How so?
    a. She refused to pay for his education.
    b. She stopped him from joining the family business.
    c. She taught him to always be good.

Passage #4: Lecture

- 50
- 480,000
- 5.6 million
- 20 million
- 600
- 69

31. How many chemicals in tobacco are known to cause cancer? ________

32. How many children alive in 2014 will die prematurely of a tobacco-related disease when they are adults? ________

33. Tobacco contains how many ingredients? ________

34. At the time of the article in 2014, how many years since had it been since the original 1964 U.S. Surgeon General's report on smoking and health? ________

35. The Surgeon General reported in 2014 that cigarettes had killed over how many users? ________

36. When did the surgeon general first report on smoking and health?
   a. 1864
   b. 1914
   c. 1964

37. What is the most dangerous way to consume tobacco?
   a. Absorption
   b. Combustion
   c. Immersion

38. The professor describes which one of the following groups as a "priority population"?
   a. Disabled people
   b. Elderly people
   c. Poor people

39. Which of the following are inhaled by cigarette smokers?
   a. Particulate matter and measles
   b. Lead and sarin
   c. Carbon monoxide and tars

40. Read the following part of the lecture again. Then answer the question.
   (Professor) Why not place the wholly preventable deaths and disease burdens of tobacco use behavior on the same priority list of scourges to be eradicated?

How would the professor answer this rhetorical question?
   a. Tobacco use behavior isn't placed on that same list because the government is corrupt.
   b. Tobacco use behavior shouldn't be on that same list because it's not a medical illness.
   c. Tobacco use behavior should be placed on that same list alongside malaria and HIV/AIDS.

Academic Test Reading

Passage #1: Biology

The following passage about the lymph system would be found in an introductory biology textbook. Read the passage and then answer the questions that follow.

[1] The lymph (lymphatic) system helps the body fight infections and other diseases. It's made up of tissue and organs:

- **Lymph**: Lymph is a clear fluid that contains white blood cells, especially lymphocytes such as B cells and T cells.
- **Lymph vessels**: The lymph system has a network of lymph vessels that carry lymph. Lymph vessels branch into all the tissues of the body.
- **Lymph nodes**: Lymph vessels are connected to small, round organs called lymph nodes. Groups of lymph nodes are found in the neck, armpits, chest, abdomen, and groin. Lymph nodes store white blood cells, which trap and remove harmful substances that may be in lymph.
- **Other parts of the lymph system**: The other parts include the tonsils, thymus, and spleen. The tonsils are in the back of the throat; the thymus is between the lungs; and the spleen is to the left of the stomach. Lymph tissue is also found in other parts of the body including the stomach, skin, and small intestine.

[2] Hodgkin lymphoma starts in the lymph system, usually in a lymph node. The disease may be found because of a swollen lymph node in the neck, chest, or other areas. The disease begins when a lymphocyte (almost always a B cell) becomes abnormal. The abnormal cell divides to make copies of itself, which continue dividing and building up. When white blood cells collect around the abnormal cells, the lymph node that contains abnormal cells becomes swollen. Abnormal cells may spread through the lymph vessels or blood vessels to other parts of the body. Although normal cells die when they get old or damaged, abnormal cells don't die off naturally. Also, unlike normal cells, abnormal cells can't help the body fight infections.

[3] In 2013, more than 9,000 Americans will be diagnosed with Hodgkin lymphoma. About 4,000 of these people will be children, teens, and adults younger than 35 years old. Most people diagnosed with Hodgkin lymphoma have the classical type. In 2013, about 8,550 Americans will be diagnosed with this type. In classical Hodgkin lymphoma, the abnormal cell is called a Reed-Sternberg cell. Other abnormal cells may also be found in people with Classical Hodgkin lymphoma. These cells are called Hodgkin cells. They are larger than normal lymphocytes but smaller than Reed-Sternberg cells.

[4] In 2013, about 450 Americans will be diagnosed with Nodular lymphocyte-predominant Hodgkin lymphoma (NLPHL). In this rare type of Hodgkin lymphoma, the abnormal cell is called a lymphocyte-predominant cell, and treatment options are different.

[5] Doctors describe the stages of Hodgkin lymphoma using the Roman numerals I, II, III, and IV. Stage I is early-stage cancer, and Stage IV is advanced cancer, such as Hodgkin lymphoma that has spread to the liver.

Stage I

[6] Lymphoma cells are in one lymph node group (such as the lymph nodes in the neck or armpit). Very rarely, Hodgkin lymphoma may start somewhere in the body other than a lymph node and, in such a case, lymphoma cells are found in only that part.

Stage II

[7] Lymphoma cells are in at least two lymph node groups, but both groups are on the same side of the diaphragm. Or lymphoma cells are in one part of a tissue or an organ, and the lymph nodes near that organ are on the same side of the diaphragm. Lymphoma cells may be in other lymph node groups on the same side of the diaphragm.

Stage III

[8] Lymphoma cells are in lymph nodes on both sides of the diaphragm. Lymphoma cells may also be found in one part of a tissue or an organ near these lymph node groups, or in the spleen.

Stage IV

[9] Lymphoma cells are found in several parts of at least one organ or tissue. Or lymphoma cells are in an organ (such as the liver, lung, or bone) and in lymph nodes on the other side of the diaphragm.

Questions 1-3: Write the name of the body part in the blank spaces below in NO MORE THAN ONE word, matching the question number to the number in the diagram.

1. ____________
2. ____________
3. ____________

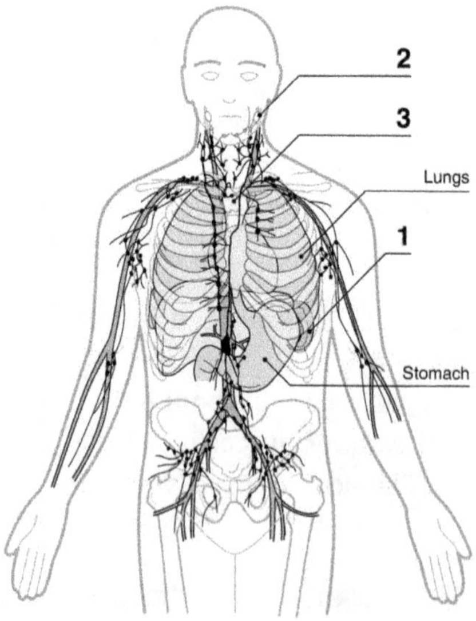

Questions 4-9: Answer the multiple-choice questions below.

4. A patient has Hodgkin lymphoma, and the lymphoma cells are concentrated in only one lymph node group. What stage is the disease in?

a. Stage I
b. Stage II
c. Stage III
d. Stage IV

5. In what stage do lymphoma cells first spread to both sides of the diaphragm?
a. Stage I
b. Stage II
c. Stage III
d. Stage IV

6. In classical Hodgkin lymphoma, what is the largest type of abnormal cell?
a. A Hodgkin cell
b. A lymphocyte-predominant cell
c. A lymphocyte
d. A Reed-Sternberg cell

7. Which of the following is a small round organ found in the neck, armpits, chest, abdomen, and groin?
a. Lymph
b. Lymph vessel
c. Lymph node
d. Lymph tissue

8. Of the Americans who it was predicted would be diagnosed with Hodgkin lymphoma in 2013, how many were expected to be children, teens, and adults younger than 35 years old?
a. 450
b. 4,000
c. 8,500
d. 9,000

9. In Nodular lymphocyte-predominant Hodgkin lymphoma (NLPHL), what is the abnormal cell called?
a. A Hodgkin cell
b. A lymphocyte-predominant cell
c. A lymphocyte
d. A Reed-Sternberg cell

Question 10 – 13: Read the definitions below and write the corresponding name of the lymphatic system part in the blank spaces using NO MORE THAN TWO words.

10. This part makes up a network that carries lymph and branches into all the tissues of the body_____________.

11. This part stores white blood cells, which removes harmful substances in lymph_____________.

12. This part is a clear fluid that contains white blood cells_____________.

13. This part refers to the cells in the lymphatic system, usually B cells or T cells_____________.

Passage #2: History

The following passage about the start of World War I would be found in an introductory history textbook. Read the passage and then answer the questions that follow.

[1] For some years prior to 1914 the great countries of Europe had been divided into two rival groups. One of these was the Triple Alliance, which comprised Germany, Austria-Hungary, and Italy. The other was the Triple Entente, which consisted of France, Great Britain, and Russia.

[2] The Triple Alliance, dominated by Germany, formed first, and was initiated by Germany as part of an ambitious plan to create a great world empire with herself at its head. In furtherance of this ambition, Germany had established close relationships with Turkey and some of the Balkan states, had extended her colonies by both peaceful means and brutal seizure, and had launched a program of military and naval expansion seeking supremacy on both land and sea.

[3] Great Britain, France, and Russia, realizing the danger posed to each country if called upon to act alone against a combination of powers such as the Triple Alliance, had formed the Triple Entente.

[4] Belgium was identified with neither the Triple Alliance nor the Triple Entente, as her neutrality had been guaranteed by all members of both groups, except Italy. Various incidents before 1914 had almost caused war between the two groups, and each incident had increased to some extent the strain which existed between them.

[5] The breaking point came when the Crown Prince of Austria, Franz Ferdinand, was assassinated on June 28, 1914 while inspecting troops in the Austrian city of Sarajevo, near the Serbian border. Austria immediately accused Serbia of having instigated the crime and adopted an aggressive attitude in the diplomatic negotiations which ensued. Serbia went to great lengths to prevent war with her powerful neighbor, and after submitting to nearly all the demands made upon her, agreed to arbitrate the others. Austria, however, confident of Germany's support in a war of aggression, refused to accept the Serbian proposals and declared war against her on July 28, 1914.

[6] Austria started mobilizing her army and Russia soon thereafter did likewise. Germany demanded that the Russian mobilization cease at once, and, at the same time, sent an ultimatum to France requiring her to state her intentions immediately in case of a Russo-German war. After receiving no reply from Russia and a statement from France declaring that she would act in her own interests, Germany declared war against Russia on August 1 and against France on August 3.

[7] Italy asserted that her agreements as a member of the Triple Alliance did not compel her to take part in a war of aggression and thus announced her neutrality. Great Britain did not enter the war until August 4, when it became certain that Germany had violated Belgian neutrality by invading it.

[8] By that point, Germany and Austria-Hungary, known as the Central Powers, were at war against the Allies, which consisted of France, Russia, Great Britain, Serbia, and Belgium. Montenegro joined the Allies a few days later. Four of these nations, France and Russia of the Allies, and Germany and Austria of the Central Powers, were able to place large, well-trained armies in the field at once. Serbia, Belgium, and Montenegro had relatively small armies, and Great Britain's main organized power was her navy, which, at that time, was the strongest in the world. Believing that, in the event of war, Russia would mobilize her forces more slowly than France, Germany, prior to the opening of hostilities, had made plans to crush the latter by a sudden and powerful offensive. According to these plans, Austrian and,

comparatively small, German forces were to engage Russia on the east until France could be defeated. After this, the combined strength of the Central Powers would be deployed against Russia.

[9] Immediately after the declaration of war, the German Army invaded France using every natural avenue of approach, including through neutral Belgium. The Belgian's displayed heroic resistance, and Great Britain's comparatively small expeditionary force supplied vital aid to the French Army. Still, the Allies were forced back rapidly to the general line of the Marne River. Making a determined stand in early September, the Allies withstood further attacks and so threatened the Germans that they retired to a position behind the Aisne River.

[10] Following this battle, both sides realized that the war would not end quickly. Therefore, each power sought to secure possession of the ports in northwestern France, which held supreme importance for future military operations. If the ports fell into German hands, not only would British military operations be hampered, but Germany would secure excellent bases for naval activities. In this famous "race to the sea," the Allies succeeded in retaining all ports southwest of Ostend.

[11] At the end of these operations, since neither contending force on the Western Front had sufficient advantage to undertake a major offensive, each began stabilizing its position by every artificial means available. Elaborate trench systems were built along the warfront to shelter troops as they fought. The armies defended their sides with unprecedented numbers of machine guns and other quick-firing weapons as well as with broad belts of barbed wire. These continuous defenses, with the hostile lines separated in many places by only a narrow strip of ground, became known as "trench warfare."

[12] The United States was a neutral nation at the beginning of the World War. While the sympathies of American citizens were, naturally, divided, the causes of the conflict were mostly considered to be of no direct concern to the United States. That is, the general attitude of the country was one of neutrality.

[13] Early in the war, however, the naval activities of the warring nations began to interfere with American maritime trade. The war's interference with American commerce caused an exchange of vigorous diplomatic notes with Great Britain, while differences with Germany over the use of the submarine became particularly irritating. It soon developed that Germany intended to disregard a fundamental principle of international law which, up to that time in history, had remained unquestioned: that neither enemy merchant vessels nor ships of neutral countries could be lawfully sunk without first taking steps to remove the passengers and crew.

[14] The first serious difficulty with Germany arose when, on February 4, 1915, the country proclaimed that she would regard the waters surrounding Great Britain and Ireland as part of the war zone. This meant that enemy merchant vessels and even neutral vessels would be destroyed without ensuring that passengers could be saved. The United States strongly protested this action because it would endanger American lives and property, reminding Germany that her sole right under international law in dealing with neutral vessels on the high seas was limited to that of visit and search.

[15] The German reply was unsatisfactory, stating that the country would not be responsible for consequences to neutral ships if they entered waters in the warzone. Soon after, Germany sunk several unarmed vessels carrying American passengers without attempting to save those on board. This violation reached a climax on the afternoon of May 7, 1915, when the British liner *Lusitania* was sunk, without warning, by a German submarine off the coast of Ireland. 1,195 lives were lost, including 124 Americans and 94 children, 35 of which were infants.

[16] During the early part of 1916, the destruction of unarmed ships continued. On April 18, President Woodrow Wilson notified Germany that, unless she ceased to use submarine warfare against commercial vessels, diplomatic relations would be severed. Germany responded by promising to avoid sinking passenger ships, to give due warning to any vessels the submarines may destroy, and to give crew members and passengers a reasonable chance to save themselves in their lifeboats.

[17] This promise temporarily relieved tensions and kept relations between the two countries diplomatic during the next nine months. However, the situation again grew critical when, on January 31, 1917, Germany revoked her pledges to the United States. The country announced that it intended to use submarines to sink every vessel which sought to approach the ports of Great Britain and Ireland, the western coasts of Europe, or any port controlled by enemies of Germany within the Mediterranean. President Wilson at once broke off diplomatic relations. He did not yet recommend a declaration of war, stating to Congress that he could not take such an extreme step unless the German Government should actually carry out its threat.

[18] Events which drove the United States into war now developed rapidly. On February 26, 1917, the President requested that Congress give him the authority to equip American merchant ships with defensive arms should it become necessary. Two days later, the President revealed to the press the contents of a telegram which had been intercepted by the British Government late in January. The "Zimmerman Telegram" had been sent by the German Secretary of Foreign Affairs, Arthur Zimmermann, through the German Embassy in Washington to the German Minister in Mexico City.

It proposed that, in the event of war between the United States and Germany, an alliance be formed between Mexico and Germany and that Mexico endeavor to persuade Japan to desert the Allies and align herself with the Central Powers. In exchange, Mexico would be allowed "to reconquer her lost territory in Texas, New Mexico and Arizona." The effect the publication of this telegram had upon the American people was instantaneous and widespread. It seemed to crystallize public opinion into a strong feeling of hostility toward Germany. The House of Representatives promptly passed the bill that would authorize the arming of merchant ships, although the measure failed to pass the Senate before its adjournment on March 4 due to a filibuster. Regardless, it was clear Congress overwhelmingly favored passage of the bill.

[19] Once German submarines began sinking American ships, the President addressed a special session of Congress on April 2, 1917. He stated:

> Vessels of every kind, whatever their flag, their character, their cargo, their destination, their errand, have been ruthlessly sent to the bottom without warning and without thought of help or mercy for those on board, the vessels of friendly neutrals along with those of belligerents. Even hospital ships and ships carrying relief to the sorely bereaved and stricken people of Belgium...have been sunk with the same reckless lack of compassion and of principle...I am not now thinking of the loss of property, immense and serious as that is, but only of the wanton and wholesale destruction of the lives of non-combatants, men, women, and children, engaged in pursuits which have always, even in the darkest periods of modern history, been deemed innocent and legitimate...

He then advised that the United States declare war against the Imperial German Government. Congress, with but few dissenting votes, approved this recommendation, and war was declared against Germany on April 6, 1917.

[20] Diplomatic relations were severed with Austria-Hungary two days later; however, war was not officially declared against her until December 7, 1917.

[21] The President took great care to announce the aims and attitude of America in his speech to Congress on April 2, 1917. He said:

> We have no selfish ends to serve. We desire no conquest, no dominion. We seek no indemnities for ourselves, no material compensation for the sacrifice we shall freely make. We are but one of the champions of the rights of mankind...We enter this war only where we are clearly forced into it, because there are no other means of defending our rights.

14. Which event changed public opinion in the United States to one of hostility towards Germany?
    a. The Zimmerman Telegram
    b. The German invasion of France
    c. The formation of the Triple Alliance
    d. The assassination of Franz Ferdinand

15. Which country sought to maintain neutrality, but nonetheless was drawn into the war via German invasion?
    a. Italy
    b. Belgium
    c. The United States
    d. Austria

16. What battle strategy was developed to shelter troops as they defended their sides with machine guns, quick-firing weapons, and broad belts of barbed wire?
    a. Naval expansion
    b. Submarine warfare
    c. Expeditionary force
    d. Trench warfare

Questions 17-22: Complete the sentences below using NO MORE THAN TWO WORDS.

17. On July 28, 1914, _______________ declared war on Serbia, starting the conflict that spiraled into World War I.

18. Early in the war, the naval activities of the warring nations began to interfere with American __________.

19. On May 7, 1915, a German submarine sunk the British liner _________ off the coast of Ireland, killing 1,195 people.

20. The Zimmerman Telegram proposed that, in the event of war between the __________and Germany, an alliance be formed between Mexico and Germany and that Mexico endeavor to persuade Japan to desert the Allies and align herself with the Central Powers.

21. ____________ had the strongest navy in the world at the start of World War I.

22. Prior to 1914, France, Great Britain, and Russia formed the _________________________.

Questions 23-28: *Write the paragraph number in the blank that most closely matches its description.*

23. The paragraph contains a quotation from President Woodrow Wilson claiming that America had no desire to conquer colonies and didn't expect to be repaid after the war. ________

24. The paragraph describes Germany's decision to dedicate more resources to invading France than Russia at the start of the war. ________

25. The paragraph states that American citizens favored neutrality during the beginning of World War I because they didn't believe the war was of direct concern to them. ________

26. The paragraph quotes President Woodrow Wilson's address to a special session of Congress and ends with the United States declaring war on Germany. ________

27. The paragraph provides the date when Germany declared the waters surrounding Great Britain a war zone, meaning that neutral ships might be targeted. ________

28. The paragraph includes information about how the assassination of the Crown Prince of Austria triggered events that led to the start of World War I. ________

Passage #3: Psychology

The following passage about stress would be found in a textbook for an introductory psychology textbook. Read the passage and then answer the questions that follow.

[1] Early life events play a powerful role in later mental and physical health, as demonstrated by the adverse childhood experiences (ACE) studies and recent work related to maternal care in animals and parental care in humans that will be explored below. Animal models have contributed enormously to our understanding of how parental care affects the human brain and body. Notable studies include the "neonatal handling" research of Levine and Denenberg and recent work by Meaney and Syzf. Epigenetic, transgenerational effects transmitted by maternal care are central to the findings in these studies. Besides the frequency of maternal care, the consistency of that care over time and the offspring's exposure to novelty are important factors, according to both rodent and monkey models. Prenatal stress impairs hippocampal development in rats, as does stress in adolescence. Abusive maternal care in rodents, specifically the surprising attachment shown by infant rats to their abusive mothers, appears to involve an immature amygdala, which causes an aversive conditioning response to emerge when activated by glucocorticoids. Maternal anxiety in the variable foraging demand (VFD) model in rhesus monkeys leads to chronic anxiety in the offspring, as well as signs of metabolic syndrome.

[2] Studies of ACE in human populations show increased inflammatory tones present in children and young adults who experienced early life abuse. Such conditions may include family instability, use of chronic harsh language, and physical and sexual abuse. According to one study, chaos in the home is also associated with poor self-regulatory behaviors and obesity. That particular ACE study focused on a middle-income population, highlighting that poverty is not the only early life stressor.

[3] Nevertheless, low socioeconomic status (SES) does increase the likelihood of stressors in the home and neighborhood. Without a determination of exact causes, it has been reported that low SES children are more likely to be deficient in language skills and self-regulatory behaviors. They are also more disposed to experience deficiencies in certain types of memory, which are likely reflections of impaired

development of perisylvian cortex language centers, prefrontal cortical systems, and temporal lobe memory systems. Low SES and family poverty reportedly correlate with smaller hippocampal volumes, overall smaller gray matter volume, and, in children, reduced prefrontal control of amygdala activity that results in impaired self-regulatory behavior. Neglect is associated with impaired white matter development and integrity. Lower subjective SES, an important index of objective SES, is associated with reduction in prefrontal cortical gray matter. Moreover, individuals reared in a lower SES environment tend to show greater amygdala reactivity to angry and sad faces; this may be a predisposing factor for early cardiovascular disease, which is more prevalent at lower SES levels. Depression is also often associated with low SES. Furthermore, children of depressed mothers, followed longitudinally, have shown increased amygdala volume but no effect on hippocampal volume.

[4] Yet, humans possess "reactive or context-sensitive alleles" that, in nurturing environments, benefit individuals and lead to better outcomes compared to less reactive alleles, although those same reactive alleles can enhance adverse outcomes in a stressful early life environment. Regarding adverse outcomes and "good and bad environments," allostatic processes adjust via epigenetic influences to optimize the individual's adaptation to, and resulting fitness for, a particular environment, whether more or less threatening or nurturing. There are physical and mental health "trade-offs" that, on the one hand, may increase the likelihood of passing on one's genes by coping with adversity, thereby enhancing mental health and overall reproductive success but, on the other hand, may impair later health, e.g., by eating of "comfort foods."

Moreover, when an individual faces a new challenge, like moving from a safe environment into a dangerous one or vice versa, there are differences of resilience in terms of the ability to show experience-related adaptation. This raises the question of plasticity, particularly in brain architecture that is so fundamental to brain and body health. There is both old and new evidence that glucocorticoids, often thought of in a negative sense in relation to stress effects, play an important role in the brain's ability to adapt to new challenges and possibly also to remediate deficits associated with stress accumulated over the lifetime.

[5] What can be done to remediate the effects of chronic, lifelong stress at both individual and societal levels? For the individual, the complexity of non-linear and biphasic interactions of the mediators of stress and adaptation, as described above, emphasizes behavioral, or "top-down," interventions (i.e., interventions that involve integrated central nervous system [CNS] activity). These may include cognitive-behavioral therapy, physical activity, and programs, such as the Experience Corps, that promote social support and integration and meaning and purpose in life. It should also be noted that many interventions that are intended to promote plasticity and slow decline with age, such as physical activity and positive social interactions that give meaning and purpose, are also useful for promoting "positive health" and "eudaimonia" independently of any notable disorder and within the range of normal behavior and physiology.

[6] In contrast, pharmacological agents, which are useful in many circumstances to redress chemical and molecular imbalances, run the risk of dysregulating other adaptive pathways, i.e., no pharmaceutical is without side effects.

[7] A powerful "top down" therapy (i.e., an activity, usually voluntary, involving activation of integrated nervous system activity, as opposed to pharmacological therapy which has a more limited target) is regular physical activity, which improves prefrontal and parietal cortex blood flow and enhances executive functioning. Moreover, regular physical activity consisting of walking one hour for five days a

week, increases hippocampal volume in previously sedentary adults. This finding complements work showing that fit individuals have larger hippocampal volumes than sedentary adults of the same age range. It is also well known that regular physical activity is an effective antidepressant and protects against cardiovascular disease, diabetes, and dementia. Moreover, intensive learning has also been shown to increase the volume of the hippocampus.

[8] Social integration and support and finding meaning and purpose in life are known to protect against allostatic overload and dementia. Programs such as the Experience Corps that promote these along with increased physical activity have been shown to slow the decline of physical and mental health and to improve prefrontal cortical blood flow in a similar manner to regular physical activity alone.

[9] Depression and anxiety disorders are examples of a loss of resilience, in the sense that changes in brain circuitry and function—caused by the stressors that precipitate the disorder—become "locked" in a particular state and thus need external intervention. Indeed, prolonged depression is associated with shrinkage of the hippocampus and prefrontal cortex. While there appears to be no neuronal loss, there is evidence for glial cell loss and smaller neuronal cell nuclei, which is consistent with a shrinking of the dendritic tree (nerve fiber branches at the end of a neuron) after chronic stress. Indeed, a few studies indicate that pharmacological treatment may reverse the decreased hippocampal volume in unipolar and bipolar depression, but the possible influence of concurrent cognitive-behavioral therapy in these studies is unclear. And yet, it is possible that a combination of a pharmaceutical or behavioral (e.g., exercise) intervention that opens up a "window of plasticity" might improve the efficacy of behavioral therapies.

[10] In this connection, it is important to reiterate that successful behavioral therapy tailored to individual needs, can produce volumetric changes in both the prefrontal cortex, in the case of chronic fatigue, and in the amygdala, in the case of chronic anxiety, as measured in the same subjects longitudinally. This reinforces the notion that plasticity-facilitating treatments should be given within the framework of a positive behavioral or physical therapy intervention. On the other hand, negative experiences during the window of enhanced plasticity may have undesirable consequences, such as a person returning to a family environment that may have precipitated anxiety or depression in the first place. Relatedly, it should be noted that BDNF, a plasticity enhancing class of molecules, also has the ability to promote pathophysiology, such as seizures.

[11] At the societal level, the most important top-down interventions are government and private sector policies that improve education and allow people to make choices that increase their chances for a healthy life. This point was made by the Acheson report of the British Government in 1998, which recognized that no public policy of virtually any kind should be enacted without considering the implications for the health of all citizens. Basic education, housing, taxation, setting of a minimum wage, and addressing occupational health and safety and environmental pollution regulations are all likely to affect health via a myriad of mechanisms. Additionally, providing access to affordable, high quality food ensures that those in both poor and affluent neighborhoods can eat well, provided they also learn what types of food to eat. Likewise, making neighborhoods safer and more congenial and supportive can improve opportunities for positive social interactions and increase recreational physical activity. However, government policies are not the only way to reduce allostatic load. For example, businesses that encourage healthy lifestyle practices among their employees are likely to gain reduced health insurance costs and, possibly, a more loyal workforce.

Questions 29-40: Complete the sentences below using NO MORE THAN THREE WORDS.

29. Along with other recent work, the adverse childhood experiences (ACE) studies found that early_________________ in parental care play a powerful role in later mental and physical health.

30. Regular physical activity is an effective_________________ and protects against cardiovascular disease, diabetes, and dementia.

31. At the societal level, the most important top-down interventions are the policies of _________________ and the private sector that not only improve education but also allow people to make choices that improve their chances for a healthy life.

32. _________________ increases the likelihood of stressors being present in the home and neighborhood, including toxic chemical agents such as lead and air pollution.

33. _________________ is tailored to individual needs, and when used to treat chronic fatigue, it can produce volumetric changes in the prefrontal cortex.

34. _________________ agents, which are useful in many circumstances to redress chemical and molecular imbalances, nevertheless run the risk of dysregulating other adaptive pathways.

35. Depression and anxiety disorders are examples of a loss of resilience, in the sense that changes in_________________ and function become "locked" in a particular state and thus need external intervention.

36. Intensive learning has also been shown to increase the volume of the human _________________.

37. Chaos in the home is associated with development of poor self-regulatory behaviors, as well as_________________.

38. Studies have shown that early life abuse, such as family instability, use of chronic harsh language, and physical and sexual abuse, cause increased _________________.

39. Businesses that encourage healthy lifestyle practices among their employees are likely to gain reduced_________________ costs and possibly a more loyal workforce.

40. A powerful _________________ therapy is regular physical activity.

General Training Reading

Section #1

The next six questions are based on the following passage:

Eating Disorders Explained

[1] Eating disorders are serious medical illnesses marked by severe disturbances to a person's eating behaviors. Obsessions with food, body weight, and shape may be signs of an eating disorder. These disorders can affect a person's physical and mental health; in some cases, they can be life-threatening. But eating disorders can be treated. Learning more about them can help you spot the warning signs and seek treatment early.

[2] Remember: Eating disorders are not a lifestyle choice. They are biologically-influenced medical illnesses.

[3] Eating disorders can affect people of all ages, racial/ethnic backgrounds, body weights, and genders. Although eating disorders often appear during the teen years or young adulthood, they may also develop during childhood or later in life (40 years and older).

[4] Remember: People with eating disorders may appear healthy yet be extremely ill.

[5] The exact cause of eating disorders is not fully understood, but research suggests a combination of genetic, biological, behavioral, psychological, and social factors can raise a person's risk.

[6] Common eating disorders include anorexia nervosa, bulimia nervosa, and binge-eating disorder. If you or someone you know experiences the symptoms listed below, it could be a sign of an eating disorder—call a health provider right away for help.

Questions 1-6: Complete the following summary below using NO MORE THAN TWO WORDS.

Eating disorders can affect people of all ages, races/ethnicities, body weights, and 1. ______________. A combination of genetic, 2. ______________, behavioral, psychological, and social factors can raise a person's risk of developing an eating disorder. Common eating disorders include anorexia nervosa, 3. ______________, and binge-eating disorder. Signs of these disorders typically include obsessions with food, 4. ______________, and shape that negatively impact physical and mental health. 5.______________ are treatable but if ignored, can lead to serious and potentially life-threatening health problems. People should call a 6. ______________ right away for help if they grow concerned about problematic thoughts and behavior related to food.

The next ten questions are based on the following passage:

<u>Tips for Preparing Healthy Snacks for Children</u>

[1] Snacks can help children get the nutrients they need to grow and maintain a healthy weight. Prepare single-serving snacks for younger children to help them satisfy their hunger. Let older kids make their own snacks by keeping healthy foods in the kitchen.

[2] Store sliced vegetables in the refrigerator and serve with dips like hummus or low-calorie dressing. Top half a whole-wheat English muffin with spaghetti sauce, chopped vegetables, and low-fat shredded mozzarella and melt in the microwave.

[3] For older school-age kids, mix dried fruit, unsalted nuts, and popcorn in a snack-size bag for a quick trail mix. Blend plain fat-free or low-fat yogurt with 100% fruit juice and frozen peaches for a tasty smoothie.

[4] A cup of low-fat or fat-free milk or milk alternative (soy milk) is an easy way to drink a healthy snack.

[5] Offer whole-wheat breads, popcorn, and whole-oat cereals that are high in fiber and low in added sugars, saturated fat, and sodium. Limit refined-grain products such as snack bars, cakes, and sweetened cereals.

[6] Choose lean protein foods such as low-sodium deli meats or unsalted nuts. Wrap sliced, low-sodium deli turkey around an apple wedge. Store hard-cooked (boiled) eggs in the refrigerator for kids to enjoy any time.

[7] Snacks shouldn't replace a meal, so look for ways to help your kids understand how much is enough. Store snack-size bags in the cupboard and use them to control serving sizes.

[8] Fresh, frozen, dried, or canned fruits can be easy "grab-and-go" options that need little preparation. Offer whole fruit and limit the amount of 100% juice served.

[9] A single-serving container of low-fat or fat-free yogurt or individually wrapped string cheese can be enough for an after-school snack.

[10] Keep healthier foods handy so kids avoid cookies, pastries, or candies between meals. Add seltzer water to a ½ cup of 100% fruit juice instead of offering soda.

[11] For homemade sweets, add dried fruits like apricots or raisins and reduce the amount of sugar in the recipe. Adjust recipes that include fats like butter or shortening by using unsweetened applesauce or prune puree for half the amount of fat.

Questions 7-16: Complete the sentences below using NO MORE THAN THREE WORDS.

7. An individually wrapped string cheese can be just enough for an ______________snack.

8. Adjust recipes that include fats like butter or ______________by using unsweetened applesauce or prune puree for half the amount of fat.

9. Use snack-size bags to control______________.

10. ______________is an alternative milk product.

11. Add seltzer water to a ½ cup of 100% ______________ instead of offering soda.

12. Store sliced vegetables in the refrigerator and serve with dips like hummus or ______________dressing.

13. For older school-age kids, mix dried fruit, unsalted nuts, and popcorn in a snack-size bag for a quick ______________.

14. Choose lean protein foods such as ______________ deli meats or unsalted nuts.

15. Limit refined-grain products such as snack bars, ______________, and sweetened cereals.

16. Fresh, frozen, dried, or canned fruits can be easy ______________options that need little preparation.

Section #2

The following work schedule should be used for questions 17-22. The schedule covers all the hours that the store is open.

<u>Store's Work Schedule</u>

Date and Shift	Hours	Team Members	Team Leader
July 1 morning	7:00 AM – 3:00 PM	Alexandra Juan Ryan Zachary	Ryan
July 1 evening	3:00 PM – 11:00 PM	Diana Richard Timothy Xavier	Xavier
July 2 morning	6:00 AM – 2:00 PM	Alexandra Latisha Ryan Xavier	Latisha
July 2 evening	2:00 PM – 10:00 PM	Freddy Diana Richard Samantha	Samantha

July 3 morning	9:00 AM – 3:00 PM	Alexandra Latisha Xavier Zachary	Alexandra
July 3 evening	3:00 PM – 9:00 PM	Diana Freddy Juan Samantha	Juan
July 4 morning	9:00 AM – 12:00 PM	Latisha Ryan Xavier Zachary	Ryan
July 4 evening	12:00 PM – 3:00 PM	Alexandra Juan Richard Samantha	Richard

17. What day does the store open earliest?
   a. July 1
   b. July 2
   c. July 3
   d. July 4

18. What day does the store close earliest?
   a. July 1
   b. July 2
   c. July 3
   d. July 4

19. Who is the only employee scheduled to open the store after closing the previous night?
   a. Alexandra
   b. Juan
   c. Xavier
   d. Zachary

20. Who is scheduled to work the most hours?
   a. Alexandra
   b. Juan
   c. Latisha
   d. Zachary

21. Who is scheduled to work the least hours?
   a. Ryan
   b. Timothy
   c. Freddy
   d. Diana

22. Who is the only employee to serve as the team leader on two different days?
   a. Juan
   b. Latisha
   c. Richard
   d. Ryan

Questions 23-30 are based on the following job listing:

Job Listing

[1] INTERVIEWER

Leaders of Tomorrow

Full-time

Remote

[2] ABOUT US

Leaders of Tomorrow publishes the premier weekly newsletter by and for entrepreneurs. Every issue explores the latest technological innovations and game-changing business strategies. Our staff consists of world-renowned experts who have all personally led a start-up company to market. We're currently looking to take our newsletter to the next level by interviewing the start-up community's biggest movers and shakers.

[3] ABOUT THE ROLE

As an interviewer, you will be responsible for identifying, researching, contacting, and, of course, interviewing, entrepreneurs who have disrupted their industry. The entrepreneur could be a founder, investor, or advisor, but they must be a visionary who has changed the way normal business is done. All interviews will be capped at 2,000 words.

[4] The interviewer will travel to their subjects, but everything else can be done from home. This isn't your typical desk job.

[5] The role is a full-time position, requiring an average of 50 hours per week, with a starting salary between $35,000 and $40,000, depending on qualifications.

[6] QUALIFICATIONS

- Bachelor's degree, communications preferred
- 5+ years professional experience writing long-form content and interviewing subjects
- 2+ years professional experience covering the start-up industry
- Once personally led a start-up to market
- Excellent communication skills with a knack for storytelling and narrative creation
- Detail-oriented and comfortable with tight turnarounds
- Ability to adopt our voice and style
- Knowledge of Microsoft Office, Google Docs, Adobe Acrobat, and several other software programs

[7] CONTACT US

Do you have what it takes to join our tribe? Find out now by emailing us your resume, cover letter, and two best published pieces. We can't wait to meet you!

Questions 23-30: Answer the multiple-choice questions below.

23. Qualified candidates will have covered the start-up industry for how many years?
    a. 2+ years
    b. 3+ years
    c. 4+ years
    d. 5+ years

24. What is the position's primary responsibility?
    a. The primary responsibility is traveling to the interviews.
    b. The primary responsibility is leading a start-up company to market.
    c. The primary responsibility is disrupting an industry.
    d. The primary responsibility is identifying, researching, contacting, and interviewing entrepreneurs.

25. What have the staff all personally done?
    a. Interviewed a visionary
    b. Disrupted an industry
    c. Led a start-up company to market
    d. Developed a game-changing business strategy

26. Which one of the following can be properly inferred based on the listing?
    a. All the interviews will take place in the United States.
    b. The right candidate will need to stay current with technology.
    c. The newsletter is published exclusively online.
    d. Every member of the staff is a college graduate.

27. What is the maximum word count for the interviews?
    a. 1,000 words
    b. 1,500 words
    c. 2,000 words
    d. 2,500 words

28. What should the interested candidate NOT send the employer?
    a. Resume
    b. Cover letter
    c. Two published pieces
    d. Social media history

29. In Paragraph 1, the three lines directly below "INTERVIEWER" provide what information?
    a. Name of company, hours, location of job
    b. Name of company, title of position, location of job
    c. Name of newsletter, hours, and title of position
    d. Title of position, location of job, available hours

30. How much does the position pay?
    a. Between $25,000 and $30,000
    b. Between $30,000 and $35,000
    c. Between $35,000 and $40,000
    d. At least $40,000

Section #3

The next ten questions are based on the following passage:

<u>The Risks of Drowsy Driving</u>

[1] Drowsy driving is a major problem in the United States. The risk, danger, and sometimes tragic results of drowsy driving are alarming. Drowsy driving is the dangerous combination of driving and sleepiness or fatigue. This usually happens when a driver has not slept enough, but it can also occur due to untreated sleep disorders, medications, drinking alcohol, and shift work.

[2] Operating a motor vehicle while fatigued or sleepy is commonly referred to as "drowsy driving." Drowsy driving poses a serious risk not only for one's own health and safety, but also for the other people on the road. The National Highway Traffic Safety Administration estimates that between 2005 and 2009 drowsy driving was responsible for an annual average of:

- 83,000 crashes
- 37,000 injury crashes

- 886 fatal crashes (846 fatalities in 2014)

These estimates are conservative, though, and up to 6,000 fatal crashes each year may be caused by drowsy drivers.

[3] How Often Do Americans Fall Asleep While Driving?

- Approximately 1 out of 25 adults aged 18 years and older surveyed reported that they had fallen asleep while driving in the past 30 days.
- Individuals who snored or slept 6 hours or less per day were more likely to fall asleep while driving.

[4] Falling asleep at the wheel is dangerous but being sleepy affects your ability to drive safely even if you don't fall asleep. Drowsiness—

- Makes drivers less attentive.
- Slows reaction time.
- Affects a driver's ability to make decisions.

[5] The Warning Signs of Drowsy Driving

- Yawning or blinking frequently.
- Difficulty remembering the past few miles driven.
- Missing your exit.
- Drifting from your lane.
- Hitting a rumble strip.

[6] If you experience any of the warning signs of drowsy driving while driving, pull over to a safe place and take a 15-20-minute nap or change drivers. Simply turning up the radio or opening the window is not an effective way to keep you alert. For more warning signs visit the American Academy of Sleep Medicine.

[7] Who Is More Likely to Drive Drowsy?

- Drivers who do not get enough sleep.
- Commercial drivers who operate vehicles such as tow trucks, tractor trailers, and buses.
- Shift workers (work the night shift or long shifts).
- Drivers with untreated sleep disorders such as one where breathing repeatedly stops and starts (sleep apnea).
- Drivers who use medications that make them sleepy.

[8] There are four things you should do before taking the wheel to prevent driving while drowsy.

1. Get enough sleep! Most adults need at least 7 hours of sleep a day, while adolescents need at least 8 hours.

2. Develop good sleeping habits such as sticking to a sleep schedule.

3. If you have a sleep disorder or have symptoms of a sleep disorder such as snoring or feeling sleepy during the day, talk to your physician about treatment options.

4. Avoid drinking alcohol or taking medications that make you sleepy. Be sure to check the label on any medications or talk to your pharmacist.

[9] Your body needs adequate sleep on a daily basis. The more hours of sleep you miss, the harder it is for you to think and perform as well as you would like. Lack of sleep can make you less alert and affect your coordination, judgment, and reaction time while driving. This is known as cognitive impairment.

[10] Studies have shown that going too long without sleep can impair your ability to drive in the same way as drinking too much alcohol.

- Being awake for at least 18 hours is the same as someone having a blood content (BAC) of 0.05%.

- Being awake for at least 24 hours is equal to having a blood alcohol content of 0.10%. This is higher than the legal limit (0.08% BAC) in all states.

[11] Additionally, drowsiness increases the effect of even low amounts of alcohol.

Questions 31-40: Complete the notes below with NO MORE THAN THREE WORDS.

- Operating a motor vehicle while fatigued or sleepy is commonly referred to as 31. _______________.

- Lack of sleep causes 32. _______________, which can reduce alertness, coordination, judgment, and reaction time while driving. Drowsiness can cause as much impairment as 33. _______________ while driving.

- Warning Signs for drowsiness include:
    - Yawning or blinking frequently
    - Difficulty remembering the past few miles driven
    - Missing your 34. _______________
    - Drifting from your lane
    - Hitting a 35. _______________

- How to Prevent Drowsiness
    - Get enough sleep
    - Develop good 36. _______________
    - Talk to your 37. _______________ after experiencing symptoms of a sleep disorder
    - Avoid drinking alcohol or taking 38. _______________ that makes you sleepy before driving.
- Someone experiencing warning signs should pull over to a safe place and take a 15-20-minute nap or 39. _______________. Simply turning up the radio or 40. _______________are not effective ways to stay alert.

First Essay

Academic Test

Prepare a response of at least 150 words on the topic below. You should spend approximately 20 minutes on this task.

Summarize the information presented on the following yogurt nutrition label. Then, make a case for whether you would recommend this product from a health standpoint. Each number corresponds to a different section of the label, as follows: 1) serving information, 2) total calories per serving, 3) nutrients, 4) daily value.

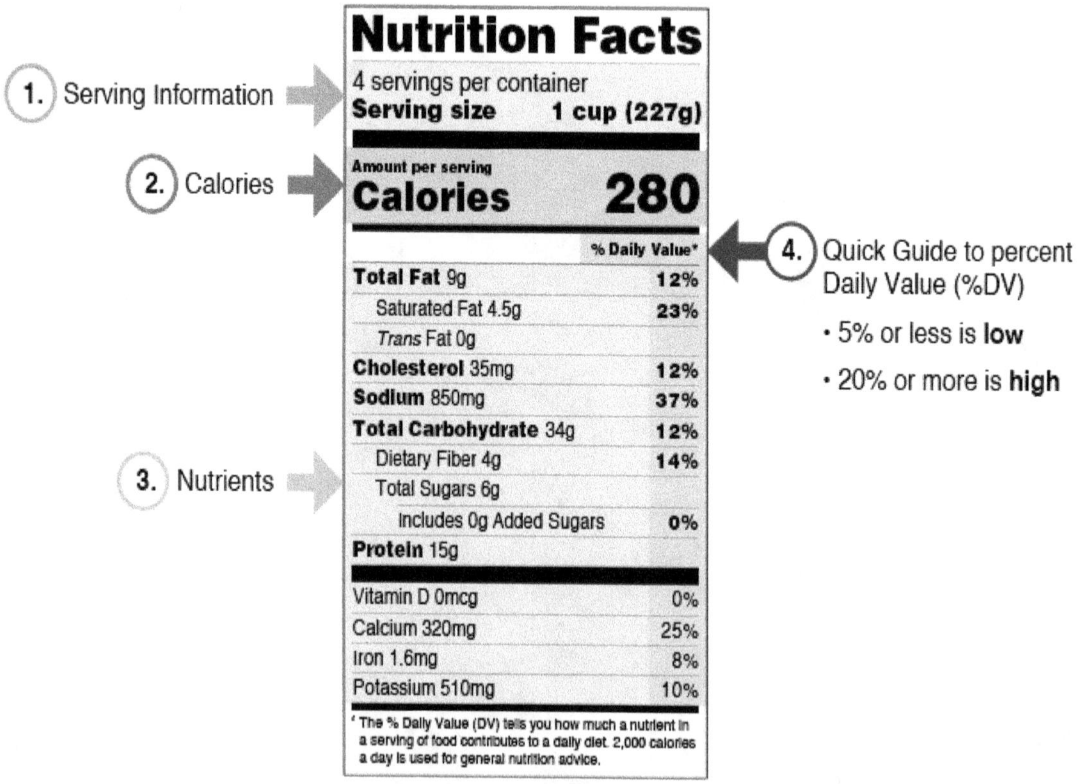

The following pages are provided for writing your essay.

General Training Exam

Prepare a response of at least 150 words on the topic below. You should spend approximately 20 minutes on this task.

You are the president's economic adviser. He wants to know how automation will generally influence the economy. Your initial research shows that automation increases efficiency and reduces costs, so companies would be more profitable. On the other hand, it's clear that automation will result in lower wages and fewer jobs, increasing unemployment. Unregulated, automation will continually advance and innovate, achieving technological breakthroughs. The president is asking whether to regulate automation. Write a memo explaining how you think automation would help or hurt the economy, then discuss what you think is the best course of action.

The following pages are provided for writing your essay.

Second Essay

Academic Test

Prepare an essay of at least 250 words on the topic below. You should spend approximately 40 minutes on this task.

> Henry David Thoreau wrote, "What does education often do? It makes a straight-cut ditch of a free, meandering brook." What do you think Thoreau meant by this statement? Support your answer with details and observations.

The following pages are provided for writing your essay.

General Training Reading

Prepare a response of at least 250 words on the topic below. You should spend approximately 40 minutes on this task.

> Write an essay detailing your experience with loss and how you dealt with it. Talk about the process of the loss and if or how it changed you. How do you view life today in light of that loss?

The following pages are provided for writing your essay.

Speaking

Task #1 (4-5 minutes)

Let's talk about your family.

- Who are the members of your family, and what are they like?
- Where did your family live when you were growing up?
- What childhood memories do you have of your family related to your hometown(s)?

Now let's talk about your hobbies

- What hobbies do you enjoy during your free time?
- What is a hobby that you have never tried, but would like to learn about?
- What activities do you enjoy with your friends when you get together?

Task #2 (3-4 minutes)

Prompt card:

You are a member of the board for the local university. The board is voting to decide on a budget issue for the upcoming school year. There's only enough money to add artificial turf to the field or renovate the auditorium. Both improvements would benefit a lot of students. The football, lacrosse, track, and soccer teams all play on the field. School plays, musicals, and concerts are all performed in the auditorium. Both projects would also be useful for certain required general education classes.

How would you vote, and why? Discuss how both projects would benefit the students in your answer.

Preparation Time: 1 minutes
Response Time: 1-2 minutes

Rounding off question:

What do you think are some of the likely consequences of leaving the auditorium and field as is?

Task #3 (4-5 minutes)

Let's consider general education requirements at universities.

- Do you think students attending university should have to take a variety of general education courses in addition to the requirements of their major? Explain why or why not.
- What are the benefits and drawbacks of general education requirements for students?
- What courses do you think should be required of all university graduates, regardless of their major?

Now let's talk about textbooks.

- An increasing number of universities are now offering students the option to rent course textbooks instead of buy them. Which do you think is a better option?
- What are the benefits and drawbacks of each option?
- Do you or would you rent or buy your books?

Answer Explanations #2

Listening

1. Luck

2. Work ethic

3. Skill

4. Ten

5. Night

6. A: The basketball fan claims every basketball team has at least one talented player. In response, the hockey fan says, "I doubt that's true, but I don't know enough to dispute you." The hockey fan believes Choices *B* and *C* to be true.

7. C: The hockey fan argues that a basketball team can easily score ten consecutive points within a few minutes of game time, which allows teams to overcome massive deficits; therefore, whoever plays well at the end of a game always wins. Choice *A* isn't part of the hockey fan's argument. Choice *B* is something the hockey fan also thinks, but it's an entirely separate issue.

8. A: The basketball fan contends that the icy conditions make hockey games dependent on luck. At the beginning of the conversation, the basketball fan says, "Hockey involves sliding a frozen puck around a sheet of ice that's constantly melting and getting cut up by skates." The other choices aren't part of the basketball fan's criticism.

9. A: After the hockey fan claims, "all of the league's talent is consolidated on a handful of teams," the basketball fan admits there are some "overpowering teams." The basketball fan disputes that only the last few minutes of a basketball game matter, and the hockey fan never claims watching basketball every night is excessive. The hockey fan claims Choice *C* as well, but the basketball fan doesn't explicitly concede that point, like what happens in the "overpowering teams" comment.

10. C: The basketball fan is agreeing to watch the next night's basketball game and attend a hockey game the following week with the hockey fan. The basketball fan asks the hockey fan to watch a basketball game, but that's not what he's saying here. The next night's basketball game is just part of the agreement. The basketball fan is doing more than acknowledging the proposal.

11. C: The lecture primarily addresses the transformation of marriage as an institution. That transformation is described as an evolution of the meaning of freedom, but the evolution of freedom in general is not the main focus. Choice *A* is incorrect for a similar reason. The lecture says that both societal changes and differences between generations caused the transformation, but the overall transformation of marriage is what is primarily being addressed.

12. C: The traditional view of marriage was created by the male-dominated society, and it placed family interests over the husband and wife's individual interests. Thus, parents' interests regarding their children's marriages often included political, religious, and financial questions.

13. C: Women gaining equal rights allowed them to pursue financial independence more fully. More political, economic, and societal freedom meant that women had more power to seek their own marital arrangements.

14. Strengthened

15. Weakened

16. Freedom

17. Generations

18. C: The professor believes the public can influence the judicial process because that's what happened during the transformation of marriage.

19. A: The new dimensions of freedom led to the transformation of marriage as an institution. Women no longer being treated as property is one such change.

20. C: The professor is describing changes that were so powerful they permanently altered the institution of marriage. Thus, the changes are significant, which has the same meaning as "not superficial."

21. Poor

22. Hill

23. Fly

24. B: John is desperate. He opens his monologue by saying, "Everything has gone wrong with me since the day I was born. Whatever I put my hand to fails utterly."

25. B: At the beginning of the dialogue, John states that he studied law, though he still apparently can't "string three words together."

26. C: When trying to win Mariana's affection, he asks her to take him "like a little child into [her] life, like a toy that [she can] play with, or a dog of which [she is] fond." John says he couldn't harm a fly, but he does not actually compare himself to a fly.

27. C: The treasure is Mariana's kindness. John delivers that line after calling Mariana's kindness the source of all his happiness despite it only having been directed toward relatively insignificant things.

28. A: John says that he needed to "save the little that remains to us after the folly of my father." We can infer that his father must have lost the family's money since the preceding sentences discuss his professional failings.

29. C: John wants Mariana's love.

30. C: John explains that his mother taught him to be good, which is undermining his ability to be unscrupulous and bold. John blames his professional failings on his lack of passion and determination, which were allegedly caused by his mother's directive to be good.

31. 69

32. 5.6 million

33. 600

34. 50

35. 480,000

36. C: The professor opens the lecture by saying the surgeon general first reported on smoking and health in 1964.

37. B: The professor repeatedly mentions the dangers of "combustible tobacco." At one point, the professor specifically names combustion as an enemy alongside tobacco. None of the other choices are mentioned in the lecture.

38. C: The professor defines priority populations as groups among which cigarette use is highest, and he provides poor people as an example of a priority population. The other choices aren't identified as priority populations or otherwise described in the lecture.

39. C: Cigarette smokers "inhale carbon monoxide, particulate matter, and more than 7,000 chemicals, commonly referred to as tars." Choice *C* is the only answer that consists of two correct byproducts of burning tobacco.

40. C: The professor is asking this rhetorical question to support his view that tobacco use behavior should be placed on the list of public health crises. He is drawing a comparison with other public health crises, like global warming, malaria, and HIV/AIDS, to argue that tobacco should receive the same attention. The professor doesn't argue that tobacco use behavior is more dangerous than global warming.

Academic Test Reading

1. Spleen: The number is pointing to an organ left of the stomach, which is the spleen (Paragraph 4).

2. Tonsils: The number is pointing to an organ in the throat, where the tonsils are located (Paragraph 4).

3. Thymus: The number is pointing to an organ between the lungs, which is the thymus (Paragraph 4).

4. A: "Lymphoma cells are in one lymph node group" during Stage I, and they spread to more lymph nodes as the stages progress (Paragraph 6).

5. C: Lymphoma cells first spread to both sides of the diaphragm during Stage III, so the correct answer is Choice *C*. They are still on the same side of the diaphragm during Stage II (Paragraphs 7 and 8).

6. D: In classical Hodgkin lymphoma, there are two types of abnormal cells: Reed-Sternberg cells and Hodgkin cells. Hodgkin cells are larger than normal lymphocytes but smaller than Reed-Sternberg cells, which are the largest type of abnormal lymph cell (Paragraph 3). Lymphocytes are white blood cells, such as B cells and T cells, and Hodgkin lymphoma develops when a lymphocyte turns abnormal

(Paragraph 2). A lymphocyte-predominant cell is only found in a rare version of Hodgkin lymphoma (Paragraph 4).

7. C: Lymph nodes are small round organs found in the neck, armpits, chest, abdomen, and groin. Lymph contains white blood cells, especially lymphocytes such as B cells and T cells. Lymph vessels are pathways that carry lymph and branch into all bodily tissue to connect the lymph system. Lymph tissue is found in the stomach, skin, and small intestine (Paragraph 1).

8: B: In 2013, it was expected that about 4,000 children, teens, and adults younger than 35 years old would be diagnosed with Hodgkin lymphoma (Paragraph 3).

9. B: In NLPHL, a rare type of Hodgkin lymphoma, the abnormal cell is called a lymphocyte-predominant cell, and treatment options are different (Paragraph 4).

10. Lymph vessels: The lymph system has a network of lymph vessels that carry lymph. Lymph vessels branch into all the tissues of the body (Paragraph 1).

11. Lymph nodes: Lymph nodes store white blood cells, which trap and remove harmful substances that may be in lymph (Paragraph 1).

12. Lymph: Lymph is a clear fluid that contains white blood cells, especially lymphocytes such as B cells and T cells (Paragraph 1).

13. Lymphocytes: Lymph is a clear fluid that contains white blood cells, especially lymphocytes such as B cells and T cells (Paragraph 1).

14. A: The British intercepted a telegram sent by German Secretary of Foreign Affairs Arthur Zimmermann through the German Embassy in Washington to the German Minister in Mexico City. The Zimmerman Telegram proposed allyship with Mexico in the event of war with the United states and supported Mexican ambitions to reconquer the American southwest, which enraged the American public (Paragraph 18).

15. B: By that point, Germany and Austria-Hungary, known as the Central Powers, were at war against the Allies, which consisted of France, Russia, Great Britain, Serbia, and Belgium (Paragraph 8).

16. D: "Elaborate trench systems, defended by unprecedented numbers of machine guns and other quick-firing weapons, were built along the front" (Paragraph 11). A narrow strip of ground was all that separated the hostile trenches, so this type of fighting came to be known as "trench warfare."

17. Austria: Following the assassination of their Crown Prince, Austria declared war against Serbia on July 28, 1914, with the expectation of receiving material support from Germany (Paragraph 5).

18. Maritime trade: Early in the war, however, the naval activities of the warring nations began to interfere with American maritime trade (Paragraph 13).

19. *Lusitania*: On May 7, 1915, German submarines sank the British liner *Lusitania* without warning off the coast of Ireland. The attack killed 1,195 people, including 124 Americans and 94 children, of which 35 were infants (Paragraph 15).

20. United States: The British intercepted a telegram sent by German Secretary of Foreign Affairs Arthur Zimmermann through the German Embassy in Washington to the German Minister in Mexico City. The Zimmerman Telegram proposed allyship with Mexico in the event of war with the United states and supported Mexican ambitions to reconquer the American southwest, which enraged the American public (Paragraph 18).

21. Great Britain: At the start of World War I, Great Britain had the strongest navy in the world, which was the primary source of its power as Europe began mobilizing (Paragraph 8).

22. Triple Entente: Prior to the outbreak of World War I, France, Great Britain, and Russia formed the Triple Entente to counter the Triple Alliance of Germany, Austria-Hungary, and Italy (Paragraph 1).

23. Paragraph 21: On April 2, 1917, President Wilson told Congress, "We desire no conquest, no dominion. We seek no indemnities for ourselves, no material compensation for the sacrifice we shall freely make." The first sentence refers to America not having a desire to conquer colonies, and the second sentence means the U.S. isn't expecting repayment.

24. Paragraph 8: At the start of the war, Germany wanted to crush France with a sudden and powerful offensive, while holding off Russia until France could be defeated. Following France's surrender, Germany planned to send the combined strength of the Central Powers against Russia.

25. Paragraph 12: The majority of Americans considered the conflict to be of no direct concern to the United States, and the attitude of the country as a whole was one of neutrality.

26. Paragraph 19: On April 2, 1917, President Wilson addressed a special session of Congress to condemn the German attacks against civilian targets and recommend a declaration of war. Congress declared war against Germany on April 6, 1917.

27. Paragraph 14: On February 4, 1915, Germany proclaimed that the waters surrounding Great Britain and Ireland would be regarded as part of the war zone. As a result, enemy merchant vessels would be destroyed, and neutral vessels were in danger of destruction without assurance that the passengers and crew could be saved.

28. Paragraph 5: On June 28, 1914, the Crown Prince of Austria was assassinated while inspecting troops in the Austrian city of Sarajevo, near the Serbian border. Austria immediately blamed Serbia, refused to resolve the crisis through diplomacy, and declared war on Serbia.

29. Life events: "Early life events related to maternal care in animals, as well as parental care in humans, play a powerful role in later mental and physical health, as demonstrated by the adverse childhood experiences (ACE) studies and recent work that will be noted below" (Paragraph 1). Maternal and paternal care are types of parental care.

30. Antidepressant: "Regular physical activity is an effective antidepressant and protects against cardiovascular disease, diabetes, and dementia" (Paragraph 7).

31. Government: "At the societal level, the most important top-down interventions are the policies of government and the private sector that not only improve education but also allow people to make choices that improve their chances for a healthy life. This point was made by the Acheson report of the

British Government in 1998, which recognized that no public policy of virtually any kind should be enacted without considering the implications for the health of all citizens" (Paragraph 11).

32. Low socioeconomic status: "Low socioeconomic status (SES) does increase the likelihood of stressors in the home and neighborhood, including toxic chemical agents such as lead and air pollution" (Paragraph 3).

33. Behavioral therapy: "Successful behavioral therapy, which is tailored to individual needs, can produce volumetric changes in both the prefrontal cortex in the case of chronic fatigue, and in the amygdala, in the case of chronic anxiety as measured in the same subjects longitudinally" (Paragraph 10).

34. Pharmacological: "Pharmacological agents, which are useful in many circumstances to redress chemical and molecular imbalances, nevertheless run the risk of dysregulating other adaptive pathways, i.e., no pharmaceutical is without side effects" (Paragraph 6).

35. Brain circuitry: "Depression and anxiety disorders are examples of a loss of resilience, in the sense that changes in brain circuitry and function—caused by the stressors that precipitate the disorder—become 'locked' in a particular state and thus need external intervention" (Paragraph 9).

36. Hippocampus: "Intensive learning has also been shown to increase the volume of the human hippocampus" (Paragraph 7).

37. Obesity: "Chaos in the home is associated with development of poor self-regulatory behaviors, as well as obesity" (Paragraph 2).

38. Inflammatory tone: "In studies of ACE in human populations, there are reports of increased inflammatory tone, not only in children, but also in young adults related to early life abuse, which includes family instability, use of chronic harsh language, and physical and sexual abuse" (Paragraph 2).

39. Health insurance: "However, government policies are not the only way to reduce allostatic load. For example, businesses that encourage healthy lifestyle practices among their employees are likely to gain reduced health insurance costs and possibly a more loyal workforce" (Paragraph 11).

40. Top down: "A powerful 'top down' therapy (i.e., an activity, usually voluntary, involving activation of integrated nervous system activity, as opposed to pharmacological therapy which has a more limited target) is regular physical activity, which has actions that improve prefrontal and parietal cortex blood flow and enhance executive function" (Paragraph 7).

General Training Reading

1. Genders: "Eating disorders can affect people of all ages, racial/ethnic backgrounds, body weights, and genders" (Paragraph 3).

2. Biological: "The exact cause of eating disorders is not fully understood, but research suggests a combination of genetic, biological, behavioral, psychological, and social factors can raise a person's risk" (Paragraph 5).

3. Bulimia nervosa: "Common eating disorders include anorexia nervosa, bulimia nervosa, and binge-eating disorder" (Paragraph 6).

4. Body weight: "Obsessions with food, body weight, and shape may be signs of an eating disorder" (Paragraph 1).

5. Eating disorders: "These disorders can affect a person's physical and mental health; in some cases, they can be life-threatening. But eating disorders can be treated" (Paragraph 1).

6. Health provider: "If you or someone you know experiences the symptoms listed below, it could be a sign of an eating disorder—call a health provider right away for help" (Paragraph 6).

7. After-school: "A single-serving container of low-fat or fat-free yogurt or individually wrapped string cheese can be just enough for an after-school snack" (Paragraph 9).

8. Shortening: "Adjust recipes that include fats like butter or shortening by using unsweetened applesauce or prune puree for half the amount of fat" (Paragraph 11).

9. Serving sizes: "Store snack-size bags in the cupboard and use them to control serving sizes" (Paragraph 7).

10. Soy milk: "A cup of low-fat or fat-free milk or milk alternative (soy milk) is an easy way to drink a healthy snack" (Paragraph 4).

11. Fruit juice: "Add seltzer water to a ½ cup of 100% fruit juice instead of offering soda" (Paragraph 10).

12. Low-calorie: "Store sliced vegetables in the refrigerator and serve with dips like hummus or low-calorie dressing" (Paragraph 2).

13. Trail mix: "For older school-age kids, mix dried fruit, unsalted nuts, and popcorn in a snack-size bag for a quick trail mix" (Paragraph 3).

14. Low-sodium: "Choose lean protein foods such as low-sodium deli meats or unsalted nuts" (Paragraph 6).

15. Cakes: "Limit refined-grain products such as snack bars, cakes, and sweetened cereals" (Paragraph 50).

16. Grab-and-go: "Fresh, frozen, dried, or canned fruits can be easy "grab-and-go" options that need little preparation" (Paragraph 8).

17. B: The store opens up at 6:00 AM on July 2, which is earlier than July 1 (7:00 AM), July 3 (9:00 AM), and July 4 (9:00 AM).

18. D: The store closes at 3:00 PM on July 4, which is earlier than July 1 (11:00 PM), July 2 (10:00 PM), and July 3 (9:00 PM).

19. C: Xavier is the only employee scheduled to open the store after closing the previous night. He is scheduled for the July 1 evening shift and July 2 morning shift.

20. A: Alexandra is scheduled to work the most hours. She is scheduled to work four shifts: two eight-hour shifts, one six-hour shift, and one three-hour shift, for a total of 25 hours. Juan is scheduled for two shifts, one eight hours long and the other six hours, for a total of 14 hours. Latisha and Zachary both work two eight-hour shifts and one three-hour shift, for a total of 19 hours each.

21. B: Timothy is scheduled to work the least hours. He is scheduled for only one eight-hour shift. Diana is scheduled for two eight-hour shifts and one six-hour shift, for a total of 22 hours. Ryan is scheduled for two eight-hour shifts and one three-hour shift, for a total of 19 hours. Freddy is scheduled for one eight-hour shift and one six-hour shift, for a total of 14 hours.

22. D: Ryan is the only employee to serve as the team leader on two different days. He serves as team leader on the July 1 morning shift and the July 4 morning shift. All the other choices were team leader only once.

23. A: The job listing asks for: "2+ years professional experience covering the start-up industry" (Paragraph 6).

24. D: The position's primary responsibility is "identifying, researching, contacting, and, of course, interviewing, entrepreneurs who have disrupted their industry" (Paragraph 3). Traveling to the interviews is required in order to carry out the primary responsibility of the job. Leading a start-up company to market is a qualification. Disrupting an industry is a quality the company wants for its interview subjects.

25. C: According to the job listing, all of the staff are "world-renowned experts who have all personally led a start-up company to market" (Paragraph 2).

26. B: It's possible to infer that the right candidate will need to stay current with technology, because the newsletter covers technological innovations (Paragraph 2). In addition, the qualifications include knowledge of software programs (Paragraph 6).

27. C: The job listing states that: "all interviews will be capped at 2,000 words" (Paragraph 3).

28. D: The job listing concludes by asking interested candidates to send their "resume, cover letter, and two best published pieces" (Paragraph 7). Social media history is not listed.

29. A: The three lines directly below "INTERVIEWER" are: "Leaders of Tomorrow / Full-time / Remote." Leaders of Tomorrow is the name of the company that posted the job listing (Paragraph 2). Full-time refers to the position's hours, and the interviewer will work an average of 50 hours per week (Paragraph 5). Remote is the position's location since nearly all the work can be done from home (Paragraph 4).

30. C: "The role is a full-time position, requiring an average of 50 hours per week, with a starting salary between $35,000 and $40,000, depending on qualifications" (Paragraph 5).

31. Drowsy driving: Operating a motor vehicle while fatigued or sleepy is commonly referred to as "drowsy driving" (Paragraphs 1 and 2).

32. Cognitive impairment: "Lack of sleep can make you less alert and affect your coordination, judgment, and reaction time while driving. This is known as cognitive impairment" (Paragraph 9).

33. Drinking: "Studies have shown that going too long without sleep can impair your ability to drive the same way as drinking too much alcohol" (Paragraph 10).

34. Exit: "The Warning Signs of Drowsy Driving...Missing your exit" (Paragraph 5).

35. Rumble strip: "The Warning Signs of Drowsy Driving...Hitting a rumble strip" (Paragraph 5).

36. Sleeping habits: "There are four things you should do before taking the wheel to prevent driving while drowsy.... Develop good sleeping habits such as sticking to a sleep schedule" (Paragraph 8).

37. Physician: "There are four things you should do before taking the wheel to prevent driving while drowsy.... If you have a sleep disorder or have symptoms of a sleep disorder such as snoring or feeling sleepy during the day, talk to your physician about treatment options" (Paragraph 8).

38. Medications: "There are four things you should do before taking the wheel to prevent driving while drowsy.... Avoid drinking alcohol or taking medications that make you sleepy" (Paragraph 8).

39. Change drivers: "If you experience any of the warning signs of drowsy driving while driving, pull over to a safe place and take a 15-20-minute nap or change drivers" (Paragraph 6).

40. Opening the window: "Simply turning up the radio or opening the window is not effective way to keep you alert" (Paragraph 6).

Speaking

Task #1

Examiner: Let's talk about your family. Who are the members of your family, and what are they like?

Test taker: Well, my family includes my mom, my dad, and my two little brothers, James and Robert. My mom is the quiet, steady matriarch of our family. She always makes sure that everyone has their needs met in our house. My dad is the family chef because he has a passion for cooking. He has a jovial, outgoing personality which, combined with his skills in the kitchen, draws friends to our house to hang out for dinner several times a week. I'm the oldest child in the family. James is the middle child, but he doesn't fade into the background like stereotypical middle children. He has so much energy, and he expends it by competing in every sport he can, including soccer, track, and weightlifting. Robert is the youngest and the complete opposite of James. He has a tranquil, easy demeanor that makes him come across as dependable, even though he mostly spends his time procrastinating other responsibilities by reading literature in his room.

Examiner: Where did your family live when you were growing up?

Test taker: My dad works for a large nongovernmental organization in South America, so we have lived in several different places across the continent. Growing up, I lived in Ecuador, then moved to Colombia for middle school, and finally ended up in Buenos Aires, Argentina for the last part of my high school education. I feel most connected to Buenos Aires because it has been my home for the longest period of time, and all of my closest friends live there.

Examiner: What childhood memories do you have of your family related to your hometown(s)?

Test taker: One of my favorite memories of Buenos Aires is going to the Japanese gardens with my family. Our house is in a barrio called Palermo, which is the same neighborhood as the gardens and a zoo. When I was younger, my dad would always cook a big breakfast on Saturday mornings. Our family, and sometimes a few friends, would all crowd around the tiny wooden table in our yellow apartment kitchen to eat and drink coffee. Afterwards, we would head out to the gardens. My family always valued proximity to nature, and I developed that same appreciation because of those Saturday outings.

Examiner: Now let's talk about your hobbies. What hobbies do you enjoy during your free time?

Test taker: I don't have much free time between work and studying, but when I do have a chance to relax, I love to read. I enjoy that reading a book can take my imagination anywhere and give me new perspectives. My favorite genre is science fiction. My favorite book is the classic *Dune* by Frank Herbert. I like that it's a complex, otherworldly storyline set on a fictional planet. But what I appreciate more is the way the book sets you up to analyze a wide range of political issues and navigate convoluted power structures in the real world. I suppose I'm a bit of a nerd at heart because I like learning in my free time. I also enjoy biographies of famous historical figures.

Examiner: What is a hobby that you have never tried, but would like to learn about?

Test Taker: I think I would like to learn something more kinesthetic, since most of my interests are more cerebral. It would be great to get out of my head more. I've been wanting to enroll in some kind of martial arts class, like taekwondo or jiu-jitsu. I think I would have a lot of fun and learn to defend myself at the same time.

Examiner: What activities do you enjoy with your friends when you get together?

Test Taker: When my friends and I hang out, we usually like to find some kind of arts event to attend, like a concert of museum opening. We usually meet before the event to grab something to eat at an inexpensive restaurant, then ride together to the venue. Afterwards, we all head to a cafe for dessert and coffee. While we enjoy dessert, we like to discuss what we thought of the event. For example, we recently attended a Halsey concert, where the artist read a poem in the middle of one her most famous songs. It was an incredibly poignant experience for me and enjoying it with my friends made the concert that much better!

Task #2

Examiner: Here is your prompt card. You have one minute to review it and then you have one to two minutes to respond. Don't worry about the need to keep time. I will alert you when the time is up.

Test taker: Okay.

Examiner: Okay. It is now time to begin speaking.

Test taker: Both proposals would definitely benefit the students. During my time in high school, I played football and ran track. I remember how annoying it was to play on a field with dirt patches and weeds. I'm sure all our teams would benefit from the artificial turf, which would probably make the field easier to maintain at high quality. At the same time, the auditorium urgently needs a renovation. The sound system and lights were cutting edge during the Korean War. The seats are so uncomfortable that nobody can concentrate on the performance. The curtains don't always work. Although it's a hard decision, I plan to vote for the auditorium renovations.

Examiner: Thank you. What do you think are some of the likely consequences of leaving the auditorium and field as is?

Test taker: Well, the auditorium is in dire straits, while the field is just less than optimal. We nearly had to cancel a dance recital last weekend due to the leaky roof. If we don't fix the auditorium soon, we won't be able to hold any of our assemblies or arts events. In contrast, our patchy fields didn't stop our girls' soccer team from winning the state championship. The field is playable, though we should probably keep the turf in mind the next time we have surplus funds. Also, the auditorium serves more students. The school assemblies and guest speakers are hosted in the auditorium and attended by the entire student body. More students also participate in the arts, like school plays, musicals, and band concerts, than sports. It'd be different if the field were also used for physical education, but it isn't.

To put it simply, the auditorium creates more opportunities and poses more challenges for students depending on how we act now. I don't think the consequences are nearly as critical for the field.

Task #3

Examiner: Let's consider general education requirements at universities. Do you think students attending university should have to take a variety of general education courses in addition to the requirements of their major? Explain why or why not.

Test taker: I think it's a good idea when universities require that all of their students take a handful of classes distributed across all major academic disciplines in addition to the specific course requirements dictated by their major. This design exposes students to a variety of fields in the social and physical sciences, the arts, and mathematics, so that all of that university's graduates have a well-rounded liberal arts education in addition to the advanced studies in their field of choice. This will help situate them well for a variety of careers and allow them to remain competitive and prepared for different types of jobs in case the economy changes or suffers and does not support their first choice.

Examiner: What are the benefits and drawbacks of general education requirements for students?

Test taker: Well, in addition to the benefits I mentioned, some students entering university haven't fully decided on their major. The general education requirements expose them to all sorts of topics and departments, so they can think about different careers, maybe even ones they didn't consider or know about. General education requirements encourage these students to dabble in different fields, which can help them find a good fit. A frequently cited drawback of general education courses is that they are a waste of time and not engaging for students who enter university confident in their education and career goals. For example, if someone is certain that she wants to be a dentist, having to take a history course will likely feel extraneous and useless.

Another drawback of programs that require too many general education courses is that each additional course mandated by the university equates to fewer courses possible in one's major, simply because of the conflict of time and scheduling demands. This can mean that students get less experience in their field of choice and do not have the opportunity to explore the finer details and advanced studies pertaining to their interests. All of this could ultimately hinder their career success or admissions opportunities for graduate programs.

Examiner: What courses do you think should be required of all university graduates, regardless of their major?

Test taker: Even though it can be argued that general education requirements are a waste for students who know what they want to study, I do think that all students should take at least one or two academic writing courses, regardless of their major. The ability to communicate effectively in an academic tone is paramount to students' future career success in virtually any field, even science and medicine. Imagine if a doctor conducts important research that will help patients improve their health. If that physician is unable to communicate it effectively and professionally in writing, his or her research won't be published, and the patients won't benefit from the work.

Examiner: Now let's talk about textbooks. An increasing number of universities are now offering students the option to rent course textbooks digitally instead of buy them. Which do you think is a better option?

Test taker: I actually think it's financially prudent and wise overall to actually combine both practices: renting some digital textbooks and purchasing some traditional textbooks at the bookstore. I think it's smart to buy physical textbooks for those classes that one is taking in his or her major and rent digital books for required general education classes outside of one's major. That way, the student can save some money by buying fewer physical books with the cheaper e-textbooks but will have the hard copy books for classes in his or her major in case the student wants to look back on them in future classes. With physical textbooks, students can highlight the material while they are reading to make sure they are really understanding the material as they study, which is important for classes in their majors.

Examiner: What are the benefits and drawbacks of each option?

Renting digital textbooks is a much less expensive option than buying them from the bookstore, and they obviously don't have the weight and bulk of real books. There also is an environmental benefit to consider: digital books reduce the number of trees that need to be cut down as well as all of the energy required to make physical textbooks in a publishing factory. Wood is a non-renewable resource, and we have an energy crisis on our hands, so any efforts—even seemingly minor—to reduce deforestation and humanity's energy footprint is a good thing. On the other hand, digital textbooks are not easy to highlight or flag for review while studying and, if they are rented instead of purchased, once the course is over, the student no longer has access to the book for future reference. The benefits and drawbacks of physical textbooks are essentially the opposite. They are more expensive, bulky, heavy, and not as environmentally-friendly, yet they permit students to study and review their material with greater ease.

Examiner: Do you or would you rent or buy your books?

Test taker: So far, none of my courses have offered digital textbooks to rent, so I have purchased paper books. I generally try to get them used to save money and reduce my environmental impact. Books for courses that are outside of my major or ones that I otherwise plan on never needing again, I try to resell after the course to recoup my costs.

Listening Transcripts #2

Passage #1: Conversation

(Narrator) Listen to the conversation between the basketball fan and hockey fan and then answer the questions.

(Basketball Fan) Hockey involves sliding a frozen puck around a sheet of ice that's constantly melting and getting cut up by skates. This means that the results are heavily influenced by luck.

(Hockey Fan) That's true, but the luck isn't determinative. The team with the higher work ethic and skill will always be in a much better position to win. Plus, the icy conditions make the games more exciting. In contrast, most basketball games don't matter until the final few minutes of play.

(Basketball Fan) What are you talking about? Of course, the entire basketball game matters. All the points count just the same.

(Hockey Fan) A basketball team can easily score ten consecutive points within a few minutes of game time, allowing teams to overcome massive deficits. So, whoever plays well at the end of the game always wins.

(Basketball Fan) I strongly disagree, and I watch basketball every night during the season.

(Hockey Fan) Why do you watch basketball every night? From the very start of the season, it's painfully obvious which team is going to win the championship every year. All the league's talent is consolidated in a handful of teams.

(Basketball Fan) There are admittedly some overpowering teams, but every team has at least one fun player to watch.

(Hockey Fan) I doubt that's true, but I don't know enough to dispute you.

(Basketball Fan) How about you come over to watch tomorrow night's game?

(Hockey Fan) I will if you come to a hockey game with me next week.

(Basketball Fan) That sounds like a plan.

Passage #2: Court Case

(Narrator) Listen to the court case and then answer the questions.

(Judge) The ancient origins of marriage confirm its centrality, but it has not stood in isolation from developments in law and society. The history of marriage is one of both continuity and change. That institution—even as confined to opposite-sex relations—has evolved over time.

For example, marriage was once viewed as an arrangement by the couple's parents based on political, religious, and financial concerns; but by the time of the Nation's founding, it was understood to be a voluntary contract between a man and a woman...As the role and status of women changed, the institution further evolved. Under the centuries-old doctrine of coverture, a married man and woman were treated by the State as a single, male-dominated legal entity...As women gained legal, political, and property rights, and as society began to understand that women have their own equal dignity, the law of coverture was abandoned...These and other developments in the institution of marriage over the past centuries were not mere superficial changes. Rather, they worked deep transformations in its structure, affecting aspects of marriage long viewed by many as essential...

These new insights have strengthened, not weakened, the institution of marriage. Indeed, changed understandings of marriage are characteristic of a Nation where new dimensions of freedom become apparent to new generations, often through perspectives that begin in pleas or protests and then are considered in the political sphere and the judicial process.

Obergefell v. Hodges, a U.S. Supreme Court decision (2015)

Passage #3: Speech

(Narrator) Listen to the actor's monologue and then answer the questions.

(Speaker) How can you expect a man to be brave when he meets with nothing in life but misfortune? Everything has gone wrong with me since the day I was born. Whatever I put my hand to fails utterly. You know it better than I do.

I was brought up to be rich, and I am poor. I studied law, and I cannot string three words together. A man must be strong in that profession, he must have vigor of body and mind, yet I am all out of breath if I walk up a hill; I have not the heart to crush even a fly. To save the little that remains to us after the folly of my father, I need to be unscrupulous and bold, yet my mother, God bless her, has taught me to be good, good, always good! Yes, laugh... but this is not living.

I don't know what I should do if it were not for you. If it were not for you... I might be the one who shot myself. But you have been so good to me, so kind... all the happiness I have ever known in my life until now, has sprung from you—it may have been only a little, now and then, in small things, trifles, help, advice. It was presumptuous of me, Mariana, but I am so accustomed to relying upon you, that I imagined that the treasure was all mine. Besides, I love you so—why should you not be all goodness, Mariana, and take me like a little child into your life, like a toy that you play with, or a dog of which you are fond? But let me be yours, all yours, because I love you! If you could love me only a little I should be satisfied. A little is enough.

Poor John by Gregorio Martinez Sierra, translated by John Garrett Underhill (1922)

Passage #4: Lecture

(Narrator) Listen to the professor's lecture and then answer the questions.

(Professor) It has now been more than 50 years since the original 1964 U.S. Surgeon General's report on smoking and health. In 2014, tobacco use, primarily the combustible tobacco products dominated by cigarettes, is estimated by the Surgeon General to prematurely kill even more users than ever before: 480,000 adults annually; furthermore, it is estimated that 5.6 million children alive in 2014 will die prematurely of a tobacco-related disease unless more is done. The Surgeon General also reports that cigarettes have killed over 20 million users, more American deaths than in any of the wars since the founding of the Nation. Moreover, the effects of combustible tobacco have been underestimated because analysts combined disease-specific causes of death rather than considering all-cause mortality...

...The enemy is the combustion or burning of tobacco...Cigarettes have approximately 600 ingredients; when burned, they create carbon monoxide, particulate matter, and more than 7,000 chemicals, commonly referred to as tars. At least 69 of these chemicals are known to cause cancer, and many are poisonous...

...A renewed call to action through the lens of social justice is needed now more than ever. This is not only for the sake of the current generation of adult tobacco users and for the current generation of vulnerable children, adolescents, and young adults who are potential users, but also especially for priority populations in whom cigarette use is highest (i.e., poor people and ethnic and racial minorities), those with comorbid mental and substance abuse disorders, and finally, for the generations to come.

There is great excitement at the prospect of the global eradication of smallpox, polio, and measles, and dramatic inroads and investments have been made into reducing the impact of malaria and HIV/AIDS, as well as increasing concerns about global warming and carbon footprints. Why not place the wholly preventable deaths and disease burdens of tobacco use behavior on the same priority list of scourges to be eradicated? We can plausibly imagine a world where our families and generations to come will all grow up free of the known preventable harms of using tobacco products, especially the lethal and addictive combustibles like cigarettes, cigars, and hookah.

"Cigarettes: The Rise and Decline but Not Demise of the Greatest Behavioral Health Disasters of the 20th Century" by David B Abrams et al. Population Health: Behavioral and Social Science Insights, edited by Robert M. Kaplan et al. (2015), published by the Agency for Healthcare Research and Quality (National Institutes of Health)

IELTS Practice Test #3

Listening

Directions: The Listening section measures your ability to understand conversations and lectures in English. In this test, you will listen to several pieces of content and answer questions after each one. The questions typically ask about the main idea and supporting details. Some questions ask about a speaker's purpose or attitude. Answer the questions based on what is stated or implied by the speakers.

Listen to all of these passages by going to testprepbooks.com/bonus/ielts or by scanning the QR code below:

SCAN ME

Note that on the actual test, you can take notes while you listen and use your notes to help you answer the questions. Your notes will not be scored.

For your convenience, the transcripts of all of the audio passages are provided after the answer explanations. However, on the actual test, no such transcripts will be provided.

Passage #1: Conversation

Questions 1–7: Complete the sentences below: Write NO MORE THAN TWO WORDS for each answer.

1. The colors of the bug on Tom's arm are ___ and _____.

2. Tom thinks if the bug bites him, he is going to ___.

3. Suzie says that red and yellow _____ are poisonous.

4. Suzie's cousin got bit by a _____ once, and he had to go to the hospital.

5. What is the emergency number Suzie mentioned? ___

6. Suzie tells Tom the hospital will send an _____ in case the bug bites him.

7. Mrs. Henderson says the bug is called a ________.

8. Which of the following statements makes a comparison?
    a. "I don't think this bug is big enough to hurt you."
    b. "His leg swelled up as big as a volleyball."
    c. "Suzie rolled her eyes at Tom."

9. Which statement creates a visual image for the reader?
    a. "She was beginning to get worried."
    b. "Sweat was starting to form on his forehead."
    c. "Maybe this bug was poisonous."

10. All except which of the following are exaggerations?
    a. "If it bites me, I'm going to die."
    b. "The doctor had to use a needle to pop his leg like a balloon before it exploded."
    c. "I don't think this bug is big enough to hurt you."

Passage #2: Court Case

Questions 11–15: Complete the sentences below: Write NO MORE THAN TWO WORDS for each answer.

11. A person in police custody has the right to remain _____.

12. A person being questioned has the right to call upon an _______.

13. TRUE/FALSE: If a person cannot afford an attorney, an attorney will be appointed to them: ____.

14. The individual may _____ their rights and agree to answer questions anyway.

15. TRUE/FALSE: Evidence can be used against the individual at trial, even if a warning or waiver is not demonstrated: ____.

16. What is the main issue that is addressed in this decision?
   a. Whether statements made by a person questioned in custody are admissible in court.
   b. Whether a detained person can waive their rights without an attorney present.
   c. Whether the government has an obligation to provide an attorney to every person detained by the police.

17. What does "deprived of freedom" mean in the context of this court decision?
   a. Undergoing police questioning
   b. Sentenced to prison
   c. Arrested without cause

18. When can a detained person's admissions be used against them?
   a. Never
   b. During ongoing threats to public safety
   c. After they waive their rights

19. What word does the judge use to describe a law enforcement officer questioning a detained person?
   a. Examination
   b. Conversation
   c. Interrogation

20. Read the following part of the lecture again. Then answer the question.

   (Judge) We hold that, when an individual is taken into custody or otherwise deprived of his freedom by the authorities in any significant way and is subjected to questioning, the privilege against self-incrimination is jeopardized.

What does "hold" mean in this context?
   a. Address
   b. Believe
   c. Disagree

Passage #3: Conversation

21. TRUE/FALSE: The museums discussed are located in Houston: ______________

22. Which location offers ice-skating? (NO MORE THAN TWO WORDS)

____

23. Which detail is correct?
   a. The Health Museum showcases hand-carved artifacts.
   b. The Kemah Boardwalk is located 45 miles away from Houston on Galveston Island.
   c. Discovery Green offers yoga classes in the winter months.
   d. Children can find gemstones in the Natural Science Museum.

Questions 24–30: Complete the summary below using NO MORE THAN ONE WORD per space.

There are lots of free parks in Houston. Memorial Park has 24. _____ and 25. _____ trails. Discovery Green offers ice skating in the winter and sessions of outdoor 26. _____ during the warmer months. At

Hermann Park, take a 27. ______ to go around the pond or play on the 28. _____. A 29. _____ is also available to ride around the park. There are many beautiful 30. ______.

Passage #4: Lecture

Questions 31–37: Complete the sentences below using NO MORE THAN TWO WORDS for each answer.

31. This passage is about _____.

32. What discovery was made by William Dutcher? _____

33. Who was shot dead by a plume hunter? _______

34. What association works to protect the bird colonies? ________

35. One of the most important colonies is on ________.

36. What type of bird was seen in eastern Massachusetts? _______

37. The professor ends the monologue with a _______ about whether the wardens can continue to hold the plume-hunters at bay.

38. Read the following part of the lecture again. Then answer the question.

> **(Professor and activist)** Today, the plume hunters who do not dare to raid the guarded rookeries are trying to study out the lines of flight of the birds, to and from their feeding-grounds, and shoot them in transit.

What is the meaning of the word *rookeries* in the text?

a. Houses in a slum area
b. A place where hunters gather to trade tools
c. A colony of breeding birds

39. What is on Bird Island?

a. Hunters selling plumes
b. An important bird colony
c. Bird Island battle between the hunters and the wardens

40. According to the passage, why are hunters trying to study the lines of flight of the birds?

a. To further their studies of ornithology
b. To help wardens preserve the lives of the birds
c. To have a better opportunity to hunt the birds

Academic Test Reading

Passage #1: Ecology

The following passage about bald eagles would be found in an introductory ecology textbook. Read the passage and then answer the questions that follow.

[1] Bald eagles were recently removed from the U.S. Fish and Wildlife Service (USFWS) federal list of threatened and endangered species. The primary risk factor identified for the bald eagle is human disturbance. In Washington, bald eagles nest primarily west of the Cascade Range, with scattered breeding areas along major rivers in the eastern part of the state. Wintering eagles find respite along the upper and lower Columbia River and its tributaries, with major wintering concentrations located along rivers with salmon runs.

[2] Breeding territories for bald eagles are established in upland woodlands and lowland riparian stands with a mature conifer or hardwood component. Territory size and configuration are influenced by factors such as density of breeding bald eagles, quality of foraging habitat, and the availability of prey. The three main factors that influence the location of nests and territories include proximity of water and availability of food; availability of nesting, perching, and roosting trees; and the density of breeding-age bald eagles in the area. Anthony and Isaacs reported that nest sites in older contiguous forest habitats with low levels of human disturbance resulted in higher levels of bald eagle productivity. Several studies have reported the importance of late-successional forests in defining quality of nesting habitat and influencing productivity of bald eagles.

[3] Reported responses of bald eagles to human disturbances have ranged from spatial avoidance of the activity to reproductive failure, although in some cases, bald eagles tolerate human disturbances. Bald eagles seem to be more sensitive to humans afoot than to vehicular traffic. Fletcher et al. reported that the abundance of bald eagles was lower in riparian habitats with nonmotorized trails compared to riparian habitats without trails. Recommended buffer distances to reduce the potential for disturbance to bald eagles during the nesting period have ranged from 984 to 2,624 ft. Grubb and King evaluated the influence of pedestrian traffic and vehicle traffic on bald eagle nesting activities and recommended buffers of 1,800 ft. for pedestrians and 1,500 ft. for vehicles.

[4] The following issues were identified during this assessment and from the published literature regarding the viability of populations of bald eagle and likely other species in the riparian family and the large tree or snag/open water group for the considerations of managers:

1. Late-successional forest had low availability within riparian source habitats.
2. Human activities reduced the effectiveness of source habitats.

Questions 1-7: Complete the summary below with NO MORE THAN TWO WORDS.

Breeding territories for bald eagles are established in upland woodlands and lowland 1. ____________ with a mature conifer or hardwood component. Territory size and 2. __________ are influenced by factors such as density of breeding bald eagles, quality of 3. ___________, and the availability of prey. The primary risk factor identified for the bald eagle is 4. __________. Reported responses of bald eagles to human disturbances have ranged from spatial avoidance of the activity to 5. __________. This assessment highlighted two issues that should be given additional attention by wildlife managers. First, there is low availability of 6. ___________ forest within riparian source habitat. Second, human activities reduced the effectiveness of 7. ___________.

8. Which of the following is NOT one of the three main factors that influences the location of nests and territories for bald eagles?

a. Proximity of water and availability of food
b. Availability of nesting, perching, and roosting trees
c. High possibility for human disturbance
d. The density of breeding-age bald eagles in the area.

9.Which of the following is a reported response of bald eagles to human disturbances?
a. Spatial interaction
b. Reproductive failure
c. Migration
d. Higher levels of productivity

10. According to the passage, how far should pedestrians stay from nesting bald eagles?
a. 1,500 ft.
b. 950 ft.
c. 2,800 ft.
d. 1,800 ft.

11. Where might one expect to find major concentrations of wintering bald eagles?
a. In a section of upland woodlands
b. Around lowland riparian stands with mature conifers
c. Along a river with a large salmon population
d. In a riparian habitat with non-motorized trails

12. What is the author's main objective in the passage?
a. To explain how human disturbance positively influences bald eagle habitats
b. To make recommendations for disturbing bald eagle populations
c. To describe habitats that make ideal bald eagle breeding territories
d. To identify and discuss issues related to bald eagle habitats and human disturbance

Passage #2: History

The following passage about the occupation of Berlin would be found in a textbook for an introductory history textbook. Read the passage and then answer the questions that follow.

[1] On 14 November 1944, while the war still raged, American, British, and Soviet representatives signed an agreement to divide Germany into three zones of occupation, each governed by the commander-in-chief of the respective power. In the same accord, they agreed to split Berlin, the German capital, into three sectors. Despite the sector lines, however, the powers contemplated no administrative division of the city. Instead, they resolved to treat it as a single area under combined rule. Thus, unlike the zones of Germany, which marked off spheres of political control, Berlin's sectors defined merely the physical location of the occupying forces.

[2] At the time, the contradiction between the principle of joint rule and the establishment of sectors was scarcely noticed. In the absence of sectors, the powers might have created an intermingled force of occupation with offices, guard posts, and quarters throughout the city, and with common facilities for communications and supplies. But the formation of sectors was the founding act of Cold War Berlin. Instead of mixed forces, cohesive national garrisons took shape in the assigned districts, and the Western areas soon became enclaves inside the Soviet sphere.

[3] The arrangements for joint rule reflected the degree of camaraderie and common cause that the wartime alliance had forged by 1945. For most leaders, whether civilian or military, the prospect of East-West conflict had scant effect on their conduct during the war or on their planning for the aftermath. At General Dwight D. Eisenhower's insistence, U.S. commanders in Europe resisted the politicization of decision-making, declined to make a race for territory, and left the capture of Berlin to the Soviets. Their goal in war was victory over Adolf Hitler's military machine, and their aim in peace was to control Germany, not the Soviet Union. These Americans had witnessed the devastation brought on by German aggression in Europe; knew the Soviets as generally reliable, if rather secretive, military allies; and believed cooperation might continue in the war's aftermath. Aside from some bickering between Washington and London, the Allies concluded decisions on Germany with relative ease. Despite ongoing suspicions and tensions over Soviet behavior in Eastern Europe, most Anglo-American leaders saw no reason to assume that wartime cooperation, nourished in the comradeship of common struggle, must abruptly cease.

[4] In October 1943, the American, British, and Soviet foreign ministers— Cordell Hull, Anthony Eden, and Vyacheslav M. Molotov—met in Moscow to prepare an agenda for the upcoming talks between the three heads of government in Tehran. In the course of these deliberations, they signed a protocol establishing a standing committee to meet in London. The mission of that body—the European Advisory Commission—would be to formulate recommendations for postwar policy, particularly in regard to Germany.

[5] When tripartite negotiators concurred on the zonal boundaries in early 1944, no one could foretell where the vise on Germany would close. The Western armies had not landed in France, and Soviet troops were still fighting on home soil. At the time of the protocol's signing in September 1944, the war's end was in sight, but none of the Allies had set foot in Germany. By February 1945, at the time of Yalta, Soviet forces had reached the Oder and held a small foothold on its western bank, only forty miles from Berlin, while Western Allied forces had yet to cross the Rhine. The decisions of the European Advisory Commission, however, had precluded an Allied race to conquer territory. Instead, the commission had struck a balance of competing interests and claims.

The agreement on Germany accorded the Soviets disproportionately greater territory in the east, when measured by surface area, while favoring the Western powers regarding the greatest concentrations of population and productive resources. It assured the same balance for Berlin. Although the Soviet Sector covered 42 percent of Berlin's surface area, the population of each of the three sectors was virtually equal, and once such factors as housing, industry, and political-administrative institutions were considered, no discernable advantage favored one party.

[6] The Soviet Sector in eastern Berlin comprised the city's administrative center, important industrial plants, and a heavy concentration of working-class slums. The district Mitte, the historical core of Berlin, was the site of national ministries, the city hall and parliament, state cultural institutions, the main university, the former residence of the Kaiser, and the headquarters of Germany's greatest banks. The residential districts of eastern Berlin were chiefly working class. In prewar parlance, they were named after their postal code, NO for *Nordost* (Northeast). The term covered a vast expanse of nineteenth- and early- twentieth-century tenements in the districts Prenzlauer Berg and Friedrichshain, home to Berlin's rough but proud industrial proletariat. It also referred to the damp and rotting slums in Mitte, some predating the seventeenth century, home to a wretched underclass.

[7] The presence of several key industrial establishments compensated somewhat for the mediocre quality of East Berlin's residential areas. Foremost among them were the AEG (*Allgemeine Elektricitätsgesellschaft*–General Electric Company) installations in the Köpenick and Treptow districts. These comprised an electrical generating plant and four huge factories producing electrical and telephone cable, transformers, broadcasting equipment, vacuum tubes, radios, electrical switches, rectifiers, and studio tape recorders. Moreover, a large Bergmann-Borsig machine tool factory was located in Pankow. Köpenick, Treptow, and Pankow were all suburban areas that had seen little war, and their factories stood ready for productive use, to the extent they had not already been dismantled by the Soviets.

[8] By contrast, the two western sectors contained Berlin's wealthiest residential districts. The grand villas of Zehlendorf, Wilmersdorf, and Tiergarten, built by Berlin's industrial bosses during an economic boom in the late-nineteenth and early-twentieth centuries, equaled or surpassed the opulence of New York's Fifth Avenue, Chicago's Gold Coast, and London's Belgravia—and extended over an area greater than all of them combined. Most had escaped serious damage. Charlottenburg, Schöneberg, and Steglitz were home to high-level civil servants, lawyers, doctors, and other prosperous professionals who resided in immense apartments with thirteen-foot ceilings, inlaid parquet, elaborate moldings, and marbled foyers. In the American Sector, the only working-class districts were Neukölln and Kreuzberg. One of two originally British districts given to France in July 1945, the so-called *Rote Wedding* (Red Wedding), was more famously proletarian, having delivered a defiant leftist majority in Berlin's last election in March 1933, despite conditions of Nazi terror. However, aside from these last exceptions, the Western powers obtained the nicest parts of town.

[9] Besides having the best amenities, the western sectors contained significant industrial establishments. Although the American sector was largely residential, it boasted an installation of utmost political and cultural value: a huge printing plant in Tempelhof belonging to the prewar Ullstein publishing empire. In addition, Tempelhof was home to Berlin's main airport.

[10] The British sectors contained the city's greatest economic gems. The *Siemensstadt* (Siemens City) in Spandau comprised one of the world's largest complexes for production of electrical goods, including a housing area for company workers. Located in the Tiergarten district was AEG's electrical turbine generator factory and repair workshop, AEG-Turbinen. This facility was of special importance because the Soviet zone's economy had no such facility for the production and repair of turbine generators, and therefore depended on this one establishment located in western Berlin.

Questions 13-17: Answer the multiple-choice questions below.

13. What was the purpose of the European Advisory Commission?
    a. To strengthen post-war Germany by centralizing legislation in Berlin
    b. To make post-war policy recommendations with regard to Germany
    c. To divide Berlin into three sectors: Russian, German, and British
    d. To negotiate a peaceful end to the tense relations that characterized Cold War Berlin

14. Eastern Berlin was home to all of the following institutions EXCEPT:
    a. Tempelhof printing plant
    b. General Electric Company installations
    c. City hall and parliament buildings
    d. Bergman-Borsig machine tool factory

15. What district was known as the historical core of Berlin and featured many academic, civic, cultural, and financial sites?
   a. Pankow
   b. Mitte
   c. Köpenick
   d. Tiergarten

16. According to this lecture, who insisted that the Allies should leave the capture of Berlin to the Soviets?
   a. Douglas MacArthur
   b. Omar Bradley
   c. Dwight Eisenhower
   d. Cordell Hull

17. Why did the United States ally itself with the Soviet Union?
   a. The United States wanted to overthrow the Soviet government.
   b. The United States feared fighting a two-front war against the Soviets.
   c. The United States supported Soviet ambitions in Eastern Europe.
   d. The United States shared a common enemy with the Soviet Union.

Questions 18-27 Write the paragraph number in the blank that most closely matches its description.

18. The paragraph describes the Soviet Sector in eastern Berlin, explaining how it included the city's administrative center, important industrial plants, and many working-class slums. ________

19. The paragraph names the printing plant and airport that were in the American sector. ________

20. The paragraph provides detailed information about the Soviet Sector's industrial capacity. ________

21. The paragraph provides details about the British Sector's economic advantages. ________

22. The paragraph includes information about why the United States valued defeating Adolf Hitler more than controlling the Soviet Union. ________

23. The paragraph concludes that the division of Berlin was equitable and didn't overly favor any one party. ________

24. The paragraph mentions the *Rote Wedding* (Red Wedding) district, which voted for the communists in Berlin's last election despite the threat of Nazi terror. ________

25. The paragraph includes the date the American, British, and Soviet representatives signed an agreement to divide Germany into three zones of occupation. ________

26. The paragraph describes why the American, British, and Soviet ministers created the European Advisory Commission ________

27. The paragraph points to the formation of sectors as the founding act of Cold War Berlin. ________

Passage #3: Economics

The following passage about state-owned enterprises would be found in a textbook for an introductory economics textbook. Read the passage and then answer the questions that follow.

[1] As hybrid creations of economics and politics, state-owned enterprises (SOEs) have always played important roles in the political economies of nation-states. There are four main categories of SOEs: (a) public utilities such as electric power, water, communications, and transport; (b) basic goods industries such as coal, oil and nuclear resources, and steel; (c) financial services such as banks, insurance companies, and social security administrations; and (d) social services such as education and health services. In addition to the often-designated natural monopolies of the public utilities, the range of commercial activities that might qualify for SOE status is rather wide. To analyze the SOEs in the context of stability operations, it is useful to subsume these four categories in two: basic utilities and commercial enterprises.

[2] The impact of SOEs on the global economy is significant. In the early 1980s, SOEs produced 10-25 percent of the manufacturing output of the developed world and more than 25 percent in developing countries. Textiles, food, beverages, tobacco, cement, automotive vehicles, ships, and aircraft comprised the principal categories. The proportion of national economic production from SOEs has varied historically according to the shifting tides of political and ideological forces. From the completely centrally managed economies of the former Soviet Union and its satellites and imitators in the developing world at one extreme, to the open market economies of the Western industrialized nations at the other, there has been movement in both directions along this spectrum, in part because, as noted by economic theorists, "the development of a positive approach has shown that government failure is as frequent as market failure." In addition to the political and ideological motivations for establishing SOEs, there generally are three other reasons for doing so: (1) market failures; (2) promotion of economic growth on the basis of long-term planning; and (3) industrial and financial bailouts resulting from irreversible crises.

[3] As national economies adapted to historical events in the 20th century, the ideological pendulum swung back and forth from one extreme to the other. On one swing, unregulated markets turned to growing state involvement (1933-80), in accordance with the economic philosophy of Keynesianism following the market failure of the Great Depression; and on the return swing, state regulation turned to minimal government and market freedom by a process of deregulation (1980-present) following the stagflation of the early 1970s and early 1980s, all in accordance with the philosophy of Friedrich Hayek, as interpreted by Milton Friedman and others, and as implemented by the government of Margaret Thatcher in the United Kingdom (UK) and by the Reagan administration in the United States. The policies at work within these two national economies strongly influenced other national economies directly as major trading partners and indirectly through international financial institutions, which required economic reforms as conditions for loans.

[4] The place of the SOEs in both national economies changed with these swings of the ideological pendulum. During the Keynesian era, "profound criticism of the capitalist system opened the way to doubt about the market economy, and liberal forces believed that stronger state control of crucial sectors of the economy could resolve the problems of market failures, with the result that an impressive first wave of nationalization began, particularly in those Western countries most affected by the Depression." State involvement in the economy seemed to be the correct path, with public enterprises being developed in the Western economies through deliberate nationalization of the enterprises. "In most Western countries, the great age of nationalization and successful public enterprise was the 3

decades following World War II," with its peak in the mid-1970s when the output of SOEs averaged 10 percent of gross national product and 16.5 percent of gross capital formation.

[5] In the United States in 1980, the economic policies associated with Reaganomics sought to reverse Keynesianism through deregulation, minimal taxes, and high interest rates to control inflation, swinging the influence and acceptance of SOEs in the opposite direction. The Reagan administration noticed the formula that banks discovered to correct the deficits of New York City's budgetary management of the 1970s: call in loans and cut payrolls through layoffs of hospital staff and school workers. The formula worked so well in restoring fiscal balance that U.S. bankers, working through the U.S. Department of the Treasury, recommended it as the standard prescription for the international financial institutions' economic reforms for developing countries. The recommendations reflected market fundamentalism which eventually be- came part of what is sometimes called the Washington Consensus. As social theorist David Harvey pointed out, while the banks had not articulated a complete theory of what they were doing in New York City, they recognized successful financial results when they saw them, and therefore decided that their method could be applied to indebted countries around the world.

[6] Much of the policy discussion regarding SOE reform has centered on the need to privatize them in order to generate the investment needed to make SOEs self-sustainable. Privatization is a complex undertaking and should be attempted only within a proper regulatory framework, however. Without proper regulation, a rush to privatization would likely lead to the kind of abuses that characterized Russia's economic reforms of the 1990s.

Questions 28-40: Complete the notes below with NO MORE THAN TWO WORDS.

- There are four main categories of SOEs:
    a. Public utilities
    b. Basic goods production
    c. Financial services
    d. 28.______________
- It is sometimes useful to subsume these four categories in two:
    a. Basic utilities
    b. 29.______________
- There are four common reasons for establishing SOEs:
    a. Political and 30. ______________ motivations
    b. Market failures
    c. Promotion of 31. ______________ based on long-term planning
    d. Industrial and financial bailouts during times of crisis
- 32. ______________ was an influential economic philosophy during the Great Depression.

- Following the 33. ______________ of the early 1970s and early 1980s, in the UK, the government of 34. ______________ reduced the British government's regulatory power to increase market freedom.

- 35.______________ sought to reverse Keynesianism through deregulation, 36. ______________, and high interest rates to control inflation.

- Nationalization and successful public enterprise peaked in the 37. ______________. SOEs averaged:

    - 10 percent of gross national product; and

    - 16.5 percent of gross 38. ______________

- Privatization should only be attempted within a proper 39. ______________.

    - Lessons can be learned from what happened when 40. ______________ rushed into privatization.

General Training Reading

The next six questions are based on the following passage:

Section #1

Food Allergy Basics

[1] Each year, millions of Americans have allergic reactions to food. Although most food allergies cause relatively mild and minor symptoms, some food allergies can cause severe reactions and may even be life-threatening.

[2] There is no cure for food allergies. Strict avoidance of food allergens—and early recognition and management of allergic reactions to food—are important measures to prevent serious health consequences.

[3] To help Americans avoid the health risks posed by food allergens, the Food and Drug Administration (FDA) enforces the Food Allergen Labeling and Consumer Protection Act of 2004 (the Act). The Act applies to the labeling of foods regulated by the FDA which includes all foods except poultry, most meats, certain egg products, and most alcoholic beverages which are regulated by other Federal agencies. The Act requires that food labels must clearly identify the food source of any ingredients that are one of the major food allergens or contain any protein derived from a major food allergen.

[4] As a result, food labels help allergic consumers identify offending foods or ingredients so they can more easily avoid them.

[5] While more than 160 foods can cause allergic reactions in people with food allergies, the law identifies the eight most common allergenic foods. These foods account for 90 percent of food-related allergic reactions and are the food sources from which many other ingredients are derived.

[6] The eight foods identified by the law are:

1. Milk

2. Eggs

3. Fish (e.g., bass, flounder, cod)

4. Crustacean shellfish (e.g., crab, lobster, shrimp)

5. Tree nuts (e.g., almonds, walnuts, pecans)

6. Peanuts

7. Wheat

8. Soybeans

[7] These eight foods, and any ingredient that contains protein derived from one or more of them, are designated as "major food allergens" by FALCPA.

Questions 1-6: Complete the sentences below using NO MORE THAN THREE WORDS.

1. The Food Allergen Labeling and Consumer Protection Act of 2004 requires that _____________ must clearly identify the food source of any ingredients that are one of the major food allergens or contain any protein derived from a major food allergen.

2. Strict avoidance, early recognition, and _____________ of allergic reactions to food are important for preventing serious health consequences.

3. The FDA doesn't have the authority to regulate _____________, most meats, certain egg products, and most alcoholic beverages.

4. Crab, lobster, and_____________ are crustacean shellfish.

5. The FALCPA designates eight foods, and any ingredient that contains _____________ derived from one or more of them, as "major food allergens."

6. Eight major food allergens account for_____________ of food allergic reactions.

The next six questions are based on the following passage:

Protecting Yourself from Predatory Lenders

[1] Most mortgage professionals are trustworthy and provide a valuable service, helping you to buy or refinance your home. But dishonest or "predatory" lenders do exist and engage in practices that can put you at risk of losing your home to foreclosure. Learn how to protect yourself from and report predatory lending and loan fraud.

[2] Learn about the types of scams that predatory lenders use to trick you. The Department of Housing and Urban Development (HUD) has counselors available across the country to help you navigate mortgage professionals, look out for scams, and choose the right loan type for you.

[3] Predatory lenders may try to:

- Sell properties for much more than they are worth using false appraisals
- Encourage borrowers to lie about their income, expenses, or cash available for down payments in order to get a loan
- Knowingly lend more money than a borrower can afford to repay
- Charge high interest rates to borrowers based on their race or national origin and not on their credit history
- Charge fees for unnecessary or nonexistent products and services

[4] Do:

- Before you buy a home, attend a homeownership education course offered by a U.S. Department of Housing and Urban Development (HUD)-approved, non-profit counseling agency.
- Interview several real-estate agents and ask for and check references before you select one to help you buy or sell a home.
- Get information about the current values and recent sale prices of other homes in the neighborhood.
- Hire a qualified and licensed home inspector to carefully inspect the property before you are obligated to buy.
- Determine whether you or the seller will be responsible for paying for the repairs.
- Shop for a lender and compare costs.
- Be suspicious if anyone tries to steer you to just one lender. Learn more about how to spot predatory lending and protect yourself.
- Become an educated consumer and learn about loans, mortgage fraud, and consumer protection.

[5] Don't:

- Don't lie about your income, age, or anything else on a home loan application.
- Don't give anyone your personal or financial information, including your Social Security number, through email or messaging.
- Don't use a lender, real-estate professional, or contractor who cannot provide you with a license number and recommendations.
- Don't fall for loans or offers that seem too good to be true.
- Don't take out a loan offered to you by telemarketers, flyers, or door-to-door sales.
- Don't feel obligated or pressured to sign up for a loan or service "today."

Questions 7-12: Answer the multiple-choice questions below.

7. What federal agency directly offers homeownership education course?
   a. Department of Health and Human Services
   b. Department of Labor
   c. Department of Housing and Urban Development
   d. Department of Justice

8. Which is NOT a common predatory lending scam?
   a. Charging fees for unnecessary services
   b. Lending more money than the borrower can afford to repay
   c. Impersonating the buyer to finalize the sale
   d. Using false appraisals to inflate the purchase price

9. What should a home buyer do while interviewing real-estate agents?
   a. Interview every real-estate agent in the area.
   b. Hire multiple real-estate agents.
   c. Determine if the real-estate agent is a college graduate.
   d. Ask for and check references.

10. Who is responsible for paying for the repairs?
   a. The real-estate agent
   b. The purchaser
   c. The seller
   d. The purchaser or the seller, depending on the agreement

11. What should people know when shopping for a home?
   a. Current values and recent sale prices in that housing market
   b. The district's current elected representatives
   c. Neighbors' prior requests for permits
   d. Average annual income for the state

12. Which of the following loan offers is suspicious?
   a. A loan offered by a telemarketer
   b. A loan offered by a mortgage company
   c. A loan offered by the government
   d. A loan offered by a bank

Questions 13-22 are based on the following apartment listing:

<u>Apartment Listing</u>

[1] OVERVIEW

Beautiful and spacious 2BR and 2BA apartment in up-and-coming neighborhood available for rent ASAP. Located at 170 Main Street, easily accessible off the E/F/N/R/Z lines, and yours for $2100/month.

[2] FEATURES

- 2 bedrooms with walk-in closets
- 2 bathrooms
- 24-hour monitored video surveillance system
- New kitchen appliances (refrigerator, stove, microwave)
- Washer and dryer
- Hardwood floors
- High ceilings
- Flooded with sunlight
- On-site super and maintenance staff

[3] RENTER REQUIREMENTS

- Credit score 650 or higher
- Current paystubs showing annual income that's 40 times the monthly rent. Incomes can be combined for a household. Guarantors also accepted.
- Application fee: $50

[4] CONTACT US

Please call Walter at (123) 456-7890 to schedule a viewing. The sooner, the better. This apartment will go FAST.

Questions 13-22: Complete the notes below with NO MORE THAN THREE WORDS.

- Location: 13. ____________
- Person to Contact: 14. ____________
- Two 15. ____________ with walk-in closets
- Rent: 16. ____________/month
- Requirements
    - Credit Score: 17. ____________
    - Annual combined income 40 times the 18. ____________

- Best Features
    - High 19. ___________
    - On-site 20. ___________
    - 21.___________ closets
    - New 22. ___________appliances

Section #2

The next nine questions are based on the following passage:

What You Need to Know About Workplace Harassment

[1] Harassment is a form of employment discrimination that violates Title VII of the Civil Rights Act of 1964, the Age Discrimination in Employment Act of 1967 (ADEA), and the Americans with Disabilities Act of 1990 (ADA).

[2] Harassment is unwelcome conduct that is based on race, color, religion, sex (including pregnancy), national origin, age (40 or older), disability or genetic information. Harassment becomes unlawful where 1) enduring the offensive conduct becomes a condition of continued employment, or 2) the conduct is severe or pervasive enough to create a work environment that a reasonable person would consider intimidating, hostile, or abusive. Anti-discrimination laws also prohibit harassment against individuals in retaliation for filing a discrimination charge; testifying, or participating in any way in an investigation, proceeding, or lawsuit under these laws; or opposing employment practices that they reasonably believe discriminate against individuals, in violation of these laws.

[3] Petty slights, annoyances, and isolated incidents (unless extremely serious) will not rise to the level of illegality. To be unlawful, the conduct must create a work environment that would be intimidating, hostile, or offensive to reasonable people.

[4] Offensive conduct may include, but is not limited to, offensive jokes, slurs, epithets or name calling, physical assaults or threats, intimidation, ridicule or mockery, insults or put-downs, offensive objects or pictures, and interference with work performance. Harassment can occur in a variety of circumstances, including, but not limited to, the following:

- The harasser can be the victim's supervisor, a supervisor in another area, an agent of the employer, a co-worker, or a non-employee.
- The victim does not have to be the person harassed but can be anyone affected by the offensive conduct.
- Unlawful harassment may occur without economic injury to, or discharge of, the victim.

[5] Prevention is the best tool to eliminate harassment in the workplace. Employers are encouraged to take appropriate steps to prevent and correct unlawful harassment. They should clearly communicate to employees that unwelcome harassing conduct will not be tolerated. They can do this by establishing an effective complaint or grievance process, providing anti-harassment training to their managers and

employees, and taking immediate and appropriate action when an employee complains. Employers should strive to create an environment in which employees feel free to raise concerns and are confident that those concerns will be addressed.

[6] Employees are encouraged to inform the harasser directly that the conduct is unwelcome and must stop. Employees should also report harassment to management at an early stage to prevent its escalation.

[7] The employer is automatically liable for harassment by a supervisor that results in a negative employment action such as termination, failure to promote or hire, and loss of wages. If the supervisor's harassment results in a hostile work environment, the employer can avoid liability only if it can prove that: 1) it reasonably tried to prevent and promptly correct the harassing behavior, and 2) the employee unreasonably failed to take advantage of any preventive or corrective opportunities provided by the employer.

[8] The employer will be liable for harassment by non-supervisory employees or non-employees over whom it has control (e.g., independent contractors or customers on the premises), if it knew, or should have known about the harassment and failed to take prompt and appropriate corrective action.

[9] When investigating allegations of harassment, the Equal Employment Opportunity Commission looks at the entire record, including the nature of the conduct and the context in which the alleged incidents occurred. A determination of whether harassment is severe or pervasive enough to be illegal is made on a case-by-case basis.

[10] If you believe that the harassment you are experiencing or witnessing is of a specifically sexual nature, you may want to see EEOC's information on sexual harassment.

23. Which of the following is NOT a basis for harassment under the law?
   a. Age
   b. National origin
   c. Genetics
   d. Qualifications

24. What legal standard is used to determine whether the conduct is severe or pervasive enough to create a work environment that is intimidating, hostile, or abusive?
   a. Beyond a reasonable doubt
   b. Reasonable person standard
   c. Clear and convincing evidence
   d. Preponderance of the evidence

25. What violates Title VII of the Civil Rights Act of 1964?
   a. Wage theft
   b. Workplace harassment
   c. Affirmative action
   d. Disability fraud

26. What federal agency directly investigates allegations of harassment?
    a. Equal Employment Opportunity Commission
    b. Federal Bureau of Investigations
    c. Department of Commerce
    d. Department of Health and Human Services

27. How should an employee respond when subject to harassment?
    a. Ignore the harasser until the employer independently discovers the harassment.
    b. Retaliate against the harasser.
    c. Inform the harasser directly that the conduct is unwelcome and must stop.
    d. Request an accommodation from the employer to avoid working with the harasser.

Questions 28-31: Complete the following summary below using NO MORE THAN TWO WORDS.

Harassment is unwelcome conduct that is based on race, color, religion, sex, national origin, age, disability, or 28. ____________. To be unlawful, the conduct must be more than an isolated nuisance; it must create a work environment that would be intimidating, hostile, or offensive to 29. ____________. The employer is automatically 30. ______________ for harassment by a supervisor that results in a negative employment action and harassment by 31. ______________ employees when the employer knew or should have known about the harassment.

Questions 32-35 are based upon the following passage:

This excerpt is an adaptation from Charles Dickens' speech in Birmingham in England on December 30, 1853 on behalf of the Birmingham and Midland Institute.

> My Good Friends,—When I first imparted to the committee of the projected Institute my particular wish that on one of the evenings of my readings here the main body of my audience should be composed of working men and their families, I was animated by two desires; first, by the wish to have the great pleasure of meeting you face to face at this Christmas time, and accompany you myself through one of my little Christmas books; and second, by the wish to have an opportunity of stating publicly in your presence, and in the presence of the committee, my earnest hope that the Institute will, from the beginning, recognise one great principle—strong in reason and justice—which I believe to be essential to the very life of such an Institution. It is, that the working man shall, from the first unto the last, have a share in the management of an Institution which is designed for his benefit, and which calls itself by his name.
>
> I have no fear here of being misunderstood—of being supposed to mean too much in this. If there ever was a time when any one class could of itself do much for its own good, and for the welfare of society—which I greatly doubt—that time is unquestionably past. It is in the fusion of different classes, without confusion; in the bringing together of employers and employed; in the creating of a better common understanding among those whose interests are identical, who depend upon each other, who are vitally essential to each other, and who never can be in unnatural antagonism without deplorable results, that one of the chief principles of a Mechanics' Institution should consist. In this world a great deal of the bitterness among us arises from an imperfect understanding of one another. Erect in Birmingham a great Educational Institution, properly educational; educational of the

feelings as well as of the reason; to which all orders of Birmingham men contribute; in which all orders of Birmingham men meet; wherein all orders of Birmingham men are faithfully represented—and you will erect a Temple of Concord here which will be a model edifice to the whole of England.

Contemplating as I do the existence of the Artisans' Committee, which not long ago considered the establishment of the Institute so sensibly, and supported it so heartily, I earnestly entreat the gentlemen—earnest I know in the good work, and who are now among us, —by all means to avoid the great shortcoming of similar institutions; and in asking the working man for his confidence, to set him the great example and give him theirs in return. You will judge for yourselves if I promise too much for the working man, when I say that he will stand by such an enterprise with the utmost of his patience, his perseverance, sense, and support; that I am sure he will need no charitable aid or condescending patronage; but will readily and cheerfully pay for the advantages which it confers; that he will prepare himself in individual cases where he feels that the adverse circumstances around him have rendered it necessary; in a word, that he will feel his responsibility like an honest man, and will most honestly and manfully discharge it. I now proceed to the pleasant task to which I assure you I have looked forward for a long time.

32. Read the following passage again, then answer the question.
You will judge for yourselves if I promise too much for the working man, when I say that he will stand by such an enterprise with the utmost of his patience, his perseverance, sense, and support.

Which term most closely aligns with the definition of the term *working man* as defined in the passage?

a. Plebian
b. Viscount
c. Entrepreneur
d. Bourgeois

33. Which of the following statements most closely correlates with the definition of the term *working man* as it is defined in Question 32?

a. A working man is not someone who works for institutions or corporations, but someone who is well versed in the workings of the soul.
b. A working man is someone who is probably not involved in social activities because the physical demand for work is too high.
c. A working man is someone who works for wages among the middle class.
d. A working man is someone who works for wages among the middle class.

34. Based upon the contextual evidence provided in the passage above, what is the meaning of the term *enterprise* in the third paragraph?

a. Company
b. Courage
c. Game
d. Cause

35. The speaker addresses his audience as *My Good Friends*—what kind of credibility does this salutation give to the speaker?
   a. The speaker is an employer addressing his employees, so the salutation is a way for the boss to bridge the gap between himself and his employees.
   b. The speaker's salutation is one from an entertainer to his audience and uses the friendly language to connect to his audience before a serious speech.
   c. The salutation gives the serious speech that follows a somber tone, as it is used ironically.
   d. The speech is one from a politician to the public, so the salutation is used to grab the audience's attention.

Section #3

The next five questions are based on the following passage:

Tips for Saving Energy Costs in the Spring

[1] Today marks the beginning of spring and the end of a long, brutal winter for much of the United States. With the start of a new season comes a fresh opportunity to find ways to save energy and money. Here, we suggest a few simple things you can do to improve the energy efficiency and comfort of your home as warmer temperatures arrive.

[2] Easy maintenance such as routinely replacing, or cleaning, air filters can lower your cooling system's energy consumption by up to 15 percent. Also, the first day of spring could serve as a reminder to check your air conditioner's evaporator coil, which should be cleaned annually to ensure the system is performing at optimal levels.

[3] Opening windows creates a cross-wise breeze, allowing you to naturally cool your home without switching on air conditioners. This is an ideal tactic in spring when temperatures are mild.

[4] Cooling your home with ceiling fans will allow you to raise your thermostat four degrees. This can help lower your electricity bills without sacrificing overall comfort.

[5] On warmer spring days, keep the heat out of your home by using an outdoor grill instead of indoor ovens.

[6] Energy efficient window treatments or coverings such as blinds, shades, and films can slash heat gain when temperatures rise. These devices not only improve the look of your home but also reduce energy costs.

[7] Using low-cost caulk to seal cracks and openings keeps warm air out of your home—and cash in your wallet.

[8] During daylight hours, switch off artificial lights, and use windows and skylights to brighten your home.

[9] On warm days, setting a programmable thermostat to a higher setting when you are not at home can help reduce your energy costs by approximately 10 percent.

[10] Air loss through ducts can lead to high electricity costs, accounting for nearly 30 percent of a cooling system's energy consumption. Sealing and insulating ducts can go a long way toward lowering your electricity bills.

[11] Bathroom fans suck out heat and humidity from your home, improving comfort.

Questions 36-40: Complete the sentences below using NO MORE THAN TWO WORDS.

36. Using an ________________ instead of an indoor oven keeps the heat out of your home, lowering energy costs.

37. Opening windows creates a cross-wise breeze, allowing you to naturally cool your home without switching on ________________.

38. ________________ suck out heat and humidity from your home, improving comfort.

39. Keep warm air out by using low-cost ________________ to seal cracks and openings in your home.

40. Easy maintenance such as routinely replacing or cleaning ________________ can lower your cooling system's energy consumption by up to 15 percent.

First Essay

Academic Test

Prepare a response of at least 150 words on the topic below. You should spend approximately 20 minutes on this task.

The below chart illustrates the number of deaths among 25 – 34 year old people in the United States in 2003, categorized by cause. For people ages 35-44 who died in that same year, the percentage of homicide and suicide was 10.9%. Summarize the information in the graph, then discuss possible reasons for the lower homicide and suicide rate in the older age group.

Number of deaths by cause among 25 – 34 year old people– United States, 2003

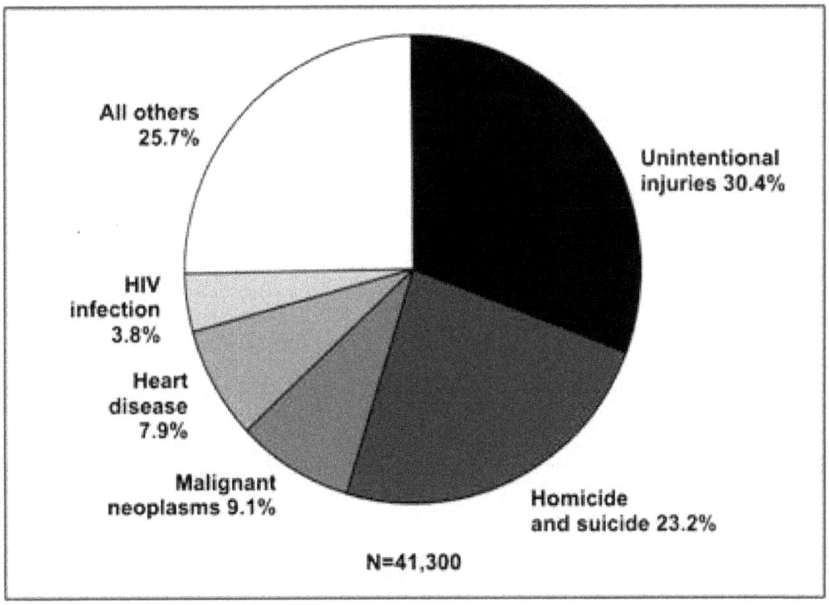

SOURCE: National Center for Injury Prevention and Control

The following pages are provided for writing your essay.

General Training Exam

Prepare a response of at least 150 words on the topic below. You should spend approximately 20 minutes on this task.

The Daily Telegraph has recently reported that UK governmental agencies have been considering issues of national security and how it pertains to Internet usage. The government feels that a structured framework for surveillance to help protect the rights and privacy of UK citizens is necessary with the public's increased reliance on social media sites, ecommerce sites, and other Internet destinations.

Write a letter to the paper's editor arguing whether you think government surveillance of online-based activity and data collection of citizens should be lawful or not and what sorts of conditions or laws would be most effective. Use specific examples to support your argument.

The following pages are provided for writing your essay.

Second Essay

Academic Test

Prepare an essay of at least 250 words on the topic below. You should spend approximately 40 minutes on this task.

> Margaret Atwood says, "war is what happens when language fails." In an essay that is going to be read by educated adults, explain whether you agree or disagree with this observation. Support your argument with details and examples.

The following pages are provided for writing your essay.

General Training Exam

Prepare a response of at least 250 words on the topic below. You should spend approximately 40 minutes on this task.

> Students and teachers alike have had mentors who have changed the course of their lives for the better. Name someone who was a mentor to you. Explain what they were like and how their experience and encouragement changed the course of your life.

The following pages are provided for writing your essay.

Speaking

Task #1 (4-5 minutes)

Tell me about your experience learning English:

- Why did you choose to study English?
- What tools have you found to be most helpful for learning the language?
- What advice would you give an exchange student moving to a country where people speak a different language than them?

Now let's talk about travel.

- What types of transportation do you prefer when you travel?
- What countries do you hope to visit one day? Why?
- What types of activities would you recommend to someone visiting your city or town?

Task #2 (3-4 minutes)

Prompt card

You are a local politician, and the legislature is considering a new proposal. The proposal is to install red light cameras on Main Street in the busiest part of your electoral district. There has been a series of accidents in this area during the last year, and studies have shown that red light cameras significantly reduce accidents. But you also know the cameras would be unpopular with most of your constituents, the people whose views you were elected to represent.

How do you vote? How will your constituency react to your decision, and what are the likely consequences?

- Preparation Time: 1 minute
- Response Time: 1-2 minutes

Rounding off questions:

What would you say to a constituent who called your office to complain about your decision?

Task #3 (4-5 minutes)

Let's discuss government:

- What do you think are the most important functions of government?
- Which responsibilities do you think should be handled locally, such as by a city or district?
- In your opinion, which duties should be carried out by the federal government?

Now let's talk about civic engagement:

- In your experience, what are some ways citizens can influence the government?
- What are some ways citizens can affect their local community?

Answer Explanations #3

Listening

1. Red, black

2. Die

3. Snakes

4. Spider

5. 9-1-1

6. Ambulance

7. Ladybug

8. B: Choice *B* compares the size of Rob's leg to the size of a volleyball, so this is the correct answer.

9. B: Choice *B* helps create a visual picture for readers—we can imagine the sweat on Tom's forehead.

10. C: Exaggeration means "to make a statement that isn't necessarily accurate in order to make a point." This is often done when telling a story. Choice *C* does not make an exaggeration.

11. Silent

12. Attorney

13. True: The passage says, "He must be warned prior to any questioning that he has the right...to the presence of an attorney, and that, if he cannot afford an attorney one will be appointed for him prior to any questioning if he so desires."

14. Waive

15. False: the passage says, "But unless and until such warnings and waiver are demonstrated by the prosecution at trial, no evidence obtained as a result of interrogation can be used against him."

16. A: The judge mentions reviewing cases in which someone admitted to a crime during questioning by police or another authority. The people questioned had no lawyers with them, and they were not told they could refuse to answer the questions. So the main issue is whether statements obtained that way can be used in court.

17. A: When the individual is subjected to questioning within the confines of custody or other deprivation of freedom. In the passage, the first sentence of the second paragraph states that "...We hold that, when an individual is taken into custody or otherwise deprived of his freedom by the authorities in any significant way and is subjected to questioning, the privilege against self-incrimination is jeopardized."

18. C: The detained person's self-incriminating statements can only be used against them after a waiver of rights.

19. C: The judge describes the police questioning as an "interrogation" three different times. The other three choices don't appear in the judge's decision.

20. B: Based on this context, "hold" means "believe," since what follows is the judge's declaration of rights for detained persons, which is what the judge believes.

21. True: Each of the museums mentioned are located in Houston, Texas.

22. Discovery Green: Discovery Green park is the place that offers ice-skating in the winter.

23. D: Children can find gemstones in the Natural Science Museum.

24. Hiking

25. Biking

26. Yoga

27. Paddleboat

28. Playground

29. Train

30. Views

31. Birds

32. Colonies

33. Warden

34. Audubon, or Audubon Association

35. Bird Island

36. Egret

37. Question

38. C: A *rookery* is a colony of breeding birds.

39. B: The previous sentence is describing "twenty colonies" of birds, so what follows should be a bird colony. Choice *A* may be true, but we have no evidence of this in the text. Choice *C* does touch on the tension between the hunters and wardens, but there is no official "Bird Island Battle" mentioned in the text.

40. C: Choice *A* might be true in a general sense, but it is not relevant to the context of the text. Choice *B* is incorrect because the hunters are not studying lines of flight to help wardens, but to hunt birds.

Academic Test Reading

1. Riparian stands: "Breeding territories for bald eagles are established in upland woodlands and lowland riparian stands with a mature conifer or hardwood component" (Paragraph 2).

2. Configuration: Territory size and configuration are influenced by factors such as density of breeding bald eagles, quality of foraging habitat, and the availability of prey (Paragraph 2).

3. Foraging habitat: Territory size and configuration are influenced by factors such as density of breeding bald eagles, quality of foraging habitat, and the availability of prey (Paragraph 2).

4. Human disturbance: "Bald eagles were recently removed from the U.S. Fish and Wildlife Service (USFWS) federal list of threatened and endangered species. The primary risk factor identified for the bald eagle is human disturbance" (Paragraph 1).

5. Reproductive failure: "Reported responses of bald eagles to human disturbances have ranged from spatial avoidance of the activity to reproductive failure, although in some cases, bald eagles tolerate human disturbances" (Paragraph 3).

6. Late-successional: "The following issues were identified during this assessment and from the published literature regarding the viability of populations of bald eagle and likely other species in the riparian family and the large tree or snag/open water group for the considerations of managers:

1. Low availability of late-successional forest within riparian source habitat.
2. Human activities reduced the effectiveness of source habitats." (Paragraph 4).

7. Source habitats: "The following issues were identified during this assessment and from the published literature regarding the viability of populations of bald eagle and likely other species in the riparian family and the large tree or snag/open water group for the considerations of managers:

1. Low availability of late-successional forest within riparian source habitat.
2. Human activities reduced the effectiveness of source habitats." (Paragraph 4).

8. C: The passage states that the three main factors that influence the location of nests and territories are "proximity of water and availability of food; availability of nesting, perching, and roosting trees; and the density of breeding-age bald eagles in the area." Therefore, the only choice that is not one of these factors is Choice *C*.

9. B: The passage lists two reported responses of bald eagles to human disturbances: spatial avoidance of the activity and reproductive failure. Choice *A* is incorrect because spatial reactions are limited to avoidance or tolerance, not active interaction. Choice *C* is incorrect because it is a reaction to weather patterns, not human disturbances. Choice *D* is incorrect because the article does not indicate that human disturbances could lead to higher productivity.

10. D: Grubb and King evaluated the influence of pedestrian traffic and vehicle traffic on bald eagle nesting activities and recommended buffers of 1,800 ft. for pedestrians and 1,500 ft. for vehicles.

11. C: Wintering eagles find respite along the upper and lower Columbia River and its tributaries, with major wintering concentrations located along rivers with salmon runs.

12. D: The main objective of this passage is to identify and discuss issues related to bald eagle habitats and the effects of human disturbance on bald eagle populations. This is evident in the concluding paragraph, which summarizes the issues discussed and positions the information as helpful considerations for managers.

13. B: "The mission of that body—the European Advisory Commission—would be to formulate recommendations for postwar policy, particularly in regard to Germany" (Paragraph 4).

14. A: The text mentions the General Electric Company installations, city hall and parliament buildings, and the Bergman-Borsig machine tool factory in the discussion of important institutions located in East Berlin. Additionally the passage says, "Besides having the best amenities, the western sectors contained significant industrial establishments. Although the American sector was largely residential, it boasted an installation of utmost political and cultural value: a huge printing plant in Tempelhof belonging to the prewar Ullstein publishing empire (Paragraph 9)." This sentence indicates that the Tempelhof printing plant was located in the Western sector. Therefore, Choice *A* could not be located in the Eastern sector and must be the correct choice.

15. B: "The district Mitte, the historical core of Berlin, was the site of national ministries, the city hall and parliament, state cultural institutions, the main university, the former residence of the Kaiser, and the headquarters of Germany's greatest banks" (Paragraph 6)." "Köpenick and Pankow were suburban areas in Soviet-controlled East Berlin, and they had productive factories left largely untouched by the war (Paragraph 7)." "Tiergarten was home to Berlin's wealthiest residential districts, and it was under Western control (Paragraph 8)."

16: C: "At General Dwight D. Eisenhower's insistence, U.S. commanders in Europe resisted the politicization of decision-making, declined to make a race for territory, and left the capture of Berlin to the Soviets" (Paragraph 3).

17. D: The United States and Soviet Union were united in their opposition to Nazi Germany. "Their goal in war was victory over Adolf Hitler's military machine, and their aim in peace was to control Germany, not the Soviet Union. These Americans had witnessed the devastation brought on by German aggression in Europe; knew the Soviets as generally reliable, if rather secretive, military allies; and believed cooperation might continue in the war's aftermath" (Paragraph 3).

18. Paragraph 6: "The Soviet Sector in eastern Berlin comprised the city's administrative center, important industrial plants, and a heavy concentration of working-class slums. The district Mitte, the historical core of Berlin, was the site of national ministries, the city hall and parliament, state cultural institutions, the main university, the former residence of the Kaiser, and the headquarters of Germany's greatest banks. The residential districts of eastern Berlin were chiefly working class."

19. Paragraph 9: "Besides having the best amenities, the western sectors contained significant industrial establishments. Although the American Sector was largely residential, it boasted an installation of utmost political and cultural value: a huge printing plant in Tempelhof belonging to the prewar Ullstein publishing empire. In addition, Tempelhof was home to Berlin's main airport."

20. Paragraph 7: "The presence of several key industrial establishments compensated somewhat for the mediocre quality of East Berlin's residential areas. Foremost among them were the AEG (*Allgemeine Elektricitätsgesellschaft*–General Electric Company) installations in the Köpenick and Treptow districts. These comprised an electrical generating plant and four huge factories producing electrical and telephone cable, transformers, broadcasting equipment, vacuum tubes, radios, electrical switches, rectifiers, and studio tape recorders."

21. Paragraph 10: "The British sectors contained the city's greatest economic gems. The *Siemensstadt* (Siemens City) in Spandau comprised one of the world's largest complexes for production of electrical goods, including a housing area for company workers. Located in the Tiergarten district was AEG's electrical turbine generator factory and repair workshop, AEG-Turbinen. This facility was of special importance because the Soviet Zone's economy had no such facility for the production and repair of turbine generators, and therefore depended on this one establishment located in western Berlin."

22. Paragraph 3: "Their goal in war was victory over Adolf Hitler's military machine, and their aim in peace was to control Germany, not the Soviet Union. These Americans had witnessed the devastation brought on by German aggression in Europe; knew the Soviets as generally reliable, if rather secretive, military allies; and believed cooperation might continue in the war's aftermath. Aside from some bickering between Washington and London, the Allies concluded decisions on Germany with relative ease. Despite ongoing suspicions and tensions over Soviet behavior in Eastern Europe, most Anglo-American leaders saw no reason to assume that wartime cooperation, nourished in the comradeship of common struggle, must abruptly cease."

23. Paragraph 5: "The agreement on Germany accorded the Soviets disproportionately greater territory in the east, when measured by surface area, while favoring the Western powers with the greatest concentrations of population and productive resources. It assured the same balance for Berlin. Although the Soviet Sector covered 42 percent of Berlin's surface area, the population of each of the three sectors was virtually equal, and once such factors as housing, industry, and political-administrative institutions were considered, no discernable advantage favored one party."

24. Paragraph 8: "One of two originally British districts given to France in July 1945, the so-called *Rote Wedding* (Red Wedding), was more famously proletarian, having delivered a defiant leftist majority in Berlin's last election in March 1933, despite conditions of Nazi terror."

25. Paragraph 1: "On 14 November 1944, while the war still raged, American, British, and Soviet representatives signed an agreement to divide Germany into three zones of occupation, each governed by the commander-in-chief of the respective power. In the same accord, they agreed to split Berlin, the German capital, into three sectors."

26. Paragraph 4: "In October 1943, the American, British, and Soviet foreign ministers— Cordell Hull, Anthony Eden, and Vyacheslav M. Molotov—met in Moscow to prepare an agenda for the upcoming talks between the three heads of government in Tehran. In the course of these deliberations, they signed a protocol establishing a standing committee to meet in London. The mission of that body—the European Advisory Commission—would be to formulate recommendations for postwar policy, particularly in regard to Germany."

27. Paragraph 2: "In the absence of sectors, the powers might have created an intermingled force of occupation with offices, guard posts, and quarters throughout the city, and with common facilities for communications and supplies. But the formation of sectors was the founding act of Cold War Berlin. Instead of mixed forces, cohesive national garrisons took shape in the assigned districts, and the Western areas soon became enclaves inside the Soviet sphere."

28. Social services: "There are four main categories of SOEs: (a) public utilities such as electric power, water, communications, and transport; (b) basic goods industries such as coal, oil and nuclear resources, and steel; (c) financial services such as banks, insurance companies, and social security administrations; and (d) social services such as education and health services" (Paragraph 1).

29. Commercial enterprises: "To analyze the SOEs in the context of stability operations, it is useful to subsume these four categories in two: basic utilities and commercial enterprises" (Paragraph 1).

30. Ideological: "In addition to the political and ideological motivations for establishing SOEs, there generally are three other reasons for doing so: (1) market failures; (2) promotion of economic growth on the basis of long-term planning; and (3) industrial and financial bailouts resulting from irreversible crises" (Paragraph 2).

31. Economic growth: "In addition to the political and ideological motivations for establishing SOEs, there generally are three other reasons for doing so: (1) market failures; (2) promotion of economic growth on the basis of long-term planning; and (3) industrial and financial bailouts resulting from irreversible crises" (Paragraph 2).

32. Keynesianism: "As national economies adapted to historical events in the 20th century, the ideological pendulum swung back and forth from one extreme to the other. On one swing, unregulated markets turned to growing state involvement (1933-80), in accordance with the economic philosophy of Keynesianism following the market failure of the Great Depression..." (Paragraph 3).

33. Stagflation: "On one swing, unregulated markets turned to growing state involvement (1933-80), in accordance with the economic philosophy of Keynesianism following the market failure of the Great Depression; and on the return swing, state regulation turned to minimal government and market freedom by a process of deregulation (1980-present) following the stagflation of the early 1970s and early 1980s, all in accordance with the philosophy of Friedrich Hayek, as interpreted by Milton Friedman and others, and as implemented by the government of Margaret Thatcher in the United Kingdom (UK) and by the Reagan administration in the United States." (Paragraph 3).

34. Margaret Thatcher: "On one swing, unregulated markets turned to growing state involvement (1933-80), in accordance with the economic philosophy of Keynesianism following the market failure of the Great Depression; and on the return swing, state regulation turned to minimal government and market freedom by a process of deregulation (1980-present) following the stagflation of the early 1970s and early 1980s, all in accordance with the philosophy of Friedrich Hayek, as interpreted by Milton Friedman and others, and as implemented by the government of Margaret Thatcher in the United Kingdom (UK) and by the Reagan administration in the United States." (Paragraph 3).

35. Reaganomics: "In the United States in 1980, the economic policies associated with Reaganomics sought to reverse Keynesianism through deregulation, minimal taxes, and high interest rates to control inflation, swinging the influence and acceptance of SOEs in the opposite direction" (Paragraph 5).

36. Minimal taxes: "In the United States in 1980, the economic policies associated with Reaganomics sought to reverse Keynesianism through deregulation, minimal taxes, and high interest rates to control inflation, swinging the influence and acceptance of SOEs in the opposite direction" (Paragraph 5).

37. Mid-1970s: "'In most Western countries, the great age of nationalization and successful public enterprise was the 3 decades following World War II,' with its peak in the mid-1970s when the output of

SOEs averaged 10 percent of gross national product and 16.5 percent of gross capital formation" (Paragraph 4).

38. Capital formation: "'In most Western countries, the great age of nationalization and successful public enterprise was the 3 decades following World War II,' with its peak in the mid-1970s when the output of SOEs averaged 10 percent of gross national product and 16.5 percent of gross capital formation" (Paragraph 4).

39. Regulatory framework: "Privatization is a complex undertaking and should be attempted only within a proper regulatory framework" (Paragraph 6).

40. Russia: "Without proper regulation, a rush to privatization would likely lead to the kind of abuses that characterized Russia's economic reforms of the 1990s" (Paragraph 6).

General Training Reading

1. Food labels: "The Act requires that food labels must clearly identify the food source names of any ingredients that are one of the major food allergens or contain any protein derived from a major food allergen" (Paragraph 3).

2. Management: "Strict avoidance of food allergens—and early recognition and management of allergic reactions to food—are important measures to prevent serious health consequences" (Paragraph 2).

3. Poultry: "The Act applies to the labeling of foods regulated by FDA which includes all foods except poultry, most meats, certain egg products, and most alcoholic beverages which are regulated by other Federal agencies" (Paragraph 3).

4. Shrimp: "The eight foods identified by the law are...crustacean shellfish (e.g., crab, lobster, shrimp)" (Paragraph 6).

5. Protein: These eight foods, and any ingredient that contains protein derived from one or more of them, are designated as "major food allergens" by FALCPA (Paragraph 7).

6. 90 percent: "While more than 160 foods can cause allergic reactions in people with food allergies, the law identifies the eight most common allergenic foods. These foods account for 90 percent of food allergic reactions and are the food sources from which many other ingredients are derived" (Paragraph 5).

7. C: "Before you buy a home, attend a homeownership education course offered by a U.S. Department of Housing and Urban Development (HUD)-approved, non-profit counseling agency" (Paragraph 4).

8. C: Predatory lenders may try to: sell properties for much more than they are worth by using false appraisals, encourage borrowers to lie about their ability to pay their down payments, knowingly lend more money than a borrower can afford to repay, charge high interest rates to borrowers based on their race or national origin, and charge fees for unnecessary/nonexistent products and services (Paragraph 3). The passage doesn't mention anything about predatory lenders impersonating buyers to finalize sales.

9. D: "Interview several real estate agents and ask for and check references before you select one to help you buy or sell a home" (Paragraph 4). Interviewing several real estate agents isn't the same as interviewing every agent in the area. The passage doesn't mention hiring multiple agents or requiring agents to hold a college degree.

10. D: "Determine whether you or the seller will be responsible for paying for the repairs" (Paragraph 4). We can infer based on this recommendation that either the buyer or lender could be responsible for repairs, and that designation depends on the agreement.

11. A: "Get information about the current values and recent sale prices of other homes in the neighborhood" (Paragraph 4). The other choices could be beneficial for prospective home buyers, but they aren't recommended or mentioned in the passage.

12. A: "Don't take out a loan offered to you by telemarketers, flyers, or door-to-door sales" (Paragraph 5). A mortgage company, government, and bank could all be appropriate lenders, depending on the individual circumstances. In contrast, a telemarketer is much more likely to be selling a scam.

13. 170 Main Street: "Located at 170 Main Street, easily accessible off the E/F/N/R/Z lines, and yours for $2100/month" (Paragraph 1).

14. Walter: "Please call Walter at (123) 456-7890 to schedule a viewing. The sooner, the better. This apartment will go FAST" (Paragraph 4).

15. Bedrooms: "2 Bedrooms with walk-in closets" (Paragraph 2).

16. $2100: "Located at 170 Main Street, easily accessible off the E/F/N/R/Z lines, and yours for $2100/month" (Paragraph 1). "Yours for" is referring to the apartment, so $2100 is the rent per month.

17. 650 or higher: "Credit score 650 or higher" (Paragraph 3).

18. Monthly rent: "Current paystubs showing annual income that's 40 times the monthly rent. Incomes can be combined for a household. Guarantors also accepted" (Paragraph 3).

19. Ceilings: "High ceilings" (Paragraph 2).

20. Super: "On-site super and maintenance staff" (Paragraph 2).

21. Walk-in: "2 Bedrooms with walk-in closets" (Paragraph 2).

22. Kitchen: "New kitchen appliances (refrigerator, stove, microwave)" (Paragraph 2).

23. D: "Harassment is unwelcome conduct that is based on race, color, religion, sex (including pregnancy), national origin, age (40 or older), disability, or genetic information" (Paragraph 2). Harassment based on qualifications isn't protected under the law.

24. B: "The conduct is severe or pervasive enough to create a work environment that a reasonable person would consider intimidating, hostile, or abusive" (Paragraph 2). Thus, the standard is what a reasonable person would think. The other evidence burdens aren't discussed or referenced in the passage.

25. B: "Harassment is a form of employment discrimination that violates Title VII of the Civil Rights Act of 1964, the Age Discrimination in Employment Act of 1967 (ADEA), and the Americans with Disabilities Act of 1990 (ADA)" (Paragraph 1).

26. A: "When investigating allegations of harassment, the Equal Employment Opportunity Commission looks at the entire record: including the nature of the conduct, and the context in which the alleged incidents occurred" (Paragraph 9). The passage doesn't describe the other departments' role in investigating allegations of harassment in the workplace.

27. C: "Employees are encouraged to inform the harasser directly that the conduct is unwelcome and must stop. Employees should also report harassment to management at an early stage to prevent its escalation" (Paragraph 6).

28. Genetic information: "Harassment is unwelcome conduct that is based on race, color, religion, sex (including pregnancy), national origin, age (40 or older), disability or genetic information" (Paragraph 2).

29. Reasonable people: "To be unlawful, the conduct must create a work environment that would be intimidating, hostile, or offensive to reasonable people" (Paragraph 3).

30. Liable: "The employer is automatically liable for harassment by a supervisor that results in a negative employment action such as termination, failure to promote or hire, and loss of wages" (Paragraph 7).

31. Non-supervisory: "The employer will be liable for harassment by non-supervisory employees or non-employees over whom it has control (e.g., independent contractors or customers on the premises), if it knew, or should have known, about the harassment and failed to take prompt and appropriate corrective action" (Paragraph 8).

32. D: *Working man* is most closely aligned with Choice *D, bourgeois.* In the context of the speech, the word *bourgeois* means *working* or *middle class*. Choice *A, plebian*, does suggest *common people*; however, this is a term that is specific to ancient Rome. Choice *B, viscount*, is a European title used to describe a specific degree of nobility. Choice *C, entrepreneur*, is a person who operates their own business.

33. C: In the context of the speech, the term *working man* most closely correlates with Choice *C*. Choice *A* is not mentioned in the passage and is off-topic. Choice *B* may be true in some cases, but it does not reflect the sentiment described for the term *working man* in the passage. Choice *D* may also be arguably true. However, it is not given as a definition but as acts of the working man, and the topics of *field, factory,* and *screen* are not mentioned in the passage.

34. D: *Enterprise* most closely means *cause*. Choices *A, B,* and *C* are all related to the term *enterprise*. However, Dickens speaks of a *cause* here, not a company, courage, or a game. "He will stand by such an enterprise" is a call to stand by a cause to enable the working man to have a certain autonomy over his own economic standing. The very first paragraph ends with the statement that the working man "shall...have a share in the management of an institution which is designed for his benefit."

35. B: The speaker's salutation is one from an entertainer to his audience and uses the friendly language to connect to his audience before a serious speech. Recall in the first paragraph that the speaker is there to "accompany [the audience] ... through one of my little Christmas books," making him an author there to entertain the crowd with his own writing. The speech preceding the reading is the passage itself, and, as the tone indicates, a serious speech addressing the "working man." Although the passage speaks of employers and employees, the speaker himself is not an employer of the audience, so Choice *A* is incorrect. Choice *C* is also incorrect, as the salutation is not used ironically, but sincerely, as the speech addresses the wellbeing of the crowd. Choice *D* is incorrect because the speech is not given by a politician, but by a writer.

36. Outdoor grill: "On warmer spring days, keep the heat out of your home by using an <u>outdoor grill</u> instead of indoor ovens" (Paragraph 5).

37. Air conditioners: "Opening windows creates a cross-wise breeze, allowing you to naturally cool your home without switching on <u>air conditioners</u>" (Paragraph 3).

38. Bathroom fans: "<u>Bathroom fans</u> suck out heat and humidity from your home, improving comfort" (Paragraph 11).

39. Caulk: "Using low-cost <u>caulk</u> to seal cracks and openings in your home keeps warm air out—and cash in your wallet" (Paragraph 7).

40. Air filters: "Easy maintenance such as routinely replacing, or cleaning, <u>air filters</u> can lower your cooling system's energy consumption by up to 15 percent" (Paragraph 2).

Speaking

Task #1

Examiner: Tell me about your experience learning English. Why did you choose to study English?

Test taker: At first, it wasn't my choice to study English. My parents signed me up for four years of high school English classes in Argentina, where I'm from. Once I got into college, I became enamored with my native language, Spanish, and began studying Latin American literature and writing. My department offered a study abroad opportunity as part of a partnership with New York University in New York City. I thought the program would be a great way to gain a new perspective on my chosen field, explore a fascinating, foreign city, and improve the English skills I had learned in high school. I became much more interested in English once my everyday life required it.

Examiner: What tools have you found to be most helpful for learning the language?

Test taker: I didn't know very much English when I moved to New York City to study Spanish literature at NYU. We spoke Spanish in the classroom, but, everywhere else, I tried to speak only English. It helped a lot that my roommates were bilingual students who spoke English as a first language. I could always ask them questions, and I had a ton. Some of the biggest difficulties weren't even related to language. They were more cultural, like where to stand in the subway or on escalators. The pace of life was much faster than I'd ever experienced before. Plenty of strangers were nice enough to point me in the right direction, but the vast majority didn't have time to answer my questions as they rushed around. Still, this type of immersion is what worked the best for me. I did have a safety net at NYU, especially with my roommates, but otherwise I had to fend for myself. Learning English wasn't just my goal, it was a requirement to function every day. And I did just that. I learned more English in those three months than I did in four years of high school English classes.

Examiner: What advice would you give an exchange student moving to a country where people speak a different language than them?

Test taker: I would tell them not to be afraid of making mistakes. It can feel embarrassing to attempt to speak a language that you don't know out in public, but immersion is the best way to learn. It's important to maintain a good sense of humor and a curiosity about the language you are learning. For example, when I started learning English, I had a difficult time with the word "refrigerator." I would make my roommates repeat the word over and over while I mimicked them. Imagine three college students rolling around laughing at the refrigerator – I thought it was hysterical, and through the experience, I cultivated a patience towards my own mistakes. I would also advise an exchange student to gather and engage with as much material in their target language as possible. Read books. Listen to podcasts. Watch television. Ask native speakers out to coffee or dinner, writing down unfamiliar words and phrases as you converse.

Examiner: Now let's talk about travel. What types of transportation do you prefer when you travel?

Test taker: I enjoy taking the train when I travel. There is something exhilarating about buying a ticket from a booth inside a train station, then boarding one of the trains waiting between platforms. I always try to sit in a window seat. That way, I can appreciate the views as the locomotive speeds through the cities, towns, and countryside. The experience triggers a pleasant sense of nostalgia for me because it reminds me of times I traveled by train with my parents in my younger years.

Examiner: What countries do you hope to visit one day? Why?

Test taker: I have never traveled to Europe before, and I would like to sometime in the next five years. Specifically, I would love to visit Norway and Spain. Oslo seems like such a mysterious, culturally interesting city. I have seen some gorgeous photos of the mountains, waterfalls, and glaciers throughout the Norwegian countryside and I would like to encounter that beauty for myself. Hopefully, I could witness the Northern Lights, too. I want to go to Spain because I grew up in Argentina and I think it would be interesting to experience a completely different culture that speaks the same language as me. I am most excited by the prospect of visiting the crystal palace inside of the main park in Madrid, as well as the royal palace and the Plaza Mayor. I would also like to explore Seville and Granada. The Alhambra also intrigues me because I've recently cultivated an interest in Moorish architecture and design.

Examiner: What types of activities would you recommend to someone visiting your city or town?

Test taker: For someone visiting Buenos Aires, I would recommend checking out the Plaza de Mayo, which is a gorgeous, centralized square in the city. It's composed of grand historical buildings, including the main government building. Next, I would suggest that visitors check out Recoleta Cemetery. It's a unique cemetery in that it hosts the most famous mausoleum in the country, where important Argentinian historical figures are buried. After visiting the cemetery, visitors should check out Caminito, a colorful open-air street museum created by artist Benito Quinquela Martín. Don't miss the empanadas at nearby restaurant Patagonia Sur! Finally, for dinner, I would suggest that visitors check out Café Tortoni to enjoy a delicious meal and live tango performances. Some of these places can feel touristy, but not without good reason!

Task #2

Examiner: Here is your prompt card. You have one minute to review it and then you have one to two minutes to respond. Don't worry about the need to keep time. I will alert you when the time is up.

Test taker: Okay.

Examiner: Okay. It is now time to begin speaking.

Test taker: I will vote yes on the pending proposal to install red light cameras on Main Street. Our community has recently suffered a series of tragic accidents. Studies have shown that red light cameras significantly reduce accidents, and our law enforcement officers think that red light cameras likely would've prevented those recent accidents. People are less likely to run a red light when they know it'll cost them money. It's the same reason people generally obey parking rules, except in the case of red lights, it's even more imperative to do something because people are getting hurt. I don't want anyone to lose a loved one because we refuse to safeguard against known dangers. I know many of my constituents will not be happy with this decision. Despite these disagreements, I hope they can at least understand where I'm coming from. I expect that my opponent will use this against me in the next election, but I stand by my decision. I will always support policies that protect the people I'm elected to represent.

Examiner: Thank you. What would you say to a constituent who called your office to complain about your decision?

Test taker: I would first thank them for their interest in and commitment to the community. I would then listen to their concerns, making sure to acknowledge the ways the new red light cameras may pose an inconvenience to them. However, I would then explain the reasoning behind the decision, focusing on the accidents the community could have avoided through a more aggressive red light policy. I would let the community member know that my interests lie firmly with keeping each and every one of the citizens of our district safe.

Task #3

Examiner: Let's discuss government. What do you think are the most important functions of government?

Test taker: To me, the most important function of government lies in protecting the life and liberty of citizens. This responsibility can take on many different expressions, extending to issues such as transportation, economics, public health, public welfare, food security, individual privacy, and numerous individual freedoms.

Examiner: Which responsibilities do you think should be handled locally, such as by a city or district?

Test taker: Local governments tend to have a better idea of the values and needs of the people living in the community, so I think they should have control of the institutions that affect citizens on a daily basis. For example, in my opinion, school policy should lie largely in the hands of local government. By that, I mean that school districts should have authority over school funding choices, dress codes, policy decisions, cafeteria programs, and curriculum. Traffic planning should also be a local government responsibility, albeit one that must be congruent with surrounding local governments to streamline transportation. Local leadership should also reserve the right to allocate local tax dollars to the needs of the community; this gives citizens a voice in determining what causes they value and would like to buoy. Such localized power provides communities with the ability to support things like children's food programs, continuing education opportunities, library resources, and mental health supports.

Examiner: In your opinion, which duties should be carried out by the federal government?

Test taker: The federal government should serve to manage larger programs aimed at protecting the life and liberty of citizens. Because the national government usually has more funds available, it should focus on distributing money to help people reach more stable, higher-quality living situations while protecting freedoms. For example, federal governments have the resources to help students support themselves as they seek improvement through education. The government can disperse funds through grants, reduce costs through food programs, and set welfare policies that target specific populations that need the most help. Another important duty of the federal government lies in managing uniform policies and programs across the country. For example, the United States Department of State manages international travel for all Americans by centralizing the process of passport acquisition. If local governments maintained the responsibility of setting passport policy, air travel in the United States would become much more fractured and confusing.

Examiner: Now let's talk about civic engagement. In your experience, what are some ways citizens can influence the government?

Test taker: In my experience, protesting is one of the most effective ways citizens can enact government change. Protest remains a powerful tool for average people to voice dissatisfaction with the status quo and influence powerful officials toward creating new policies, adjusting existing laws, or abolishing oppressive structures. In countries all over the world, people organize protests to make their voices heard on the national level. Running for office and voting also serve as key mechanisms that elevate the interests of average citizens.

Examiner: What are some ways citizens can affect their local community?

Test taker: Citizens can affect their local community through organizing. Organizing can take lots of different forms, such as petitions, protests, charities, fundraisers, voting drives, and volunteerism. Volunteering can make a huge difference for community members, especially when it is geared toward meeting specific needs of other citizens. For example, if one person in the community requires a new wheelchair ramp because of a recent accident, volunteers can work together to build one, thus reducing and redistributing the costs of the project.

Listening Transcripts #3

Passage #1: Conversation

(Narrator) Listen to the conversation and then answer the questions.

(Tom) Ahhh!

(Suzie) What's wrong?

(Tom) There's a bug on my arm!

(Suzie) Bug? What kind of bug?

(Tom) Don't touch it! If you make it mad, it might bite me. It's red and black. Don't the colors red and black mean an animal is poisonous? If it bites me, I'm going to die!

(Suzie) Don't be silly, Tom. You're thinking of snakes. Red and yellow snakes are poisonous. I don't think this bug is big enough to hurt you.

(Tom) I think you're wrong. I'm pretty sure the color red on its back means it's poisonous!

(Suzie) You're right! I think the spots are a bad sign. My cousin, Rob, got bitten by a spider once. It had spots on its back. His leg swelled up as big as a volleyball. My Aunt Becky had to take him to the hospital. The doctor had to use a needle to pop his leg like a balloon before it exploded. Don't cry, Tom. I'll go get Mr. Henderson and tell him to call 9-1-1. They will send someone to get this bug. And they will send an ambulance in case it bites you.

(Tom) Don't get too close, Mr. Henderson! If you make it mad, it might bite me!

(Mr. Henderson) Why, Tom! Don't be afraid. I don't see any hospitals in your future. This innocuous little cutie is a ladybug!

Passage #2: Court Case

(Narrator) Listen to the court case and then answer the questions.

(Judge) The constitutional issue we decide in each of these cases is the admissibility of statements obtained from a defendant questioned while in custody or otherwise deprived of his freedom of action in any significant way. In each, the defendant was questioned by police officers, detectives, or a prosecuting attorney in a room in which he was cut off from the outside world. In none of these cases was the defendant given a full and effective warning of his rights at the outset of the interrogation process. In all the cases, the questioning elicited oral admissions, and in three of them, signed statements as well, which were admitted at their trials...

...We hold that, when an individual is taken into custody or otherwise deprived of his freedom by the authorities in any significant way and is subjected to questioning, the privilege against self-incrimination is jeopardized. Procedural safeguards must be employed to protect the privilege, and unless other fully effective means are adopted to notify the person of his right of silence and to assure that the exercise of this right will be scrupulously honored, the following measures are required. He must be warned prior to any questioning that he has the right to remain silent, that anything he says can be used against him in a court of law, that he has the right to the presence of an attorney, and that, if he cannot afford an attorney one will be appointed for him prior to any questioning if he so desires. Opportunity to exercise these rights must be afforded to him throughout the interrogation. After such warnings have been given, and such opportunity afforded him, the individual may knowingly and intelligently waive these rights and agree to answer questions or make a statement. But unless and until such warnings and waiver are demonstrated by the prosecution at trial, no evidence obtained as a result of interrogation can be used against him.

Miranda v. Arizona, U.S. Supreme Court decision (1966)

Passage #3: Conversation

(Narrator) Listen to the conversation and then answer the questions.

(Tourist) Hello, I was wondering if you could give me some information about Houston, Texas?

(Travel Agent) Houston, Texas is a city with many exciting things to do and places to visit. Its museums and monuments provide a great historical background of the area. There are several amusement parks with plenty of games and rides to provide a day of fun for people of all ages. In addition, the city is home to many beautiful parks that host events year-round.

(Tourist) Can you tell me more about the museums and if they are worth checking out?

(Travel Agent) Houston's museums are certainly worth checking out. The Natural Museum of Science showcases a variety of dinosaur skeletons, gemstones, and hand-carved artifacts. The Health Museum houses life-size animated organs to teach visitors about healthy lifestyles. Participants can also test their strength and play learning games at the museum. The Children's Museum is an interactive museum for children.

(Tourist) That all sounds great! You mentioned amusement parks earlier. Can you tell me more about the entertainment side of the area?

(Travel Agent) The Houston area is home to several amusement parks. You can spend the day at the Kemah Boardwalk riding a variety of rollercoasters, or ride the Bullet, a high-speed boat that makes a big splash. Pleasure Pier is located 45 miles away on Galveston Island. Carnival rides, games, and restaurants extend out over the water for a thrilling time. Typhoon Texas is an amusement park that offers only water rides. Splash in the wave pool, whoosh down slides, or relax by the pool.

(Tourist) Great, thanks! I'm working within a budget, so can you tell me more about activities that might be free of cost?

(Travel Agent) If cost is a concern, there are plenty of free parks to visit during a trip to Houston. Memorial Park is known for its miles of hiking and biking trails. Discovery Green is a park that offers seasonal citywide events. During the warmer months, enjoy a session of outdoor yoga. In the winter, a temporary ice-skating rink is built for all to enjoy. Hermann Park is located in the Houston Medical Center. Take a paddleboat in the pond or hang around at the playground. You can also ride a miniature train around the park and enjoy the beautiful views.

(Tourist) That all sounds fun! Thanks so much for the information!

Passage #4: Lecture

(Narrator) Listen to the lecture and then answer the questions.

(Professor and activist) Three years ago, I think there were not many bird-lovers in the United States who believed it possible to prevent the total extinction of both egrets from our fauna. All the known rookeries accessible to plume-hunters had been totally destroyed. Two years ago, the secret discovery of several small, hidden colonies prompted William Dutcher, President of the National Association of Audubon Societies, and Mr. T. Gilbert Pearson, Secretary, to attempt the protection of those colonies. With a fund contributed for the purpose, wardens were hired and duly commissioned. As previously stated, one of those wardens was shot dead in cold blood by a plume hunter. The task of guarding swamp rookeries from the attacks of money-hungry desperadoes, to whom the accursed plumes were worth their weight in gold, is a very chancy proceeding. There is now one warden in Florida who says that "before they get my rookery, they will first have to get me."

Thus far the protective work of the Audubon Association has been successful. Now there are twenty colonies, which contain all told, about 5,000 egrets and about 120,000 herons and ibises which are guarded by the Audubon wardens. One of the most important is on Bird Island, a mile out in Orange Lake, central Florida, and it is ably defended by Oscar E. Baynard. Today, the plume hunters who do not dare to raid the guarded rookeries are trying to study out the lines of flight of the birds, to and from their feeding-grounds, and shoot them in transit. Their motto is—"Anything to beat the law and get the plumes." It is there that the state of Florida should take part in the war.

The success of this campaign is attested by the fact that last year a number of egrets were seen in eastern Massachusetts—for the first time in many years. And so, today the question is, can the wardens continue to hold the plume-hunters at bay?

Excerpt from *Our Vanishing Wildlife* by William T. Hornaday, 1913

Dear IELTS Test Taker,

We would like to start by thanking you for purchasing this study guide for your IELTS exam. We hope that we exceeded your expectations.

Our goal in creating this study guide was to cover all of the topics that you will see on the test. We also strove to make our practice questions as similar as possible to what you will encounter on test day. With that being said, if you found something that you feel was not up to your standards, please send us an email and let us know.

We would also like to let you know about other books in our catalog that may interest you.

TOEFL iBT Study Guide

This can be found on Amazon: amazon.com/dp/1637750153

GRE Study Guide

amazon.com/dp/1637752261

GMAT Study Guide

amazon.com/dp/1637758847

MCAT Study Guide

amazon.com/dp/1637755465

We have study guides in a wide variety of fields. If the one you are looking for isn't listed above, then try searching for it on Amazon or send us an email.

Thanks Again and Happy Testing!
Product Development Team
info@studyguideteam.com

FREE Test Taking Tips Video/DVD Offer

To better serve you, we created videos covering test taking tips that we want to give you for FREE. **These videos cover world-class tips that will help you succeed on your test.**

We just ask that you send us feedback about this product. Please let us know what you thought about it—whether good, bad, or indifferent.

To get your **FREE videos**, you can use the QR code below or email freevideos@studyguideteam.com with "Free Videos" in the subject line and the following information in the body of the email:

a. The title of your product

b. Your product rating on a scale of 1-5, with 5 being the highest

c. Your feedback about the product

If you have any questions or concerns, please don't hesitate to contact us at info@studyguideteam.com.

Thank you!

SCAN HERE

Printed in the USA
CPSIA information can be obtained
at www.ICGtesting.com
LVHW011804121023
760795LV00010B/146

9 781637 75489